Praise for
Opt-In Marketing

"Currently, most companies do not have a measurable, repeatable process for building solid relationships. However, if we demonstrate to the customer we care, they will trust us. Roman and Hornstein's Consensual Marketing is the breakthrough process for establishing a powerful consensual relationship built on delivering value per customer's individual requirements. It is an important book."

—Horst H. Schulze
President and Chief Executive Officer
The West Paces Hotel Group, LLC
Former CEO, Ritz Carlton Hotels

"Roman and Hornstein continue to perfect a system for bringing value to potential customers through well-planned communications. In an era where purchasers are bombarded with communications that are often irritating, this approach can set a company apart. They describe a process for high-quality communication that sparks a consensual relationship which develops into a preferred provider status. Must reading if your goal is to be the quality and market leader."

—Elaine J. Heron, Ph.D.
Chief Executive Officer
Labcyte Inc.

"This book is not only a sobering warning against the indiscriminate use of e-mail, mail, and telemarketing, it is chock-full of sound marketing wisdom and quantifiable techniques for significantly increasing profits through effective communications with customers."

—John A. Hunter
Senior Vice President
QVC

"The enactment of the CAN-SPAM and Do Not Call legislation has changed the customer engagement landscape. Customers now have the legal right to opt in or opt out of your marketing communications. Consensual Marketing provides marketers with a proven strategy for approaching customers with true value. Equally important, this book makes the case for enacting significant change within corporate marketing organizations."

—Bruce Thompson
Marketing Manager
Worldwide Small and Medium Business Group
Microsoft Corporation

"Customers have changed. Traditional marketing hasn't. Consensual customer relationships are essential for success. *Opt-In Marketing* clearly points the way with processes, methodologies, but most of all, detailed case studies proving this approach delivers!"

—Don Schultz
Professor Emeritus
Northwestern University, Medill School of Journalism
Founder of consultancy Agora, Inc.

"There is no more urgent priority than for marketers to wake up to the skyrocketing consumer resistance to marketing. And then to do something about it. The principles behind Consensual Marketing are all about putting the customer in complete control, which is the only basis on which profitable marketing will suceed in the future."

—J. Walker Smith
President
Yankelovich Partners, Inc.
Bestselling author of *Rocking the Ages: The Yankelovich Report on Generational Marketing*

"If you have been disappointed by your CRM or permission marketing initiatives, this book is for you. *Opt-In Marketing* is a powerful guide for how to communicate with your customers profitably. It demystifies the marketing process. It shows the insights gained by listening to your customers. As a bonus, there are step-by-step instructions on how to overcome your toughest challenge—bringing a new way of thinking to your company. This book will take its place among the classic texts of Kotler and Ries and Trout."

—Jim Rochford
Marketing Communications Manager
QIAGEN Inc.

"Consensual Marketing is an insightful path to marketing nirvana, where sellers and buyers voluntarily enter into relationships of trust built upon ongoing exchanges of timely, relevant information. Marketing clutter is replaced by the right messages to the right decision makers at the right moments via the media they prefer. It's a solidly documented relationship-building strategy that deserves wide exposure."

—Mitchell Orfuss
Vice President, Marketing
Harte-Hanks, Inc.

"This book is just the 'cup of tea' needed for the marketers of today. Roman and Hornstein's Consensual Marketing gives us a wake up call on effectively communicating with our customers in order to build strong and lasting relationships. Both marketing novices and seasoned professionals will benefit greatly from this book's practical examples."

—Don Vultaggio
Chairman
AriZona Beverages

"Consensual Marketing defined the way we do our marketing. It is an extremely effective marketing process and proves that our customers want to create a dialogue with us and choose how we communicate with them. It also taught us that providing high value and one-to-one communications is the most effective way for us to differentiate ourselves from our competition."

—Marianne W. Gaige
President and COO
Cathedral Corporation

"Here's a must read for every student and practitioner of Direct Marketing—a handbook for turning database marketing, traditional CRM, Integrated Direct Marketing, permission, and 1:1 marketing techniques into the most powerful marketing tool available. In simple, easily understood terms, Roman and Hornstein explain how to use Consensual Marketing to establish and nurture a long-term, profitable relationship with our customers that yields the highest customer satisfaction, the highest returns, and therefore the best chance for the highest profits. Consensual Marketing is where we all want to be."

—Harvey Markovitz
Lecturer in Marketing
Zicklin School of Business, Baruch College and Mercy College

"The Consensual Marketing Opt-In Process is an important concept for corporate leaders who formulate marketing strategies. Consensual Marketing strengthens customer relationships by engaging with customers per their content, timing, and media preferences. The reader also learns the latest techniques for deploying an integrated media mix, databases, and other tools of contemporary management. This book gives practical wisdom to every member of the management team."

—Barrett Hazeltine
Professor of Engineering Emeritus
Brown University

—Dennis W. Michaud
Director, Program in Global Commerce
Brown University

"The future of marketing is consent-based, and this book provides a powerful process for the essential goal of engaging customers. In the multichannel marketplace of today and tomorrow, students and marketing professionals can learn from Consensual Marketing how to increase value for customers while increasing customers' Life-Time Value. This one's on my list of need-to-read."

—Marjorie Kalter
Clinical Professor of Direct and Interactive Marketing
New York University

"*Opt-In Marketing* is a fascinating and astute book about improving the relationship between marketers and customers. The strength and uniqueness of this book lie in the authors' remarkable awareness of the psychological needs of buyers. Roman and Hornstein demonstrate quite convincingly how attention to these needs can dramatically improve marketing campaigns. The rich and abundant case material makes learning both pleasurable and satisfying."

—Barry A. Farber, Ph.D.
Professor and Program Coordinator, Clinical Psychology Program
Teachers College, Columbia University

"Direct Marketing is in crisis. Opt-out rates are soaring. How do you get customers to opt-in to a relationship? How do you maximize the return on your marketing budget? This book answers these questions with vision and proven processes."

—Ichak Adizes, Ph.D.
Founder and CEO
Adizes Institute

"Consensual Marketing is the key to long-term marketing profitability. At last we have a guidebook that tells us not only what to do, but how to establish a consensual relationship using direct mail, tele-strategies, e-marketing, and field sales. The checklists alone will keep this book open on the astute marketer's desk. Here is expert advice aimed squarely at the bottom line."

—Herschell Gordon Lewis
President
Lewis Enterprises

"An absolute gold mine for all managers who seriously believe in investing in their customers. Rarely can we find as rich a wealth of *whats, whys,* and *hows.* This book introduces not only a revolutionary way of marketing thinking, but also highly implementable methodologies presented in a very friendly manner—supplemented by tons of real-life cases."

—Hermann Chan
Chief Executive
Times Direct Asia Limited

Opt-In Marketing

Increase Sales
Exponentially with
Consensual Marketing

Opt-In Marketing

Increase Sales
Exponentially with
Consensual Marketing

ERNAN ROMAN

SCOTT HORNSTEIN

McGraw-Hill

New York   Chicago   San Francisco   Lisbon   London   Madrid
Mexico City   Milan   New Delhi   San Juan   Seoul
Singapore   Sydney   Toronto

1 2 3 4 5 6 7 8 9 0   DOC/DOC   0 9 8 7 6 5 4

ISBN 0-07-143528-X

IDM is a registered trademark of Ernan Roman Direct Marketing.
Consensual Marketing is a service mark of Ernan Roman Direct Marketing.

McGraw-Hill books are available at special quantity discounts to use as premiums and sales promotions, or for use in corporate training programs. For more information, please write to the Director of Special Sales, McGraw-Hill Professional, Two Penn Plaza, New York, NY 10121-2298. Or contact your local bookstore.

This book is printed on recycled, acid-free paper containing a minimum of 50% recycled, de-inked fiber.

Library of Congress Cataloging-in-Publication Data

Roman, Ernan.
    Opt-in marketing : increase sales exponentially with consensual marketing / by Ernan Roman and Scott Hornstein.
        p.   cm.
    Includes bibliographical references.
    ISBN 0-07-143528-X (hardcover : alk. paper)
    1. Database marketing.   2. Customer relations.   3. Relationship marketing.   I. Hornstein, Scott.   II. Title.
HF5415.126.R653   2004
658.8'72—dc22
                                                                        2003028279

For Sheri, Elias, and Helaina, whose love, support, and counsel made this possible.

Ernan Roman

For Kellie, Mollie, and Rachel—my sun and moon, my earth and stars.

Scott Hornstein

Contents

Preface

Writing the first book on Consensual Marketing presented us with two challenges.

The first was to distill 10 years of testing and R&D into a structured, repeatable, and scalable process that you could implement at your company. To that end, we created the Seven Step Consensual Opt-In Marketing Process, which will provide you with the rationale, strategies, and proven "how to" guidelines.

The second challenge was to structure in-depth case studies that would provide you with very detailed, real-world examples, without disclosing proprietary aspects of the strategies we created for our clients.

We worked hard to meet these challenges and provide you with detailed guidelines for implementing the power of Consensual Marketing at your company.

We know that your discipline and perseverance in implementing all the components of the Seven Step Consensual Marketing Opt-In Process will reward you with an exponential increase in sales.

Should you have any questions or wish to share your ideas about Consensual Marketing, please feel free to contact us at Ernan@erdm.com or 718-225-4151.

Ernan Roman
Scott Hornstein

Acknowledgments

The best of business ideas cannot succeed without the opportunity for real-world testing and refinement.

We are grateful for the trust of these innovative clients who gave us the opportunity to test and implement the Consensual Marketing Opt-In Process: Mike Lawrie (Senior Vice President and Group Executive, Worldwide Sales and Distribution, IBM), Yvonne Brandon (former Direct Marketing Manager, Worldwide e-Business on Demand, Operating Environmental Initiatives at IBM), Garry Dawson (Manager of Marketing Communications Strategy, Hewlett-Packard, US Enterprise Systems Group), Andy Grim (Vice President Sales and Marketing, Golden Rule Insurance), and Stephen Kimmerling (Conference Program Manager, the Direct Marketing Association).

We would also like to acknowledge: Norma and Bob Hornstein; Steve, Frieda, Noah, and Julie Fenn; Tom Elliott, Curtis Gunn, Nicholas Pliakis, David Sable, and Randy Smith.

With gratitude for the contributions over the years from Eva Haller, Yoel Haller, and Murray Roman.

Thanks to Elias Roman, who took time from college (and the Call Center) to bring a Generation X perspective to the manuscript.

A special word of thanks to Vince Amen (former Vice President of Public Programs, Franklin Covey; President of Growth Coach) for his insightful review of the manuscript.

We are also grateful to Paula Lepanto for her dedication and help with research and formatting of the book.

Our gratitude to Kelli Christiansen (Acquisitions Editor, McGraw-Hill Trade) for her insights and editorial guidance.

Opt-In Marketing

Increase Sales
Exponentially with
Consensual Marketing

The Powerful Case for Consensual Marketing

THIS BOOK WILL introduce you to one of the most powerful marketing strategies today: the Consensual Marketing Opt-In Process. This methodology responds to the rapidly rising tide of consumer dissatisfaction by changing the basic paradigm of direct marketing: from unsolicited communications that are interruptive and perhaps annoying, to solicited messages that arrive with the expectation of value.

The Consensual Marketing Opt-In Process provides both immediate and long-term value to the customer. Short term, customers begin to receive more relevant and useful communications. Over time, marketers have the ability to provide increasingly focused and targeted exchanges of information that will raise each customer's satisfaction and lifetime value.

This process rewards marketers with an immediate increase in their return on investment (ROI) and the ability to exponentially increase revenue and ROI over time.

We have written this book to provide you with the rationale, strategies, case histories, and proven "how to" guidelines for helping you to bring Consensual Marketing to your company.

Customers Give the Best Advice

The origins of Consensual Marketing come from our work with some brilliant marketers and their customers. We are strong believers in combining the best thinking of both parties. No matter how good the idea sounds in the boardroom, we always run it up the flagpole to see what customers think—to make sure they are saluting before marketing budgets are spent.

Having grown dissatisfied with the accuracy of results from focus groups (often polluted by strong personalities) and quantitative surveys (you get the facts, but little in-depth insight or coloration), we developed the process of Voice of Customer (VOC) Messaging and Communication Research to round out the picture of customer likes and dislikes regarding the marketing process. Chapter 3 will provide further detail regarding this process and its value to marketers.

We have now conducted over 55 VOC Research efforts representing almost 1,600 hours of research interviews on behalf of clients such as IBM, Agilent Technologies, Hewlett-Packard, Applied Biosystems, AT&T, Golden Rule Insurance, and Franklin Covey. With every implementation of VOC Research there have been important lessons. Over the past few years we have heard firsthand the increasing customer/consumer discontent with marketing messages and tactics. Comments include:

- "You are not providing me with the information I need to make an informed decision."
- "Most of the stuff you send me is superficial and irrelevant."
- "No apparent targeting of person or message. It's the spaghetti theory of marketing (throw enough against the marketplace and some is bound to stick)."

While conducting VOC Research for a major Information Technology (IT) manufacturer, one particular interview provided an epiphany. It was with the CIO of a multinational company—a powerful individual controlling millions of dollars of purchasing power. At a certain point in the interview, she said, "Hold on just a moment. I have something to share with you." She continued:

Your client is an important supplier of hardware, software, and information. We respect your client greatly and wish to continue doing business with them for many years.

But because I am the CIO, you IT marketers think that all the materials, information, and offers you put together should be sent to me. That's not how we make decisions around here. In fact, you are using me as an executive mailroom, and I do not appreciate it!

Decision making in this department is distributed. I have many talented people working for me, each within an area of specialization. They are the ones that need to hear from you. Instead, I get hundreds of e-mails a day that I must route to the proper individual. When the mail cart comes by, there are trays of mail addressed to me. I have to skim the content and forward the information to the person responsible. A poor use of my time and a source of increasing irritation.

What I'd rather do is tell you who in my department is responsible for what decisions, what information they need, when they need it, and via which medium. If you speak to them directly it will be better, more effective for all parties. In fact, because priorities change here often, I will invite you back quarterly to update the list of who should be receiving what information when and via which medium.

We Will Hold You to a Higher Standard

"But," she added, "bringing you in and making you a partner means we will hold you to a higher standard. If you understand our information wants and needs, we expect you to satisfy them. Irrelevant or 'mass marketing' techniques will be obvious and will reflect badly on our new partnership. We expect you to live up to our expectations."

This was the germ of a profound idea, born from frustration, but with the potential to change our industry. A relationship, perhaps a partnership, between company and customer that is based on how the customer defines value, with both parties dedicated to sharing, understanding, and delivering that value over time.

This sounds like marketing nirvana, a situation where much of the guesswork is removed from the marketing process. But recognize that both the customer and the marketer enter into this relationship with significant expectations:

- Customers expect marketers to satisfy their information requirements by adhering to their needs regarding frequency and content and to deploy media in accordance with their likes and dislikes (media preference and media aversion).
- Marketers, in turn, can expect to quickly increase response and decrease waste. Instead of trying to guess who needs what and when, customers will tell them. Plain and simple.

These expectations must come to fruition for both parties or there is no relationship. All we would have is an empty promise.

Road-Testing the Concept

Most of the world's greatest ideas are deceivingly simple. To determine whether this simple idea would resonate with other executives in other industries, we tested it by conducting additional VOC Research. The results were astounding:

- Nine out of 10 executives fully endorsed the concept—stating that they would consider it a benefit if key suppliers knew exactly what to send them, when, and how.
- Nine out of 10 executives volunteered to be their department's contact—to regularly review and refresh their list of decision makers and their requirements.

This led to the development and testing of the Consensual Marketing Opt-In Process (CMO).

And lest CMO appear as academic theory, two IBM Consensual case histories will be reviewed in detail. The first is in Chapter 1 and shows how the IBM Focus 1:1 program generated $594 million over the control group. The second is in Chapter 8 and concerns IBM's Software Premier Club—which built on the lessons of Focus 1:1—and how it generated $310 million in incremental revenue.

Defining the Consensual Marketing Opt-In Process

CMO is both a philosophical point of view and a strategic process that challenges management to reexamine how we *value a customer* and engage with the customer, both long and short term. To truly value customers, companies must expand corporate goals from just sales and revenue to also include customer retention and lifetime value as strategic measures.

CMO stimulates customers to participate in a dialogue in which they define their unique needs, requirements, and preferences, populating the database with their:

- Information needs
- Timing requirements
- Contact information
- Media preference and aversion issues

In exchange, the marketer must provide value that meets the customer's requirements. This consensual relationship extends over time and provides both parties with uniquely rich in-depth information. At the heart of this relationship is a bond of trust.

The success of the process is based upon obtaining customers' consent and ongoing input to the marketing process.

Think for a moment about the enormous competitive advantage created by the resulting Consensual Database. The quality, accuracy, and depth of this database are unprecedented. No longer are we overlaying data and inferring information from third-party sources. Instead, we are acting upon information supplied directly by the customer—information knowingly supplied as input to the marketing process. That is why the Consensual process holds the promise of immediate return.

CMO is not simply asking customers to opt in to or opt out of a specific medium. Consensual Marketing asks customers to agree to participate in an ongoing, evolving relationship based on the increasingly focused and relevant exchange of information and value.

CMO is focused on increasing Customer Lifetime Value—the component parts of which are:

- Increasing customer longevity or the length of time the customer remains a customer
- Increasing customer loyalty or the breadth of products and services they purchase from your company
- Customer satisfaction that increases the most powerful marketing medium—word of mouth
- Customer revenue contribution
- Lower cost per order because marketing waste has been minimized

As we become more in tune with customers' needs and requirements, we are better able to efficiently and effectively deliver the messages and benefits required to increase Customer Lifetime Value.

Let's take a moment and check in with some of the industry's important thinkers and innovators regarding the Consensual Marketing Opt-In Process.

Philip Kotler, S. C. Johnson Distinguished Professor of International Marketing, J. L. Kellogg School of Management:[1]

> **I like Consensual Marketing very much. Permission marketing simply says you can reach me; I am letting you reach me. However, I am not supplying you with information about myself, what kind of products I'm interested in, how you should communicate with me, and so on. Consensual Marketing is a richer process— real business process innovation, consistent with the view of great marketing, which is to really meet customers' needs and satisfy them and not harass them or manipulate them. I applaud what you are doing. I am definitely a believer.**

Yvonne Brandon, former Direct Marketing Manager, Worldwide e-Business on Demand, Operating Environment Initiatives, IBM:

> **Customers are overwhelmed by marketing messages. Consensual Marketing is the only reasonable go-to-market model that will ensure that your messages are read, seen, and heard. For a company with as many products and services as IBM, profile-based targeting is the only way to assure that the right messages are getting to the right people at the right time.**

Garry Dawson, Manager of Marketing Communications Strategy, Hewlett-Packard, agrees. "Consensual Marketing is mandatory for industry leading firms," he says. "We no longer have the luxury to 'spray and pray' our marketing messages."

How and Why the CMO Process Is Different

The Consensual Marketing Opt-In Process, or CMO, is an evolution versus a revolution. It is an evolution because it builds upon the accumulated knowledge of direct marketing and adds an extra dimension by responding to the rising tide of customer dissatisfaction. Specifically, CMO is built upon some strong pillars of knowledge:

- Customer Relationship Management
- Permission Marketing
- Opt-Out

Customer Relationship Management

The concept behind Customer Relationship Management (CRM) is solid and time-tested. Think back a hundred years and imagine yourself the proprietor of the corner grocery store. You knew each customer by name and had a good understanding of their wants and needs. Every time a customer came in, it gave you a chance to renew the relationship and see how those wants and needs had changed. Your objective was to keep your customers happy and returning to your store. Single transactions were just milestones within a long-term relationship.

But as the world became more complex, we became more distant from the individual customer. CRM provides the technological enablers to reconnect. Thus, in practice, CRM has often been primarily a technology (hardware and software) statement.

Many sources point to Siebel's acquisition of Scopus in the late 1990s as the formal beginning of CRM. Siebel was the industry leading provider of sales force automation. Scopus was the expert in call center automation. The combination of the two formed the technological framework that enabled, and defined, CRM.

Two working definitions of CRM are:

CRM—industry shorthand for customer relationship management— operates on a simple premise: by setting up a system that tracks a customer's every move, you can speed up the time it takes to deliver a service or keep a promise.[2]

CRM (customer relationship management) is an information industry term for methodologies, software, and usually Internet capabilities that help an enterprise manage customer relationships in an organized way. For example, an enterprise might build a database about its customers that described relationships in sufficient detail so that management, salespeople, people providing service, and perhaps the customer directly could access information, match customer needs with product plans and offerings, remind customers of service requirements, know what other products a customer had purchased, and so forth.[3]

Today, the front counter of our grocery store is often "virtual." Our customer base has grown exponentially. We lack physical proximity. Thus, we tell customers about what we have to offer from a distance—via a specific medium, like an ad during the Super Bowl broadcast. This enables us to talk to many customers at one time, but it inhibits our ability to personalize the message to the needs and requirements of the individual, as we used to do at the corner grocery store. But how do we listen to a customer, distribute the information about their needs and requirements, and act upon it? CRM solutions provide the technological enablers, and they are not cheap.

> *"Customer Relationship Management (CRM) has proven to be an expensive technological solution that is marketer driven rather than customer driven. CRM projects that I have been involved with are more concerned about enterprise-wide data gathering and tracking customer contacts without asking the customer the kind, timing or value of the marketing process they are currently experiencing."*— Vincent J. Amen, former Vice President of Public Programs, Franklin Covey; President, Growth Coach

Peppers and Rogers provide an ideal view of the CRM world-to-be:

Eco-sys-tem: the complex of a community of organisms and its environment functioning as an ecological unit. That Merriam-Webster definition also applies to Customer Relationship Management. . . . Where CRM is concerned, an ecosystem is a community that functions as one connected whole, where each of the parts is synergistic, and where the sum of those parts—once connected—brings greater value to the whole. In an ideal CRM ecosystem, for instance, one company's SAP system could "talk" to its partner's Siebel or PeopleSoft system.[4]

However, CRM implementations have experienced astonishing failure rates. Gartner and Meta Group, two technology consulting companies, have estimated the failure rate to be 50 to 75 percent. But a recent study found that the actual failure rate is 35 percent, and, as stated in a CRM report, 45 percent of Customer Relationship Management implementations produce definite payback, and the remaining 20 percent are generating some revenue.[5]

No matter how you define a failure, no organization can support huge technological investments without returns in a relatively short period of time.

There is a feeding frenzy to place the blame for these failures. Is it the developers, the vendors, the value-added resellers (VARS), the hype, the promises, the support organizations? Our view regarding the CRM failures is that corporations have failed at:

- Integration—from the top of the corporation to the bottom, aligning goals, funding, departments, compensation, and channels of communication
- Effective planning and empowerment of the integrated organization to bring the planning to fruition
- Implementing an effective, repeatable, go-to-market process
- Developing and implementing comprehensive bottom-line metrics, enabling real-time improvements

CMO forces us to rethink the parameters and methodology of customer engagement—to engage, learn, and act upon individual preferences. CRM provides the technological tools. To illustrate: A large high-tech manufacturer committed the organization to CRM, acquired the technology, and invested in the internal research to determine what existing customer information they had and what additional information they might need. The result, the "Achilles' heel," was evident:

- Analysis determined that a desirable data field would be what technology a decision maker is currently interested in. Management determined that it would be too expensive to ask customers this question and record the answers. Instead, the field is populated with information about the most recent purchase. The data is thus incorrect per the definition of that data field and will mislead marketers. This was a very expensive mistake!
- Analysis also indicated that as contact frequency increased, customer satisfaction and response rates decreased. Thus management determined a threshold for each medium regarding how frequently a customer could be contacted. Management also named an internal "customer advocate" who would review all marketing plans per these thresholds. However, rather than a revenue-generating "line" executive, the customer advocate had a staff function. Moreover, the advocate has only the power to suggest changes regarding content, frequency, or if the communication should not be sent to a particular customer group. Advocates cannot enforce the changes.

Permission Marketing

The next reference point is Permission Marketing. Seth Godin, an early proponent of this concept, if not the founder, offers the following:

Steps to Permission Marketing
1. The marketer offers the prospect an incentive for volunteering.
2. Using the attention offered by the consumer, the marketer offers a curriculum over time, teaching the consumer about the product or service.
3. The incentive is reinforced to guarantee that the prospect maintains the permission.
4. The marketer offers additional incentives to get even more permission from the consumer.
5. Over time, the marketer leverages the permission to change consumer behavior and turn it into profits.[6]

The concept was revolutionary in that it focused on the customers and treated them as individuals, as opposed to B-52 media bombing runs where the objective is to keep hammering them until someone gives up and buys. Unfortunately, in practice, today's permission marketing is applied primarily to the "e" medium and usually means, "May I please have your e-mail address because I want to send you stuff?" Permission also seems to be transferable—you responded to a survey, so I can sell your name and then you receive generic Viagra ads.

Don Schultz, Professor Emeritus at Northwestern University, Medill School of Journalism, and founder of the Agora, Inc., consultancy, says:

> **Permission marketing is nothing more than saying: yeah, it's okay to bombard me. I've got a bomb shelter here so come drop whatever you want on me. It doesn't matter. There are many people who are now saying, I don't want to hear from you at all. Those numbers are growing and the reason they're growing is because the things marketing people are sending out and bombing them with are not relevant to them. They're only relevant to the marketer who wants to sell something. The old model is: if I keep bombarding you with this stuff, eventually you'll give up and say okay. But today, people are saying there is too much of this stuff going on. I'll figure out what's relevant and just ignore all the other stuff.**

CMO builds further on the foundation of permission marketing in the following key ways:

- It covers all media.
- The incentive offered is value. Value as the customer defines it. It is that delivery of value over time that creates the competitive advantage.
- This is a closer relationship, defined per the customers' terms.
- The burden is on the marketer to provide the ongoing value and nurture the relationship.

Opt-Out

The third reference point for CMO is opt-out. Unquestionably, a legitimate opt-out option should be part of every correspondence, no matter what the medium. If we have crossed the line and annoyed, irritated, or repeatedly presented no value to a customer or prospect, they should have the right to say "Stop."

This appears so basic that, from a moral point of view, it is unbelievable that we need legislation and penalties to ensure that marketers take this step. But promoting national opt-out lists, regardless of the medium, is not the long-term answer. Opt-out lists put the burden on the customer. The message is that marketers have the right to send you anything they want at any time and that you, Mr. or Ms. Consumer, must take the initiative to stop the flow. This does not address the root cause—it is a Band-Aid. If marketers continue on the current path of irresponsibility, each new opt-out list will vie with the National Do Not Call Registry for supersonic growth.

Instead, the burden should be on the marketer. This is the Consensual Marketing Opt-In Process. If marketers wish to attract and keep customers, they must learn their needs and requirements and deliver value over time.

"There is sensory overload in all aspects of life, and consumers feel the need to control what they can. Consumers realize that technology and the momentum of public opinion give them more control over whether, when, and how marketing messages reach them."— Stephen J. Kimmerling, Conference Program Manager, Direct Marketing Association

Why Commit to CMO: What's in It for Me?

In the short term, CMO will generate improved results and increased revenue. The incredible depth and quality of the database will generate an immediate payback. Longer term, you should expect:

- Minimum 15 percent reduction in marketing waste
- A 12 to 19 percent response, or higher
- A 100 percent increase in field follow-up to leads
- Minimum 21 percent increase in sales
- Minimum 15 percent increase in customer satisfaction

And while our crystal ball is a little cloudy, we believe that Consensual Marketing will substantially increase Customer Lifetime Value and correspondingly decrease marketing waste.

This is a "how to" book—how to take this new process of Consensual Marketing and implement it at your company. As you implement—push the borders and innovate! It requires hard work, vision, and some risk because you will be swimming against the current.

Certainly, there are innumerable pressures on you, the marketer, to continue with the status quo, to take this as an interesting interlude, then go back to your office and do the same old, same old. Please, we encourage you to read on and to test the components of the Consensual Marketing Opt-In Process. Let the results speak for themselves.

What This Book Will Do for You

We believe the process of Consensual Marketing will transform direct marketing and open up many new paths to profitability. Thus, we wrote this book not just to tell you about the concept, but to give you a manual for implementing it.

This book will provide you with:

- The rationale for, and complete explanation of, the Consensual Marketing Opt-In Process
- The strategies and tactics for implementation
- A step-by-step "how to" manual
- Real-world case studies with the statistics and results, as well as the lessons from stumbles and missteps

An Overview of What's to Come

We'll take the Consensual Marketing Opt-In Process and break it down into its component parts. For each step in the CMO process we will provide the rationale and "how to" instructions.

Chapter 1 Bringing the Benefits of CMO to Your Company
- The rationale for CMO
- The state of the industry today
- Understanding and leveraging the Customer Life Cycle

- Speed bumps on the road to Consensual Marketing
- Is Consensual Marketing for you?
- Seven Steps for Achieving Breakthrough Marketing

Chapter 2   Step One: Focus on the Customer Relationship and Increase Your Profitability Now, and Over Time

The first step in the CMO process revolves around the customer. We will discuss concepts that appear basic but are bedrock—concepts that must be in place to ensure successful implementation. And while they may appear simple, you will find them to be 180 degrees from much of the marketing thinking currently in practice. The chapter provides "how to" and implementation guidelines regarding:

- Focusing on the relationship versus the immediate sale
- Defining a customer relationship
- The concept of Customer Lifetime Value, and an easy, quick formula
- Identifying customers with the highest propensity to buy
- Determining the propensity to buy of prospects—starting with the first contact
- Guidelines for building the Consensual Database

Chapter 3   Step Two: Voice of Customer Research

The second step in the CMO process is implementing Voice of Customer (VOC) Messaging and Communication Research. This chapter will explain this specialized research technique, how it differs from other forms of research, its value to you, and its contribution to the Consensual Marketing Opt-In Process. Concepts covered include:

- The rationale for this technique and its benefits to you
- Validating critical marketing issues per VOC
- Setting research goals
- Establishing the Research Matrix
- Important questions you should consider asking your customers and prospects
- Significant lessons from previous VOC Research

Chapter 4   Step Three: How to Integrate Media and Message

The third step in the CMO process is understanding and applying the Integrated Direct Marketing methodology. IDM concentrates on surrounding customers with an effective mix of media and informed choices to create the most relevant, compelling, and competitively differentiating customer experience. This chapter provides insights and lessons from more than 20 years of testing and rolling out IDM implementations to help you reduce waste and dramatically increase response. Our focus will be how to select, sequence, and integrate your media mix and message so you will generate a double-digit response every time.

In this chapter we will discuss:

- The rationale for and definition of IDM
- Dangers of the traditional "two percent solution"
- Organizational silos
- Surrounding the customer with an effective mix of media and response options
- The art and science of integrating and synchronizing media and message

Chapter 5   Step Four: Let's Get Real about E-marketing

The fourth step in the CMO process concerns the logical and profitable deployment of the Internet—Web sites and e-mail—as part of the IDM Media Mix. The chapter will provide the "how to" information to help you integrate this important medium to its greatest value and return on investment.

Concepts we will cover to help you increase the effectiveness of e-mail include:

- Let's get real about e-mail
- E-mail is primarily a retention tool
- Prospect by affinity
- Substitute trust for permission
- Develop and deploy e-mail per CMO best practices

Concepts we will address to help you increase the value of the Internet include:

- Integrating the Internet
- Maximizing the value of the Internet's customer experience
- Primary uses of the Internet
- Generating and updating the Consensual profile via the Web
- Retail and the Web
- Search Engine Marketing (SEM)

Chapter 6   Step Five: Rethinking Customer Care

The fifth step in the CMO process focuses on proactive customer service as a powerful competitive differentiator. Additionally, this chapter will discuss the Customer Care Center and how the highest quality of inbound and outbound telecontact can deliver exceptional customer value and service.

Concepts we will cover include:

- Customer care as a powerful competitive differentiator
- The Customer Care Center
- A single, empowered point of contact
- Implementing the customer care process
- Elevating the status of the rep
- Creating the inside/outside partnership with field sales
- Requirements for the successful integration of inbound into the media mix
- Interactive scripting
- Guidelines for achieving IDM and CMO quality telesales

Chapter 7   Step Six: Metrics That Fuel Continuous Improvement

The sixth step in the CMO process involves the metrics that enable the marketer to make real-time improvements to the marketing process—essential to the overall efficiency of Consensual Marketing. This chapter will provide you with the productivity and quality metrics, and identify the key indicators that leverage the greatest response. We also will offer recommendations regarding analysis and next steps—how to turn data into information and what to do with that information.

Concepts we will cover include:

- The rationale for productivity and quality metrics
- Source coding as a prerequisite

- Metrics and key indicators for:
  - PR
  - Direct response print advertising
  - Direct mail
  - Fax
  - Inbound and outbound telecontact
  - E-mail and Internet
  - Field sales
- The Marketer's Daily Dashboard Report
- Guidelines for constructing a Projectable Testing Matrix
- Constructing a Response Curve as a forecasting tool
- Expense to Revenue (E:R) Guidelines

Chapter 8   Step Seven: Checklists to Help You Implement Consensual Marketing

There are two parts to the seventh and last step in the CMO process, both of which are essential to bringing this new discipline to your company and "going live" with CMO:

Part I, "A Checklist for Managing Organizational Change," will address the following issues:

- How to handle the "rubber band" effect of corporate change
- Increasing your effectiveness as a change agent
- Why CMO programs fail (and how to succeed)
- The psychology of change management: four conditions for changing mindsets

Part II is a step-by-step outline for building your own CMO plan and focuses on the 15-point Executive Checklist for implementation.

Throughout the book, we will include comprehensive case studies with the details and the results to show you how Consensual Marketing works in the real world and the benefits it can bring to your company.

To finish off this introduction to the book it's fitting to consider the real-world view of David Sable, Vice Chairman and President, Worldwide Operations, Wunderman:

Consumers are bombarded with advertising messages. Our customers spend more time filtering and editing out messages than

they do listening, reading, or reacting to them. Some marketers believe that technology is the answer to the problem—technology that "manages" the contacts and through this management pushes more sales. It's not working. I'm a consumer, and the only technology I obsess about is technology that can empower the user to keep all marketing messages out of their life from print to the Web to broadcast.

Consensual Marketing is the only answer. Give the participant the power to create their own speed and rhythm of dialogue, and give them equal or better value for every move they make.

Bringing the Benefits of CMO to Your Company

Indisputable Truths, but We Are Not Paying Attention!

The key to creating a successful customer relationship and lengthening that relationship is the delivery of value, initially and over time. And it is an indisputable truth that the only arbiter of value is the customer.

Here are three other indisputable truths:

- We need customers more than they need us.
- They have many choices besides us.
- Loyalty cannot be taken for granted . . . it must be earned every day.

Yet that's not how we treat customers. The following is an oversimplification of the behavior of most marketers:

- Assume that the universe revolves around us and our products
- Take customers for granted
- Focus on getting more new customers versus retaining existing customers
- Approach marketing through the Pasta Principle, i.e., throw enough marketing messages against the marketplace and hope that something sticks

- Focus on making the next sale versus increasing Customer Lifetime Value
- Create confusion by sending buyers everything under the sun that's for sale, regardless of their needs (don't worry—they'll figure it out)

The Fastest Way to Be Forgotten Is to Buy

What do customers say about all this? Here are a few examples from ERDM's Voice of Customer Messaging and Communication Research:

- "The fastest way to be forgotten is to buy."
- "What's the value of your communications?"
- "You flood me with mail instead of taking the time to understand what information you should be sending."
- "Please, no more e-mails that take a year to download."
- "I get one garbage can a day of unsolicited, irrelevant information."
- "You are not providing me with the information I need to make an informed decision."

The scenarios are familiar. We sold a customer a large ticket item. Now, the customer can't get the time of day from the rep. Why? Because we need new sales and this person already bought.

Someone buys, and their name hits our legacy database like a bullet! Because our company is organized (and marketing is funded) by product, each product manager includes this new customer on his or her list plan. The logic is sound—select the hot list of proven buyers. But we forgot the relevancy issue—we forgot who this customer really is. So we punish the customer with a barrage of communications that conflict and confuse. ("If I just invested and bought product A from you, why in the world would I then turn around and buy product B?")

The road to increasing long-term profitability is built by identifying our best customers and focusing our attention on increasing their lifetime value. Of course, we must always prospect because there is always customer attrition. We must also realize that a good customer is a goose laying golden eggs. How many eggs are reasonable to expect?

Let's take off our marketing hats for a moment and be consumers. Consider the following examples, drawn from our own lives and how we experience the dissonance of today's marketing communications:

When we remodeled our kitchen our family decided to take out a long-term repair policy with GE, the manufacturer of our appliances. We felt that the expense of insurance against high repair costs was worth it. So when we received a notice (Figure 1.1) that it was time to renew, we did just that. Then, several weeks later, we got a similar notice—it's time to renew! To make sure our renewal hadn't been lost, we called customer service. They informed us that five mailings are sent

Service Protection Plus™

P.O. Box 100
Rapid City, SD 57709-0100
www.GEAppliances.com

Service Protection Plus Renewal

Roman Ernan

Respond Today!
1-800-626-2224
www.GEAppliances.com/spp

Don't lose your protection against costly appliance repairs!

Dear Roman Ernan:

You're about to lose valuable coverage provided under your Service Protection Plus™ plan.

The protection you've had against service or repairs to your dryer is about to lapse. Your dryer is now 6 year(s) old, and is more likely than ever to require service or repairs. Without Service Protection Plus, the cost of any labor or replacement part will come out of your own pocket.

There's still a short time to continue your coverage!

It's still possible to renew your Service Protection Plus plan, but you must act immediately. If you respond now, your coverage will be extended.

When you renew your Service Protection Plus plan, you will continue to receive these benefits:

- **Professional service by experienced technicians**. When your appliance needs service or repairs, you're assured that the work will be performed by highly-skilled technicians familiar with your specific appliance.

- **Personal financial protection**. Your Service Protection Plus plan will continue to cover the expense of both functional parts and labor on all operating components that fail during normal use. So – even if your appliance needs major repairs – you won't pay an extra cent.

- **Unlimited quality customer service**. With Service Protection Plus, you can tell us as often as necessary, whenever you need help.

Don't lose your benefits! Renew your Service Protection Plus plan today.

For your convenience we now offer an automatic payment option. Never worry about missing a payment! Your payments are paid automatically through your checking or credit card.

(Over, please)

GE Service Protection Plus™ is a trademark of the General Electric Company. See enclosed terms and conditions for complete details.
FW18D19M 1401

Figure 1.1 GE Appliance Letter: Service Protection Plus Renewal

in the renewal series and it doesn't matter whether or not we buy or when we buy. Everyone gets all five!

Following 9/11, we received this letter (Figure 1.2), which we believe talks about sorrow and the commitment to make things better. However, no one here speaks Spanish!

While reading the *Wall Street Journal* we were struck by the offensive scare tactics of this full-page ad for term life insurance (Figure 1.3).

While reading the mail (snail) we came across a catalog. On the cover was one of those terrific Bose radio/CD players. And the deal was terrific! Pay for it over 12 months—zero percent interest. So, on an impulse we called to purchase. The rep answered, and we asked for the special offer. The rep said, "What are you looking at?" The latest catalog, we told him. "Hold on." After several minutes the rep returned and said, "You're right. I just got a copy and I see the offer on the cover, but it's not in my computer." He suggested we look for the offer on their Web site. Not there. Not my problem—I'd like to buy and go on about my day. "I'm sorry, sir, but I can't enter the order if it's not in my computer." We asked to speak to a supervisor. Same story. We asked to speak with their supervisor. "I'm sorry, sir; we are unable to sell you this item at this time. If you would please call back later . . . " It took under a minute to find a competitor with a similar offer.

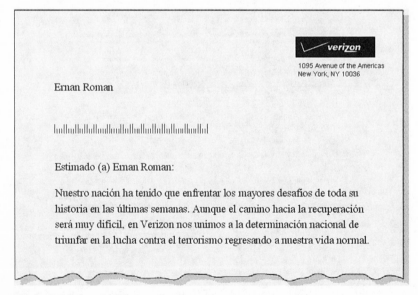

Figure 1.2 Spanish Verizon Letter

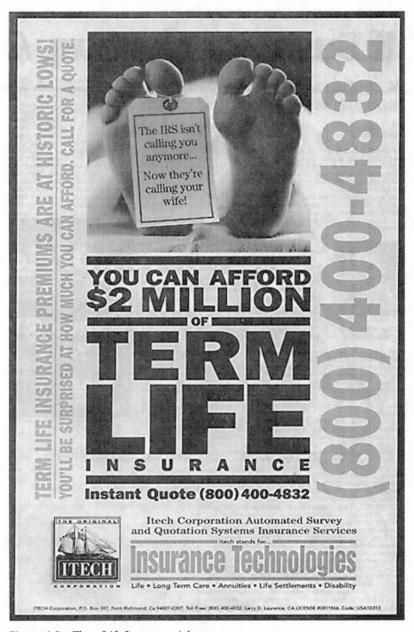

Figure 1.3   Term Life Insurance Ad

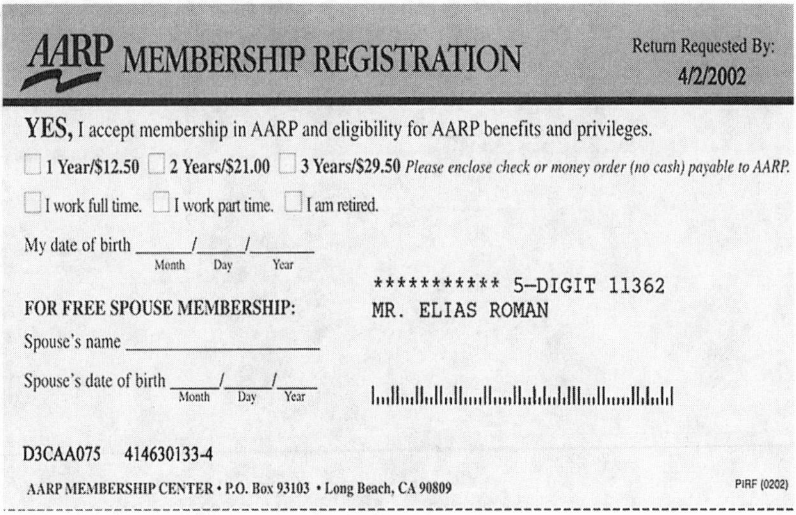

AARP MEMBERSHIP REGISTRATION

Return Requested By:
4/2/2002

YES, I accept membership in AARP and eligibility for AARP benefits and privileges.

☐ 1 Year/$12.50 ☐ 2 Years/$21.00 ☐ 3 Years/$29.50 *Please enclose check or money order (no cash) payable to AARP.*

☐ I work full time. ☐ I work part time. ☐ I am retired.

My date of birth _____/_____/_____
　　　　　　　 Month　 Day　 Year

FOR FREE SPOUSE MEMBERSHIP:

Spouse's name _____

Spouse's date of birth _____/_____/_____
　　　　　　　　　 Month　 Day　 Year

*********** 5–DIGIT 11362
MR. ELIAS ROMAN

|ııllııllıllııllııllııllıılıılıllllııllıııllılılıl|

D3CAA075　414630133-4

AARP MEMBERSHIP CENTER • P.O. Box 93103 • Long Beach, CA 90809

PIRF (0202)

Figure I.4 AARP Membership Registration

When our son Elias turned 18 it was a unique life moment. We probably celebrated for a week. Cards, letters, and good wishes came in from relatives all over the world. Included was this invitation (Figure 1.4) for Elias to join AARP (formerly known as the American Association of Retired Persons).

Predatory, Arrogant, and Insular

Customers have reached an unprecedented level of suspicion and alienation. They see marketers as predatory, arrogant, and insular. Take a look at Figure 1.5. It is one of the most unbelievable scams we've seen. It's an unsolicited fax—titled, if you will: THE BEST OFFERS YOU'LL EVER GET BY FAX.

If you want the services they promote, you have to call a 900 number. If you want to opt-in to their service, you have to call a 900 number. If you want to opt-out, it's a 900 number. The small print says: "Calls to 1-900 numbers cost $3.95 per minute and should take between 1 and 2 minutes in standard mode." So if we can stay in standard mode and don't flip our lid, we could pay Info4U Ltd. $7.90 for the privilege of not receiving their insulting stuff ever again!

Figure 1.5 Unsolicited Fax Ad

Companies rally under the flag of Customer Relationship Management, but in most cases CRM is confined to back office technology. Right now we have more technology than we know what to do with.

Despite the hoopla and promises surrounding CRM, marketers remain focused on the immediate sale, not the relationship. Customers aren't fooled.

To address this crisis, we need to focus on the customer. Technology is, at best, an enabler. It is not a substitute for strategy.

We Are No Longer in Charge

Which brings us to the last indisputable fact. The rules of the game have changed. We're no longer in the driver's seat. The customer is now in charge and calling the shots. Don Schultz, of the Medill School of Journalism, Northwestern University, helps us to see the forest in spite of all the trees:

Here's the situation: Technology has essentially taken away any kind of product differentiation. Everybody's using the same communication techniques. Everybody's selling through the same sales channels. And because the customer now has so many alternatives and so many choices, the customer really is the one that is driving the marketplace. The customer is now in charge.

We continue to use a model that was developed in the 1950s . . . the four Ps—product, price, place, and promotion. But the customer is never mentioned—it's all internally focused. It makes the assumption that if the marketers can control those four things, customers will fall in line and do whatever the marketer wants them to. Back when that model was developed, right after WWII, it worked. The marketer had control over everything. Marketers decided what to make, when to make it, how many to make, what colors to put them in, how to price it, how to communicate it. The marketer controlled the entire system. That's not true today. Easy access to information and product and service alternatives totally destroy the marketing control model.

The marketer says I want to buy a whole lot of television and I'm going to throw it at you. But the customer is sitting there saying most of this stuff is irrelevant to me. It doesn't matter. You're not talking about things that are interesting to me and you're not talking about things that are valuable to me. And as a result, customers are just screening it out.

Everything today is built on a supply chain model. I make a bunch of stuff, I think I add value by adding things to it as it goes through the chain. But, I really have no clue as to what the customer wants, so I don't know how they even consider value. We need to look at demand chains. What do customers want and how do I match my organization to what they want and what they need? The customer today is managing you to fit you and your products into what things work for them. You're really not managing anything but a distribution system. The customer is managing you in their lifestyle.

Testing has shown that the answer to this conundrum is the Consensual Opt-In Marketing Process.

10 Percent, 160 Percent, 176 Percent

Customers are actively communicating their displeasure by opting out of the marketing process.

The Direct Marketing Association, the trade association for the direct marketing industry, compiles three "Preference" lists. One is for direct mail, one is for telemarketing, and one is for e-mail. People who are averse to a particular medium send their name to the DMA and ask to be included on the list. So, if, as a consumer, you become irate at receiving calls during dinner and of asking each caller to remove your name from their list, you would ask the DMA to include your name on their Telephone Preference File. Responsible marketers use this list to suppress or remove these names from their calling files.

The process is the same for direct mail and e-mail. If you no longer wish to receive promotional mail or e-mail, you send your name to the DMA and opt out of the marketing process.

Scary indicators in one year:[1]

- The DMA's Mail Preference File increased *10 percent.* The trend has been steady, 10 percent per year, for several years.
- The Telephone Preference File increased by *65 percent.* The year before, it increased 25 percent.
- The E-mail Preference (Opt-Out) List increased by *176 percent.*

These facts illustrate the explosion in customer dissatisfaction.

The experience of some of our clients and their internal reports tells us that the rate of name removal is growing at 600 percent per year! The opt-out rate for some promotions can match or exceed the sales rate. Customers are increasingly opting out because they are not finding value in the communication process. Communication is the gatekeeper: without it, no relationship.

30 Million Opt-Outs in Five Weeks

It's not just that there is a disconnect—there is a chasm between the marketer and the customer. The customer is calling to us from the other side telling us what they want, but we choose not to listen. The customer then turns to the government for protection from our predatory practices. Legislation speaks very loudly and paints with a very broad brush.

The best example is the National Do Not Call Registry. State-sponsored do not call lists and the DMA's Telephone Preference File did not stop the tsunamic surge of robotic telemarketers calling us during dinner because of loopholes and lack of enforcement. So consumers went to Capitol Hill for relief—specifically the Federal Trade Commission.

Now, violators will be subject to a fine of $11,000 per violation.

According to the Associated Press in 2003: "The FTC expects people to register up to 60 million phone numbers in the first year. There are about 166 million residential phone numbers in the United States."[2]

On June 28, 2003, nearly 250,000 consumers registered to stop telemarketing calls within the first two hours that the service was available. Servers were swamped. By July 9 over 23 million requests had been logged. By August 6 the list topped 30 million. That's 30 million in about five weeks.

Direct Newsline, a daily marketing newsletter, reports that Vertis, a provider of marketing technology, conducted a survey to gauge consumer reaction to and usage of the new National Do Not Call Registry. Eighty percent of the respondents were aware of the national DNC list; 30 percent had actually signed up. But 68 percent said they planned to register in the future.[3]

It seems that the FTC's prediction of 60 million in the first year is fairly conservative.

The details in the DMA chart (Figure 1.6, beginning on page 30) on making a sale via telemarketing under the FTC's new regulations are intricate and well laid out. However, as we read through, we can't help but wonder: Did we need the government to tell us how to do this? If we were focused on the customer relationship, not just the immediate sale, wouldn't we take all these steps anyway?

A recent study from InsightExpress conducted after the implementation of the National Do Not Call Registry determined that 83 percent of consumers would like to see similar legislation enacted to curb spam.[4]

But the United States is nowhere near as restrictive as Europe. Charles A. Prescott, Vice President, International Business Development & Government Affairs for the Direct Marketing Association, fills us in:

The European Data Protection Directive of 1995 has had a major impact on the use of direct marketing. That Directive requires each of the member states to adopt legislation that sets a mini-

mum standard of privacy as described in the Directive itself. And all member states, except France, have adopted legislation in accordance with that requirement. The Directive states that a member state will not capture, use, or manipulate personal information about individuals unless there is a legal basis for doing so. There are two aspects to this basis. The first is consent—if the individual formally consents to your using their name and address for marketing. The second is if there is a legal requirement that the data be gathered, such as employee information, social security number, etc.

Here's how all this legislation works in the real world. For instance, you need information to fulfill a commitment you've made to somebody when you enter into a contract. So, if I call up a company and ask them to please deliver a new suit to me, they will ask me for my name, address, and credit card, and are perfectly justified in doing so. But usage of the name ends there—the company cannot use the name for any other purpose without gaining another level of consent. If you get personal information, under the Directive you have to use it only for the purpose for which you gathered it. Now that goes to the very core of the building of prospect databases. In the United States, once you have given a company your name and address, that information is considered to be fair game for marketing. Not the case in Europe under the Data Protection Directive.

The Directive also gives each country a little leeway as far as direct marketing is concerned. In practical terms, if a name and address is collected by a magazine, they can let someone else make an offer to that individual provided within that offer there is a very clear indication of the legal right to opt out. Many European countries have legislated the DMA's privacy promise. A couple of countries have been even more stringent than that. Italy and Spain have said we don't care about the Directive—you can't market to people through any media—telephone, e-mail, fax, even letters—unless that individual has affirmatively expressed their permission.

Making A Sale
Under The FTC's New
Telemarketing Sales Rule

KEY

Existing/Unchanged TSR Requirements

Additional/New TSR Requirements

Are You Covered by the Rule?
- Any plan, program, or campaign to sell goods or services through interstate calls,
- Inbound & outbound telemarketing calls,
- Sellers that provide or arrange to provide goods/services to consumers in exchange for payment,
- Most business-to-business calls are exempt, and
- Does not apply to common carriers, airlines, some financial institutions, and insurance companies to the extent regulated under state law. *But the FTC has indicated that the TSR will apply to third party call centers making calls on behalf of exempt entities.*

YES

Make Sure Your Call is Received Between 8 A.M. - 9 P.M.
Sec. 310.4(b)(4)(c) p. 254
(This is also required by the FCC for all marketers who market by phone.)

Honor In-House Suppress Requests
By scrubbing numbers of consumers (prospects & customers) who don't want to be contacted by your company from your company's telephone marketing list.
(This is also required by the FCC for all marketers who market by phone.)

Honor National Do-Not-Call (DNC) Registry
Effective Fall 2003

Calling Customers?

Calling Prospects?

THE
DMA
Direct Marketing Association
Department of Ethics & Consumer Affairs

30

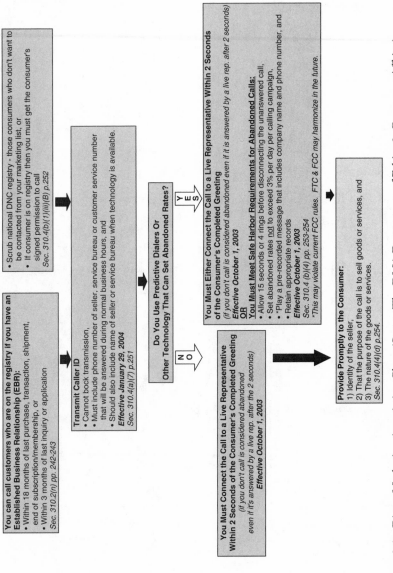

You can call customers who are on the registry if you have an Established Business Relationship (EBR):
- Within 18 months of last purchase, transaction, shipment, end of subscription/membership, or
- Within 3 months of last inquiry or application
  Sec. 310.2(n) pp. 242-243

- Scrub national DNC registry - those consumers who don't want to be contacted from your marketing list, or
- If consumer is on registry then you must get the consumer's signed permission to call
  Sec. 310.4(b)(1)(iii)(B) p.252

Transmit Caller ID
- Cannot bock transmission,
- Must include phone number of seller, service bureau or customer service number that will be answered during normal business hours, and
- Should also include name of seller or service bureau when technology is available.
  Effective January 29, 2004
  Sec. 310.4(a)(7) p.251

Do You Use Predictive Dialers Or Other Technology That Can Set Abandoned Rates?

NO

YES

You Must Connect the Call to a Live Representative Within 2 Seconds of the Consumer's Completed Greeting
(if you don't call is considered abandoned even if it's answered by a live rep. after the 2 seconds)
Effective October 1, 2003

You Must Either Connect the Call to a Live Representative Within 2 Seconds of the Consumer's Completed Greeting
(if you don't call is considered abandoned even if it is answered by a live rep. after 2 seconds)
Effective October 1, 2003
OR
You Must Meet Safe Harbor Requirements for Abandoned Calls;
- Allow 15 seconds or 4 rings before disconnecting the unanswered call,
- Set abandoned rates not to exceed 3% per day per calling campaign,
- *Play a pre-recorded message that includes company name and phone number, and
- Retain appropriate records
  Effective October 1, 2003
  Sec. 310.4 (b)(4) pp. 253-254
  This may violate current FCC rules. FTC & FCC may harmonize in the future.

Provide Promptly to the Consumer:
1) Identity of the seller,
2) That the purpose of the call is to sell goods or services, and
3) The nature of the goods or services.
  Sec. 310.4(d) p.254.

Figure 1.6 Direct Marketing Association Chart (*Source:* The DMA Department of Ethics & Consumer Affairs.)

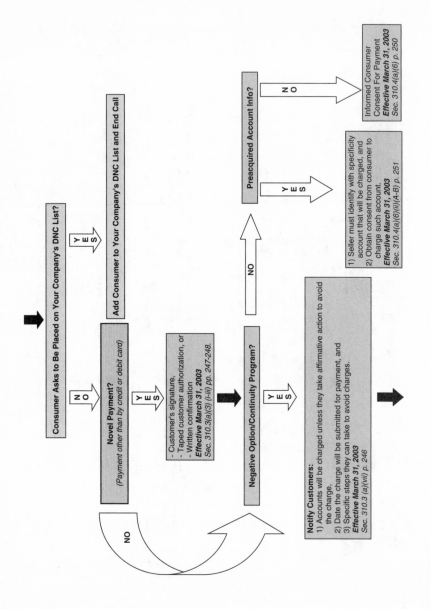

Consumer Asks to Be Placed on Your Company's DNC List?

YES → **Add Consumer to Your Company's DNC List and End Call**

NO →

Novel Payment?
(Payment other than by credit or debit card)

YES →
- Customer's signature,
- Taped customer authorization, or
- Written confirmation
Effective March 31, 2003
Sec. 310.3(a)(3) (i-iii) pp. 247-248.

NO

Negative Option/Continuity Program?

YES →
Notify Customers:
1) Accounts will be charged unless they take affirmative action to avoid the charge,
2) Date the charge will be submitted for payment, and
3) Specific steps they can take to avoid charges.
Effective March 31, 2003
Sec. 310.3 (a)(vii) p. 246

NO

Preacquired Account Info?

YES →
1) Seller must identify with specificity account that will be charged, and
2) Obtain consent from consumer to charge such account.
Effective March 31, 2003
Sec. 310.4(a)(6)(ii)(A-B) p. 251

NO →
Informed Consumer Consent For Payment
Effective March 31, 2003
Sec. 310.4(a)(6) p. 250

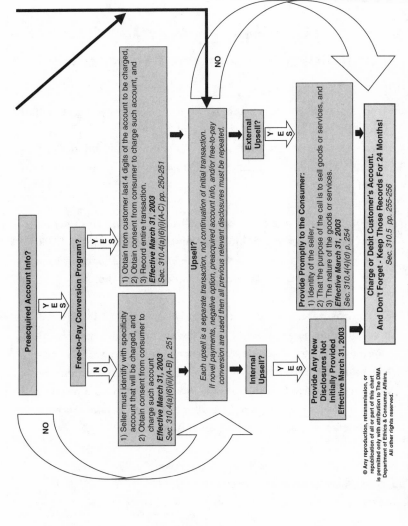

Preacquired Account Info?

Free-to-Pay Conversion Program?

YES

1) Obtain from customer last 4 digits of the account to be charged,
2) Obtain consent from consumer to charge such account, and
3) Record entire transaction.
Effective March 31, 2003
Sec. 310.4(a)(6)(i)(A-C) pp. 250-251

NO

1) Seller must identify with specificity account that will be charged, and
2) Obtain consent from consumer to charge such account
Effective March 31, 2003
Sec. 310.4(a)(6)(ii)(A-B) p. 251

Upsell?
Each upsell is a separate transaction, not continuation of initial transaction.
If novel payments, negative option, preacquired account info, and/or free-to-pay conversion are used then all previous relevant disclosures must be repeated.

NO

External Upsell?

YES

Internal Upsell?

YES

Provide Any New Disclosures Not Initially Provided
Effective March 31, 2003

Provide Promptly to the Consumer:
1) Identity of the seller,
2) That the purpose of the call is to sell goods or services, and
3) The nature of the goods or services.
Effective March 31, 2003
Sec. 310.4(d) p. 254

Charge or Debit Customer's Account.
And Don't Forget - Keep Those Records For 24 Months!
Sec. 310.5 pp. 255-256

Figure 1.6 Direct Marketing Association Chart (*Continued*)

Germany, since the 1950s, has in their constitution a very strange phrase—"Informational self-determination." By which they mean an individual has the right to determine what can be done with their personal information. Interestingly, direct marketing in Germany is extraordinarily healthy.

The Rationale for CMO: Indisputable Facts We Are Ignoring

There is an urgent need for a real breakthrough in marketing. Budgets are shrinking, costs are rising, and, to top it off, response rates are falling.

The only indicator that is showing phenomenal growth is opt-out rates. In short, we are in a crisis. Garry Dawson of Hewlett-Packard's Marketing Communication, Enterprise Systems Group, has an opinion on this subject:

> Hewlett-Packard, like many companies, contributed to the rising tide of e-mail programs. Spam complaints rose dramatically. Click-through rates declined over time. The cost per lead increased to equal or exceed other Marketing Communication choices.
>
> E-mail was perceived to be inexpensive and fast to implement. It's something new to do over the old standard of direct mail. This follows the trend of additional telemarketing done over the past few years. Unfortunately, we found that broadcast communications are perceived as increasingly intrusive and have a negative effect on orders and loyalty. The allure of quick results sacrifices the benefits of customer retention and loyalty.

Dianne J. Lucca, former Senior Interactive Marketing Manager, IBM Americas, shares her thoughts regarding the effects of marketing short-sightedness:

> The need for consensual database marketing has never been greater than it is today with e-mail marketing. Our weakened economy has put the squeeze on corporate budgets, and companies have turned to e-mail to stretch those budgets. E-mail has been recognized as fast and flexible. You can cut the com-

munications-response cycle drastically and have the flexibility to test and make mid-campaign corrections in a fraction of the time required for direct mail.

The result? Overflowing e-mail in-boxes, increased competition for attention, increased frustration, and an overused medium in need of redirection.

Customers are responding by rescinding their e-mail permissions. At IBM, opt-outs for general marketing have nearly doubled from a year ago.

Our e-mail acquisition efforts also are producing significantly lower results.

In June 2000 we had an e-mail acquisition rate of 16.4 percent. A year later we were still adding new e-mail permissions at a rate of 8.0 to 9.3 percent. But our most recent efforts produced a rate of 4 percent.

Is "Faster, Cheaper, Easier" Better?

If we are to remain in business and grow our businesses, we must turn the tide on these dangerous trends.

Companies have certainly invested in all sorts of new technologies that have done their job well. It is now faster, cheaper, and easier to get the messages out, especially with e-mail.

We have learned through experience that the investment in doing direct mail the right way pays off. That means spending the extra money for personalization, for paragraphs that can be varied or changed to address customers' specific needs, for laser printing, for a larger format (e.g., 9 by 12 inches versus a No. 10 package), for first-class postage, etc. For argument's sake, let's say that cost per piece, in the mail, for a traditional B-to-B package may be $3.50. (For insights on direct mail, see Chapter 4.) This expense may appear high, but it has been proven to bring in the revenue.

Interestingly, *Direct Newsline* reports that according to the Vertis survey cited earlier, "some 31 percent of consumers polled said they would prefer to receive a company's product or service information through direct mail . . . 10 percent chose e-mail."[5]

In contrast, we received an e-mail recently that states: "Broadcast e-mail your ad to 28 million for $149." Click through and it offers a turnkey e-mail program, including list rental and everything it takes to get the e-mail out, short of creative input. For argument's sake, let's say creative costs were $1,000. Total cost is then $1,149. Cost per piece is $0.000041!

As we compare the direct mail and e-mail scenarios, companies tend to focus only on expense. We must recognize that faster, cheaper, easier is addictive. And like most addictions, it's taking us down a rat hole. We begin to focus on the "faster, cheaper, easier" and not on the relationship. When discussing a potential e-mail campaign, we overheard one consultant say, "Let's send it to everybody—it's so cheap!" That is seductive when you're in the throes of the addiction. But in the light of day, where's the value to the customer? What is the damage to your customer list?

The Customer Life Cycle

Figure 1.7 represents our view of the Customer Life Cycle. Undoubtedly you will see it again in this book, since it is a core concept.

Traditionally, the relationship with a customer begins with presale communications. The need to provide value here is obvious. We want to close the sale!

However, after the sale, companies often lose interest (sell and run). And then they're usually too busy prospecting for new customers to pay attention to a customer who has just bought.

It's important to remember the results of a study that AT&T did in 1918 and has refreshed periodically: It is five times more expensive to sell to a prospect than to sell to an existing customer.

Thus, the sale begins one of the most crucial communication periods. As customers live with our product or service, they are satisfied or dissatisfied—we are meeting their needs or we are not. And over time, their needs and requirements change. Unless we are in an interactive dialogue with them, where both parties listen and learn, we won't know if they are satisfied or dissatisfied. We won't know if and how their needs and requirements have changed. And we will be stuck with the high cost process of chasing new customers.

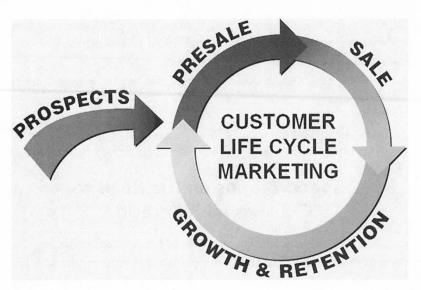

Figure 1.7   Customer Life Cycle

Consensual Marketing keeps us in a real-time dialogue with our customers throughout their life cycle.

CMO Represents an Enormous Opportunity to Improve

We are fortunate as an industry—the financials are such that we can make money on a "typical" 2 percent response rate. Or less.

However, for every 2 percent who say yes, there are 98 percent who said no. So out of every 100 customers, 98 do not respond. The vast majority of customers finds our messages irrelevant, at best, and throw us in the garbage. That is not relationship building.

In 2003, the DMA did a study of 152 e-mail campaigns[6] that found e-mail response rates averaged 1 percent. The highest response rate, of 1.8 percent, was from retail. Other response rates, by segment: travel (1.5 percent), financial products/services (1.1 percent), catalog and publishing (each at 0.8%), and computer/electronic products (0.4 percent).

Web site conversion rates also appear anemic (conversion is defined as a sale). A recent study[7] found that:

- 39 percent of marketers report a conversion rate of 3 percent or less.
- 37 percent experience conversion rates of 3 to 10 percent.
- Only 9 percent have conversion rates over 10 percent.
- 14 percent of executives interviewed did not know their conversion rate.

It certainly seems as if there is enormous opportunity to improve.

Speed Bumps on the Road to Consensual Marketing

All these statistics and facts add up to a cold shower for marketers. No matter how good our intentions, our customers are not happy with our communications and messages. Our targeting is wide of the mark. We are causing customer dissatisfaction, which is antithetical to increasing Customer Lifetime Value.

Aside from the external world, there are internal forces we must reckon with as well.

Corporate Warfare

We understand from the 1,600 hours of VOC Messaging and Communication Research interviews that when customers communicate with us, they see *one* company. They don't envision multiple profit centers, support organizations, and political agendas. It's not their responsibility. They see one company and expect us to be responsive to their needs as one company.

However, the way we are organized prevents us from seeing one customer. This is the first speed bump and leads to many of the others.

The modern corporation is organized by departments—each a silo of information and expertise. All of the component parts of communicating with and servicing the customer are in these separate organizations, or silos: product, management, marketing, telemarketing, and sales, just to name a few.

Each silo is measured differently, which causes a constant state of competing priorities. Marketing is often measured by the amount and cost of the gross leads it produces. They throw the leads over the wall to

Sales, which are measured by net revenue. They catch the leads and pronounce them worthless (competitors and low level functionaries).

Each department or silo thus behaves like a city/state—fortifying its perimeters, posting sentries, always at the ready for armed combat. This leaves little time or energy to focus on the customer.

Funding the Wrong Behavior

The next speed bump on the road is funding by product line versus funding by customer set.

Funding by product line causes two reactions:

1. The acquisition of new customers is more important than retention of existing customers. Existing customers already bought. We need new sales. Now.
2. Customers are viewed more as numbers or demographics than individuals. We are content to infer data from third parties and outside lists versus talking directly to our customers. We use technology to manufacture communications faster, easier, and cheaper, and send them out en masse.

The ultimate measure of success of funding by product line is often a 1 to 2 percent response rate (and some would be grateful for that).

Funding by customer set encourages the logical combination and sequence of messages that are focused on retention and customer satisfaction. Some product promotions may be suppressed or bundled to meet the requirements of the individual customer. The measure of success here is double-digit response.

Culture and Lunch

Which brings us to the most formidable speed bump of them all: corporate culture. A wise man once told us, "Culture eats change for lunch." And he was right.

No matter how good or how necessary change is within an organization, our experience is that corporate culture will fight it tooth and nail. Every single employee may be more successful and make more money once change is implemented, yet most will resist change either openly or subversively.

There are many theories on how to manage cultural change. They all boil down to the fact that change does not happen from the bottom up. Change only happens from the top down.

The "rubber band" theory on corporate change seems to be the simplest and truest: Suspend a rubber band between your thumb and index finger. With your other hand, pinch the middle of the rubber band and pull it to one side. The rubber band represents corporate culture. Without visible consistent management support from the very top, all we can do is stretch the culture. The minute we let go, the rubber band returns to its original state.

In Chapter 8 we go in depth into the change process and how you can successfully manage the "rubber band."

Is Consensual Marketing for You?

Consensual Marketing is not for everyone. If your goods or services are true commodities and compete solely on the basis of price, there may be other go-to-market strategies you want to consider.

If, however, yours are value-added goods or services that do not or should not compete on the basis of price alone, there are few strategies that will be more effective in increasing profitability—immediately and over the long term.

Implementation, however, is complex. Hence, the purpose of this book is to provide you with a "how to" manual to help you implement the Consensual Marketing Opt-In Process.

This book presents the concepts and frameworks for implementation—the *why*, the *how*, and the *what* in terms of expected results. You will learn a better way of marketing, which:

- Is far less wasteful.
- Makes more money, achieving substantial immediate and long-term incremental revenue.
- Solidifies relationships with customers so they stay longer and buy more!

"With Consensual Marketing your company is like a waiter in a restaurant. You've already got the customer, you know they're hungry, and you have a selection of meals for them to choose from. So there you are listening and making special offers on a one-to-one basis.

This is really what direct marketing should aspire to."—Charles A. Prescott, Vice President, International Business Development & Government Affairs, Direct Marketing Association

$594 Million over the Control Group

Now we'd like to share with you the first of the crown jewels of the Consensual Marketing Opt-In Process—world-class case history number one: IBM Focus 1:1, which generated $594 million over the control group. One of IBM's brightest stars, Yvonne Brandon, former Direct Marketing Manager, Worldwide e-Business on Demand, Operating Environment Initiatives at IBM, was a key executive and will share her insights and lessons throughout this section.

This case study proves that the CMO process works, that it is more than just theory. The following chapters will provide you with the "how to" information for implementing CMO at your company.

Case History: IBM Focus 1:1

IBM divides the United States into distinct geographic "trading areas," each with its own marketing and sales teams. The company measures (and compensates) its trading areas not only by sales and profits, but also by customer satisfaction. IBM has done many studies to quantify how many millions of dollars hinge on each percentage point of satisfaction. There is healthy competition among the trading areas for the highest sales and the highest customer satisfaction scores.

Yvonne Brandon notes that:

During a senior manager's meeting for the Great Lakes trading area (Area 4), led by Area General Manager J. Michael Lawrie (who is now IBM's Senior Vice President and Group Executive, Sales and Distribution), the Area Quality Manager had the unenviable task of presenting the trending of the area's Customer Satisfaction or Net Satisfaction Index (NSI) measurement. It looked as though Area 4 was on track to miss its objective for the year.

Analysis revealed that 221 of our largest customers with older mainframe systems processors installed were tracking two points

below where we needed to be. Furthermore, it looked as though their satisfaction was trending down and would be at least another basis point lower during the next quarter.

IBM had commissioned an extensive study to understand the impact of customer satisfaction on revenue. The study concluded that a 1 percent increase in customer satisfaction translated into $500 million in incremental revenue to IBM over a three-year period.

Mike gave us a simple mission: find the causes of our satisfaction index decline among these customers and fix it!

Voice of Customer Messaging and Communication Research was implemented to probe the causes of dissatisfaction. (Chapter 3 provides the guidelines for implementing VOC Research at your company.) Interviews were conducted by members of the executive management team for two important reasons:

- To let these dissatisfied customers know that IBM recognized their dissatisfaction and took it very seriously
- To send the message that, given IBM's commitment to these customers, the person listening to and probing these issues was the executive in charge of fixing the problems

Yvonne Brandon continues:

We discovered four primary issues:

1. Lack of continuity of coverage
2. A lower than average rating as a solutions provider
3. Too much nonrelevant mail
4. Too many divergent/often conflicting organizations/messages

Specifically, customers were saying:

"You [IBM] change coverage in my account so often that I am consistently reeducating your people on my business and on my business problems."

"You flood me with mail instead of taking time to understand what information you should be sending that is relevant to my business and to my specific needs."

"It is very difficult for me to get answers to my questions and solutions to my problems because I don't know who to call at IBM anymore."

IBM conducted a "test case" investigation into the flow of communications—not from their point of view, but from the point of view of a customer. One example was a Director of Engineering whose responsibilities included the installed RS 6000 computer, graphics, and applications development. Figure 1.8 illustrates the findings:

Within a specific quarter, this Director of Engineering received a blizzard of communications consisting of 35 different categories of messages. Some of the categories spanned several different communication touch points. When these were analyzed in reference to the director's specific computer installation and responsibilities, only 4 of the 35 categories were relevant. Some were outright irrelevant. This led to the term "marketing waste"—the marketing investment in communications and messaging was a waste for both IBM and the customer. As the Director of

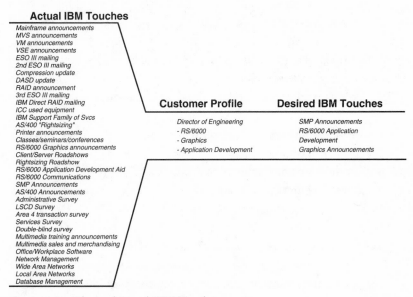

Figure 1.8 Chart of Actual IBM Touches

Engineering put it: "If I'm working on your RS 6000, why are you sending me messages about the AS 400 and mainframe computers? There's nothing I can do with this information."

Yvonne Brandon argues that one of the keys to understanding the frustration caused by receiving large quantities of communications is "the pressure these customers feel to keep on top of technological changes and developments. Many expressed resentment regarding the large amount of irrelevant pieces because it made it difficult and time consuming to get to the ones that would be worthwhile for them."

Here are some examples of customer reactions:

- "If they send too much to me, the things I'm really interested in might be buried and I'll never get to it."
- "I'm sure there is stuff I could use that I never get to because it's buried in the junk."

IBM addressed the two primary areas of customer dissatisfaction (targeting of messages and IBM's lack of responsiveness) through the Focus 1:1 pilot.

Testing the Consensual Marketing Opt-In Process

As explained earlier, there were 221 companies in this initial phase of Focus 1:1, each a major IBM customer. Within these companies, the cross-functional team (including Field Sales) identified five to seven key decision makers. These executives were reached via a mini-IDM campaign of direct mail, e-mail, and face-to-face Field Sales in order to:

- Introduce them to the Consensual concept, set expectations, and gain their buy-in
- Sign them up and complete their initial Customer Interest Profile
- Gain agreement to use their endorsement to get the second level of executives to participate

Yvonne Brandon reveals how it worked at IBM:

Our General Manager insisted that the most effective way to do this was to have the Client Executive or Client Rep for that

account make a face-to-face call on every customer they had nominated, to ask that customer to self-declare their preferences by completing an interest profile.

To help facilitate the face-to-face call, the Direct Marketing team developed a script that the Client Executive was encouraged to use. The purpose of the script was to help the rep articulate to their customer that IBM recognizes we have a communications problem that we had caused, and to let them know how and why we were changing the way we interact with them in order to provide better service. The reps were able to follow the script, giving consistency to what every customer heard about the consensual program that was being planned.

Within each of the 221 targeted companies, IBM involved decision makers and influencers in self-selecting their communication stream by supplying detailed customer information such as:

- Their media preferences and aversions
- Areas of immediate interest
- Areas of future interest
- The desired frequency of communication

IBM needed to find out what kinds of information customers perceived as valuable. Yvonne Brandon says her team asked key questions:

Did their needs involve conceptual, business process, or technical information? Customers had told us that the best way to get this information was to ask them. We developed a profile that mapped to the vast portfolio of hardware products, software, middleware, and services that IBM has to offer. We organized these offerings into logical categories for the purposes of the customer profile and so we could deliver what we promised.

Figure 1.9 is a sample of the initial Interest Profile. It was built with cooperation from the 15 software, product, and services Brand Managers in our Area. The Project Manager for the Focus pilot held regular conference calls with these Brand Managers prior to each mailing to update

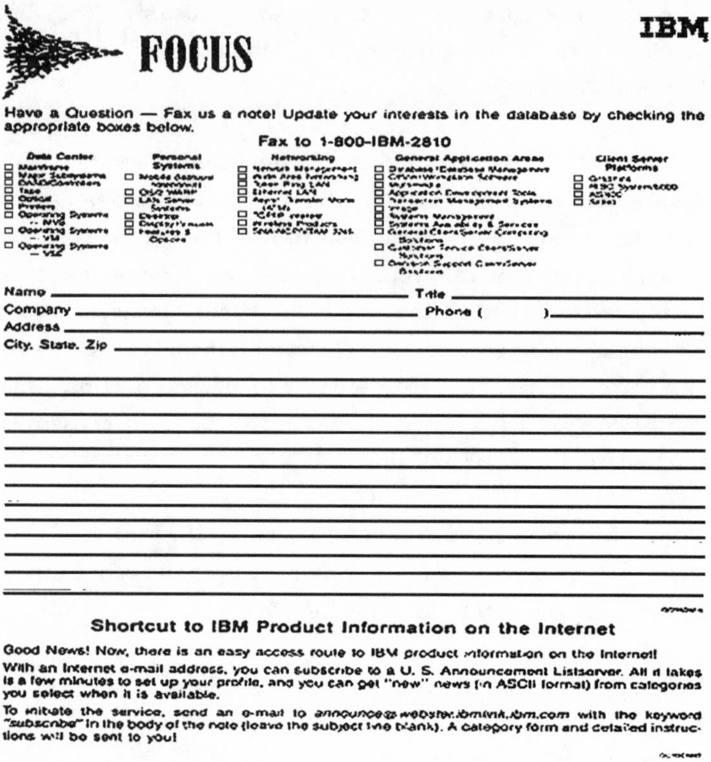

FOCUS

IBM

Have a Question — Fax us a note! Update your interests in the database by checking the appropriate boxes below.

Fax to 1-800-IBM-2810

Data Center | Personal Systems | Networking | General Application Areas | Client Server Platforms

Name ______ Title ______
Company ______ Phone ( ) ______
Address ______
City, State, Zip ______

Shortcut to IBM Product Information on the Internet

Good News! Now, there is an easy access route to IBM product information on the Internet!

With an Internet e-mail address, you can subscribe to a U. S. Announcement Listserver. All it takes is a few minutes to set up your profile, and you can get "new" news (in ASCII format) from categories you select when it is available.

To initiate the service, send an e-mail to announce@webster.ibmlink.ibm.com with the keyword "subscribe" in the body of the note (leave the subject line blank). A category form and detailed instructions will be sent to you!

Figure 1.9 Initial Interest Profile

them on responses and results from the last mailing and to ask them to select meaningful materials to populate the cooperative mailers. Figure 1.10 is a sample of the improved, more modular Interest Profile that evolved from greater participation by the brands, as the project matured.

With this intelligence, IBM was able to develop a personalized calendar of communication. Inherent to this calendar was the concept that each customer would have access to his or her profile at any time. They could change their input and criteria as their responsibilities and interests changed, and their calendar of communications would be updated accordingly.

Customers stated that their areas of interest change over time and that they would appreciate a periodic call from IBM to see if profile changes were required.

Development and implementation of the communications plan came with significant challenges:

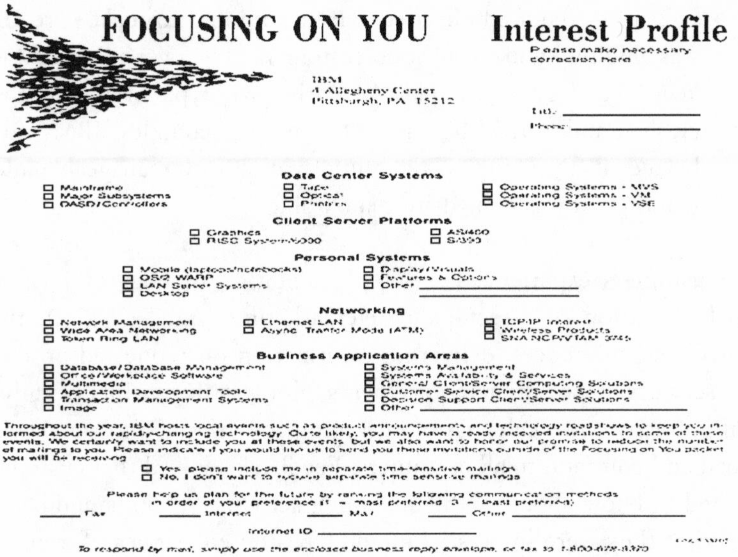

Figure 1.10   Improved Interest Profile

- Developing an effective contact management plan meant negotiating with different profit centers to potentially combine or forgo some communications. Previously, relevancy was in the eyes of the profit center—they were free to touch whomever they wished. Now, relevancy was in the eyes of the customer. IBM promised these customers that they would abide by their wishes. Therefore, when negotiation didn't work, senior management arbitration was called for to limit the messages in accordance with the customer's profile. The message to the profit centers: "We're measuring the Focus 1:1 pilot against a control group to establish bottom line results. Let's see what's better for business."

- Developing an effective coverage plan, or inside/outside partnership between the Marketing Sales Rep or MSR (Field Sales) and an inside telecontact component. The inside rep would always be available for the customer. The outside rep's job was to be out seeing customers. The mechanics and communication flow between the two sides of the partnership had to be worked out to establish an effective, seamless, interactive dialogue with the customer.

- Execution required effective database mining to make sure IBM was abiding by its promise to customers. The overriding rule was keep the database simple. An early prototype of the database crashed and burned because it became too complex. IBM had to balance its thirst for customer information with manageable information that was immediately applicable.

Customers experienced the implementation of Focus 1:1 via the synchronization of direct mail, telemarketing, and "e," given their individual preferences, delivering information on requested products and services as per their requirements, along with reprints of important publicity and a calendar of upcoming activities. This calendar was broad and common to all customers. Feedback showed that customers wanted to know about all the upcoming activities, picking and choosing what they were interested in and advising colleagues of events of particular importance.

Yvonne Brandon explains how "full wave" pieces worked for IBM:

> **To keep the promise of sending only relevant information but at the same time keeping customers informed of other events and products that they might need to know about, we developed a number of what we called "full wave" pieces that were sent to everyone. Those pieces included: a three-month calendar of events, a registration device for those events, and a "Come surf the Web with us" piece listing relevant IBM URLs.**

Creating a Single Point of Entry

IBM learned that their customers wanted one-on-one marketing from a dedicated IBM resource. Customers clamored for one person within IBM whom they could call, someone who would navigate the IBM infrastructure for them rather than simply give them another number to call.

This single point of entry was created specifically for this pilot and for this customer set. Staffed with teams of experienced, empowered IBMers dedicated to customer service, the single point of entry (SPOE) agents were there whenever the customer called.

Yvonne explains how thinking about SPOE forced changes at IBM:

Previously, these accounts were accustomed to having an IBM representative and systems engineer dedicated to covering them. Proposing a telecoverage model was of concern. Nearly 80 percent agreed to this and didn't care who covered them as long as the person assigned could get their questions answered or could deploy the right resource at the right time to solve their specific problem. Later in the project, nearly all the customers selected the telecoverage.

These agents were technologically savvy, so they were conversant in the technical jargon and challenges the customers were experiencing. They knew, within IBM, where to go for information and help. Their mission was to take ownership of whatever issue the customer presented and stay with it until the issue was resolved. And then they followed up to ensure customer satisfaction.

Results of Phase I

As measured against a control population of like accounts, the IBM Focus 1:1 pilot achieved:

- 80 percent increase in sales over the control group
- 75 percent decrease in marketing waste
- 841 percent increase in qualified response
- 82 percent conversion from responses to qualified leads
- 17 percent of the market in presale activity, versus 8 percent previously
- 6 point increase in Customer Satisfaction

The average response rate to any of IBM's tactics with a call to action was 12.5 percent. An unplanned benefit of eliminating unwanted mail to customers was a reduction in direct marketing mailing costs.

Phase II

In Phase II, IBM expanded CMO to embrace a new target market—their top "general business" customers. General business is a catchall phrase signifying those customers who are smaller than IBM's top echelon and rely on mid-sized computers (versus mainframes) to drive their mission-critical applications. This customer set had the same issues with IBM—and IBM was hoping for the same magnitude of improvements from the implementation of the Consensual Marketing Opt-In Process.

Given the success of the Focus 1:1 pilot, an objective was established by senior management to increase membership and include the top general business customers.

Enrollment in the pilot was accomplished via direct mail invitations sent to key contacts. The response rate and pattern are interesting and challenge cost-based skepticism (i.e., those who doubt the effectiveness of direct mail because of its cost). The invitation generated a 33 percent initial response:

- 78 percent via direct mail
- 17 percent via fax
- 4 percent via Internet
- 1 percent via inbound

Also included in the mailing was the provocative question: "What would it take to make you a very satisfied customer?" Customers were not shy about responding. Nor was management reticent in taking immediate, forceful action.

Yvonne explains how it worked:

Senior members of the Area management team were assigned responsibility for personally contacting customers who responded within 24 hours of receiving their complaint or comment. Our goal was to learn what we needed to do to create and maintain very satisfied customers in order to achieve our objective of closing the gap with "best of breed" competition.

In addition to feedback regarding technological and business concerns, IBM found a ringing endorsement of the goals of the Focus 1:1 pilot—to involve customers in self-selecting the content, frequency, and media mix of their communications stream. Specific comments and insights were used in training for the SPOE agents and in subsequent customer communications.

Results of Phase II

- Best of Breed Customer Satisfaction scores (outdistancing all other IBM regions)
- Incremental $594 million over control group

The balance of this book is structured to provide you with the insights, the guidelines, and the "how to" information to implement the Consensual Marketing Opt-In Process at your organization and achieve similarly outstanding results. Please read on.

2

Step One: Focus on the Customer Relationship and Increase Your Profitability Now, and Over Time

T HE FIRST STEP in the Consensual Marketing Opt-In Process revolves around the customer. We will discuss concepts that appear basic but are bedrock. These concepts must be in place to ensure successful implementation. And while they may appear simple, you will find them to be 180 degrees from much of the marketing thinking currently in practice. We will provide you with "how to" and implementation guidelines regarding:

- Focusing on the relationship versus the immediate sale
- Defining a customer relationship
- The concept of Customer Lifetime Value—an easy, quick formula
- Identifying customers with the highest propensity to buy
- Determining the propensity to buy of prospects—starting with the first contact
- Guidelines for building the Consensual Database

And throughout, we will present comprehensive case studies with the details and the results to show you how Consensual Marketing works in the real world.

What's a Relationship?

The Consensual Marketing definition of a relationship is very practical: a pattern of ongoing purchases reinforced by the mutual exchange of value and satisfaction throughout the customer life cycle. Similarly, we define the notion of loyalty in practical terms: an increase in Customer Lifetime Value. LTV is the value of all the current and future revenue realized from a customer relationship.

While many of the direct marketing theorists describe relationships and loyalty in flowery, futuristic terms, we like dealing with the cold, hard facts, thus removing the emotion from the definition. Lester Wunderman's definition[1] is terrific:

> **We have so many buzzwords in this business—for example, loyalty and relationships. I've said this before: Loyalty suggests the willingness to sacrifice. I'm loyal to my country. I'm loyal to my family. If someone breaks into my house, I'm going to risk my life defending them. Would I risk it for toothpaste? It's ridiculous. We don't sell our loyalty. What we're really talking about is negotiating a proclivity to repurchase—that's what it's all about. If you phrase it that way, you begin to see what to do about it. . . . Take the emotion out of it.**

Focusing on the Relationship

Moving from tactics that focus on grabbing that immediate sale to a disciplined process to increase Customer Lifetime Value requires an understanding of the stages of the Customer Life Cycle and the importance of maintaining an ongoing stream of interactive communications with your customers. This was illustrated in the previous chapter and is depicted again in Figure 2.1.

The energy and budgets of most marketers are devoted to the presale and sale phases. They prospect and close. Then their view changes. This

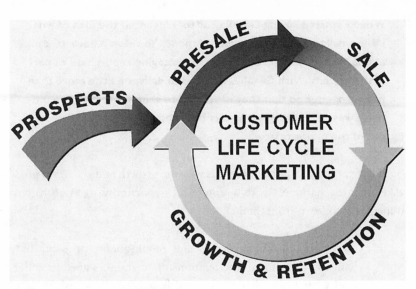

Figure 2.1   Customer Life Cycle

customer has bought. But the marketers have revenue targets to hit. *They need new sales!* So they return to the presale stage and chase new prospects.

Customers, however, continue through their life cycle. During the presale period, customers are open to the presentation of value. If they perceive sufficient value, they buy. They live and work with marketers' products or services and form their own opinions. During the growth and retention phase, marketers are often passive and reactive. Usually, the only offers made to customers during this phase are for consumables. In some cases, the only reason given to customers to purchase these consumables (the "razor blades") is a threat, i.e., "using anything other than our high-priced but otherwise comparable consumables will void your warranty."

Thus, when the customer is about to reenter the presale phase, the marketer's products and services may not look any different or better than the competition. In fact, they might look worse. However, the marketer should be the incumbent! The customer's perception of the value the marketer provides should be so strong that communications and offers from competitors do not make the customer's radar.

To get a dollar today and two dollars tomorrow, marketers must proactively provide value throughout the growth and retention phase. Lester Wunderman again provides excellent perspective:

> When I started selling Gevalia coffee, I invented the idea of what I then called automatic replenishment. You don't have to talk about brand loyalty because you're arranging repurchase as part of the system. With Gevalia, we tried to deliver a little more than people needed so that they never had to shop for coffee. The ultimate way of creating not loyalty but repurchase is to take people out of the marketplace.

There are two important reasons why the growth and retention phase also provides marketers with a wonderful opportunity to listen to customers and to learn from them:

1. Over time, customers' needs and requirements probably have changed. To maintain the relationship, marketers need to understand what those changes are and how customers wish them to respond.
2. To determine the level of customer satisfaction and take corrective action as required. This may also be a no-brainer, but the productivity of a relationship hinges on how satisfied the customer is. Dissatisfied customers rarely reach their potential for revenue generation or Customer Lifetime Value. (In fact, IBM has been able to tie customer satisfaction to bottom-line results. They can quantify how many millions of dollars are tied to each percentage point of customer satisfaction.)

A Dollar Today, Two Tomorrow—or Both

"Those who live by the quick hit will die by the quick hit."—John Hunter, Senior Vice President of Customer Services, QVC

So what do marketers want: a dollar today, two dollars tomorrow—or both? The answer seems obvious, but current marketing is absolutely focused on a dollar today. Short-term thinking for short-term gain. The Consensual process will show you how to increase your immediate and long-term revenue potential.

Here's a real-world excerpt from a meeting we had with a small manufacturing company that illustrates the required shift in thinking—from short-term commodity to long-term value:

SM (SALES MANAGER): Having a problem with a new customer. They just sent in their design. The purchase order calls for us to manufacture one design, but their design clearly specifies two drawings. I called them and they said not to worry, their design is continuous. They will cut the two apart and we should just produce the one. I said we must charge you for two. It's our policy. They are not happy and are ready to pull the job.

MM (MARKETING MANAGER): Who cares! We're really building their two designs. We should get paid for two.

PRESIDENT: How did we get this new customer?

SM: They were referred by one of our major customers.

PRESIDENT: How often do they buy?

SM: They say twice a month.

MM: We don't know that to be true. This is the first job they've sent us.

The Epiphany

PRESIDENT: Call them back and tell them we will produce their design and only charge them for one.

SM AND MM: What!!! They are ripping us off!

PRESIDENT: If we tell this customer that we must charge them for two designs, it's likely they'll be angry and place the job elsewhere. Right?

MM: Let them go. Who needs them—it's only a $100 sale.

PRESIDENT: We need them. First, we will have lost this new relationship. Someone who orders twice a month could bring in over $2,400 this year. Even if they cut apart all the orders and make five boards out of each one design, our costs and profitability are covered. Second, one of our largest customers referred them to us. This customer brings in $100,000 a year. We don't want these new guys calling the big customer saying bad things about us. Why harm that relationship?

This represents a sea change in thinking. Instead of doing battle over one sale, now this company is focusing on building long-term relationships . . . and making decisions accordingly. Focusing on and leveraging the relationship will bring in the dollar today *and* the dollar tomorrow.

What's in It for You?

The goal of the relationship is to increase Customer Lifetime Value, which is defined as the value of all the current and future revenue realized from a customer's relationship. Thus, the goal of Consensual Marketing is to forge and maintain successful relationships, and in turn to increase the Customer Lifetime Value of each of those relationships. In short—to increase sales and profits over the long term.

In researching this book, we have found many complex formulas for calculating Customer Lifetime Value. No doubt they do a good, accurate job. They are also very complex. Here's a simple approach to defining Customer LTV that may not be accurate to the penny but will give you the input you need to move quickly:

For a given customer:
- What is the dollar value of an average purchase?
- How many times a month and/or a year does this customer purchase?
- Thus, what is the monthly and yearly value of this customer?
- How many years has this customer purchased?

Stated differently:
Customer Lifetime Value = Dollar value of an average sale × Yearly frequency of purchases × Number of years of purchases

What Do Customers Want?

In a word: *value.*

Marketers define value as a motivating force—something with relative worth, merit, or importance. Perhaps it's the presentation of overwhelming benefits, or expert assistance and advice, or someone listening and taking action.

Going back to that small manufacturer we just mentioned, prior to conducting Voice of Customer (VOC) Messaging and Communication Research (this powerful research technique will be discussed in Chapter 3), the widely held belief was that customers only care about price—they will switch manufacturers at the drop of a hat to save a dollar. However, what came out of the VOC Research analysis was a "benefit hierarchy" that said customers are looking for, in order of importance:

1. Quality
2. Price
3. Delivery

This is how their customers define value. Price is important, but quality is more important. Here's a typical customer quote from the Voice of Customer Messaging and Communication Research: "Of course I look at price, but if the quality and delivery aren't there, the price means nothing."

This was what we call a BGO—a "blinding glimpse of the obvious"—and provided the manufacturer with the rationale for changing marketing messages from price to quality. The new positioning meant that they no longer had to compete as a commodity manufacturer, where one price cut is quickly met by price reductions from other competitors. (We see this as a death spiral.) Their marketing message is now one of superior quality in both manufacturing and customer service—a message that customers find truly differentiating.

During Voice of Customer Messaging and Communication Research, customers also defined what value this manufacturer should provide during the growth and retention phase:

- "It would help if you would send us ideas on how to improve our designs for manufacturability."
- "Can you tell us where technology is headed—how new equipment and processes can further improve quality?"

Let's review another case history, one that illustrates how Starwood Resorts leveraged customer relationships and achieved long-term profitability.

Case History: Starwood Resorts

Leveraging Customer Relationships

Starwood is a large hospitality conglomerate composed of many resorts and hotels nationwide. We will be discussing one of their holdings: Caesars Pocono Resorts, a luxury resort composed of four "all inclusive" unique properties. Located in the Pocono Mountains of Pennsylvania, the resort boasts the "world's most spacious and luxurious suites," including features such as in-room pools, heart-shaped tubs and their patented seven-foot-tall Champagne Glass Whirlpool.

Once a mecca for honeymooners and couples, Caesars enjoyed one of the highest occupancy rates in the industry. Increased competition from Caribbean resorts, however, eroded market share. Economic downturns caused further challenges.

While honeymooners remain a highly profitable portion of their business, vacationing couples now represent the bulk of Caesars' revenue.

The Goal

Caesars' goal and challenge: Increase occupancy and revenue without increasing marketing budgets. Here is their seven-step action plan and the results.

Step One: Start by Learning from Customers

The first step was to conduct Voice of the Customer Messaging and Communication Research. Findings indicated a substantial opportunity for enriching the relationship and generating repeat business by increasing the value and frequency of ongoing communications (during the growth and retention phase of the Customer Life Cycle). Customers wanted to know:

- What's new, what's improved, at the properties?
- What are the seasonal activities and sports?
- What are their special packages and rates?
- What big-name entertainment will be appearing and when?

Customers also expressed a great deal of interest in one of Caesars' underutilized assets: a frequent stayer program entitled "Forever Lovers."

Area Managing Director Douglas J. Wilkins explains how Caesars approached the challenge:

We initiated a Consensual Marketing process to take our marketing in a new, positive direction—to implement a customer-centric marketing focus consistent with our philosophy of building close, long-term relationships with our customers while on-property.

Step Two: Define Objectives

According to VOC findings, guests were interested in developing closer, longer-term relationships with Caesars. This supported Caesars' marketing objective to grow the relationship and thus grow Customer Lifetime Value. Specific action items were:

- Develop promotions and offers targeted to specific customer groups, focused on migrating lower tier guests to higher tiers
- Begin to capture data on customers' preferences, such as activities and entertainers
- Update Forever Lovers, the frequent stayer program, to feature the benefits guests wanted per VOC (such as special programs, pricing, etc.)
- Determine the media mix and Contact Management Calendar for each guest tier

"Our commitment to ongoing communications, to update our past customers about rooms and facilities improvements, as well as to communicate seasonal rates and big-name entertainment events [e.g., Jay Leno], and the escalating benefits of Forever Lovers was imperative," says Christopher D. Salerno, former Assistant Vice President of Sales and Marketing and Area Director of Sales and Marketing.

Step Three: Generating the Highest Return on Investment

Next was an analysis of the database and segmentation by the number of stays for each guest. Tiers or levels of stays were established to identify "best" guests—those who might have the greatest loyalty (see Figure 2.2).

Caesars conducted regression analyses to understand the historic probability of a onetime guest returning for a second stay, a two-time guest returning for a third stay, etc. Why? So the company could invest

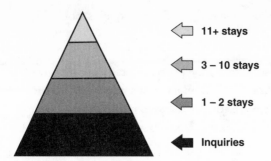

Figure 2.2 Guest Database Hierarchy

its limited marketing resources in the guests with the highest probability of returning, thus generating the greatest return on investment.

Step Four: Establishing the Testing Matrix

Doug and Chris are bottom-line marketers. Every penny spent must generate revenue. As far as they were concerned, if Caesars was going to change the "business as usual" model and embrace Consensual Marketing, it had to pay off, and in the near term. Thus, a comprehensive testing matrix was established.

Customer segments were defined by how often they stayed in the resort:

- One or two stays
- Three to ten stays
- Eleven or more stays

Each customer segment was further divided:

- One group would receive the new Caesars' communications, as outlined above.
- The other group would be the control cell—they would not experience anything new.

Additionally, baseline statistics were established for key indices:

- Response rate
- Conversion from inquiry to reservation
- Average revenue per reservation

- Return on investment measured as the ratio of marketing expense to revenue

These baseline statistics were compiled from actual results for the same time period in prior years. A great deal of care and attention went into the effort to eliminate variables, such as seasonality and economic conditions. The objective was to be able to compare the baseline statistics to the control cell in order to answer the question: Are the results we're getting now consistent with guest behavior over time?

Step Five: Getting the Word Out

To "get the word out" to customers, Caesars relied on two important methodologies: Integrated Direct Marketing (IDM) and the Consensual Marketing Opt-In Process. IDM is the proven process for helping marketers achieve a precise, synchronized, and highly relevant deployment of multiple media and field sales channels.

It is the precision deployment of multiple channels that consistently achieves *double-digit response.*

The Consensual Marketing Opt-In Process is a *strategic rethinking of how you and your customers engage.* IDM is a *disciplined go-to-market process* for achieving the precision Consensual dialogue.

The IDM Media Mix includes precision deployment of:

- Publicity/PR
- Advertising
- Internet
- E-mail
- Direct mail
- Telecontact—inbound and outbound
- Field sales channels

We discuss IDM in greater detail in Chapter 4.[2]

Customers Prefer Mail

In VOC Messaging and Communication Research, customers told Caesars their media preferences and aversions. Based on their preferences, the media mix focused on direct mail and inbound and outbound telecontact. Secondary drivers were print, Web, and e-mail. Customers said, and source code analysis proved, that TV and radio were not important to customers and would not stimulate bookings.

Customers told Caesars that they preferred direct mail for in-depth information regarding the resort (e-mail, by contrast, was seen as a vehicle for short relevant messages such as special rate promotions and was not acceptable to a sizable portion of those interviewed). Thus, direct mail was reconceived as a newsletter to feature the specific amenities guests liked most:

- Unique activities
- Upcoming entertainment
- Special offers that were versioned by customer tier

Newsletters were designed with variable sections, to minimize the cost of printing and collating while being able to present different groups with personalized messages. For instance, each newsletter featured both the upcoming big-name entertainment and improvements to rooms and facilities. However, rate offers were geared to generate reservations from target groups and to encourage them to book during historic times of lower occupancy, such as midweek.

Also in VOC Messaging and Communication Research, Caesars learned how much customers value highly skilled "Inbound Reservation Agents." These agents were so well versed in the properties, rooms, and amenities that each could paint a compelling verbal picture. But what Call Quality Monitoring also revealed was that the reservation agents were entirely reactive. A retraining initiative was begun, to have them provide *proactive expertise* and advice. This included:

- Viewing themselves as a key corporate resource—thus their job was to make the Caesars experience real and compelling for every caller
- Becoming proactive and guiding the call
- Actively listening and probing to clarify needs
- Attaching Caesars' benefits to the guests' needs
- Sending highly personalized fulfillment
- Screening and qualifying in accordance with a "propensity to visit" scoring model
- Asking for the reservation
- Determining next steps, as appropriate

Test Results

The next objective was to compare the results of the test cells to both baseline statistics and the control cell results. Without a doubt, this would tell Doug and Chris whether the Consensual Marketing methodology, including its component parts of VOC Messaging and Communication Research and IDM, was working.

The results were substantially above baseline and speak for themselves. Here are the mature results compared to those of the control cells:

- 32 percent increase in qualified response. A "qualified" response is defined as:
  - From a high-performing source (e.g., direct mail list)
  - Originating from a "feeder" market or higher potential zip code
  - A prospect with specific travel dates in mind
- 18 percent conversion rate to reservation
- 27 percent increase in average revenue per reservation
- 59 percent increase in return on marketing investment
- Expense to Revenue (E:R) under 10 percent
- 15 percent increase in revenue versus "business as usual"

Chris Salerno explains how the process worked:

The IDM process provides a discipline that can be measured and evaluated for success, or lack of success. With its concentration on comprehensive testing and bottom-line metrics, IDM also enabled Caesars to significantly reduce marketing expense by virtually eliminating nonproductive mass media such as TV and radio. This resulted in approximately a 30 percent reduction in marketing spending.

Step Six: Provide Value-Added Service

While vacationers represented the majority of reservations and revenue, honeymooners were always the most profitable. These were longer stays (five nights versus two to three nights for vacationers) and increased midweek occupancy (vacationers were primarily weekends).

To address the needs of this unique market, Doug and Chris introduced a value-added honeymoon service as a competitive differentiator. The idea for this service came from VOC Messaging and Communication Research. Subsequent VOC interviews helped develop and refine the service before marketing dollars were invested.

As honeymoon inquiries were received, their initial "propensity to buy" was calculated based on criteria that included:

- Location of the inquirer (e.g., state and city)
- Immediacy of the wedding date
- Reactions to probes concerning budget
- Source of the inquirer (e.g., what direct mail list, what bridal publication)

Later, in "Determining a Prospect's Propensity to Buy," we'll show you how to construct a "propensity to buy" scoring model for your company. For now, suffice it to say that high propensity inquirers become high priority leads. In our case study, each lead received an outbound call from a specially trained honeymoon planner who was titled the "Honeymoon Concierge." This employee offered to help the bride with every aspect of her honeymoon:

- Transportation
- What to pack
- Meeting the couple when they arrive and introducing them to the resort
- Arranging for amenities in the room, like champagne and bubble bath
- Helping them meet other newlyweds
- Ensuring a wonderful time while on-property

Honeymooners Test Results

- 38 percent conversion of all prospects contacted by the Honeymoon Concierge
- Expense to Revenue (E:R) of 4 percent

Step Seven: Introduce Line Extensions

Demographic overlays, database analysis, and common sense showed that today's honeymooners could become tomorrow's vacationers. But then, as the vacationers grew into young families, they came less frequently to

Caesars. Why? Because Caesars is a couples resort. In fact, a growing percentage of the database consisted of vacationers whose pattern of stays was declining.

To address this opportunity presented by the maturing of the database, Doug and Chris tested repositioning one of the four properties as a family-specific resort. This particular property had always enjoyed a small share of family business because of its pool and water sports and its proximity to local ski and recreation areas. Additionally, some of the rooms were spacious enough to easily accommodate parents and kids.

The risks:

- Would the increased presence of families impact the core business of honeymooners and vacationers? Clearly, loud frolicking kids might not be what these folks had in mind.
- If the test were successful, it would mean redesigning many of the honeymoon-specific rooms. The current accommodations, replete with seven-foot-tall champagne bubble baths and heart-shaped whirlpools, would be both inappropriate and a safety hazard.

The upside was significant, giving Caesars the opportunity to:

- Retain these long-term customers who had, in the past, shown a preference for Caesars.
- Capture a greater percentage of their vacation dollars.
- Minimize the cost of sale.

VOC Research confirmed that vacationers were eager to bring their young families if this would indeed be a family resort where they could expect Caesars' dedication to quality. With this information, Caesars committed to a test.

The test group received an announcement package that consisted of a letter from Doug detailing Caesars' vision and commitment to the new family resort and inviting them to bring their families. Included was a version of the regular newsletter keyed to the family resort. The control group received communications scheduled for vacationers. Results of the test and control groups were compared by week and by month over several quarters.

Line Extension Test Results

The test was remarkably successful, and created a new profit center. These families were delighted to embrace Caesars as a family resort. They identified Caesars with quality and value. The decision to bring their young families was easy. Given the following results, the investment to retrofit all rooms to be family-friendly was also easy:

- A 10 percent conversion to a family vacation
- Cost per reservation: less than $20

You May Not Be Investing Enough in Your Best Customers

As discussed earlier in this chapter, the tendency of corporations today is to chase the new sale. Sell and run. Existing customers have already bought. We need new sales. On to the next. And while this has been the tried and true way that corporations have existed and grown, it is quite wasteful over the long term.

Figure 2.3 contains two triangles. The triangle on the left represents your customer database segmented by Lifetime Value, or the total revenue contribution of customers over time. At the very top are the 10 to 20 percent of customers who contribute 80 to 90 percent of a company's revenue. These are the customers who have stayed the longest and bought the most. Yet, from a marketing budget perspective, most companies virtually ignore this group of loyalists. Marketing dollars are directed instead to finding, romancing, and closing new prospects and suspects.

Marketers always need to be prospecting, since there is always customer attrition. The bucket has a hole in the bottom and marketers must continuously refill it. But from a purely financial perspective, marketing dollars spent against your top tier customers will generate the highest return on investment (ROI). These folks are committed. They have the highest potential—the greatest propensity, or likelihood, to buy.

In Figure 2.3, the second triangle (on the right) represents the Consensual model for deployment of the marketing budget. The allocation of the marketing budget is based on the potential return on the investment. Thus, the top tier, with the potential to generate the highest ROI, receives the lion's share of investment. Lower tiers, given their lower

Figure 2.3   Investment Pyramids

potential, receive a lower percentage of the budget. And prospecting, which is always necessary, is always funded, but to a lesser extent. (As we concentrate on improving LTV from the top customer tiers, longevity of these customers will improve, mitigating—though never eliminating—the need to prospect.)

Through this focused allocation of investment and effort marketers can create and nurture the Consensual dialogue. Customer information becomes the catalyst to enable marketers to sell deeper and more consistently into the base of top tier customers, enables them—in the words of Lester Wunderman—to take them out of the market. The increase in revenue is immediate and cascades into significant increases in Customer Lifetime Value.

Are we suggesting that implementation of the Consensual Marketing Opt-In Process should begin with and concentrate on your best customers? Absolutely. It's consistent with the proven direct marketing tenet of "test with your best list." And it's the proven way of implementing Consensual Marketing to bring the greatest return.

The lesson: marketing investment must vary in agreement with the propensity to buy.

Determining a Prospect's Propensity to Buy

Which leads us to a dilemma: how can we apply this learning to prospecting?

Not all prospects are created equally. They do not come to your company with the same expectations, needs, or revenue potential. Yet, they all look and sound somewhat alike during the "first date." And because they're relatively undifferentiated, we tend to spend the same on each, undeservedly.

The answer is to develop and test a simple "propensity to buy" formula, or scoring model, which we'll detail below.

Experience says that propensity to buy increases or decreases according to four major variables: source, need, timing, and budget. Information regarding each can be gathered either electronically (see the explanation of source that follows) or during the first interactive exchange of information:

Source encompasses the mailing list, magazine, Web site, or referral the prospect came from. Thus, source is enormously important to the concept of propensity to buy. For instance, a prospect or lead that comes to you via a referral is gold—they should convert to a sale at a higher rate than prospects from any other list.

Need is just that: How important is this product or service to the customer? Is the software mission critical? Is the service essential to the smooth operation of the customer's business? The greater the need, the greater the propensity to buy.

Timing: When does the customer need this? Obviously, the sooner they need it, the higher the propensity.

Budget is, of course, the litmus test. Purchase cannot be imminent if the money is not available.

A Formula or Scoring Model

We'll use our four major variables to devise a propensity-to-buy formula, or scoring model. Assuming we have a likely prospect within an interactive conversation, perhaps on the phone, let's assign a numeric value to the possible outcomes of each variable.

Source:
- If the prospect comes from a referral, let's assign them 3 points
- If the source is a proven list, 2 points
- An untested or compiled list, 1 point

Need:
- Mission-critical, 3 points
- Important add-on that will bring increased benefits, 2 points
- "Nice to have," 1 point

Timing:
- Important to have it now, 3 points
- Want it in zero to six months, 2 points
- Just shopping, 1 point

Budget:
- Budget is approved and established, 3 points
- Budget has been requested, 2 points
- No budget at this time, 1 point

At the end of the conversation we add up the points, and here's how we interpret the score:

12 points: We have a white-hot candidate or an AA lead.

10 or 11 points: This may qualify as an A lead. Perhaps not a slam-dunk sale, but a bona fide lead that is worthy of additional follow-up.

8 or 9 points: We have an interested party who should be nurtured via alternate media (e.g., e-mail, direct mail) until they're ready for field follow-up.

In summary, this formula provides you with the information that will drive the most efficient allocation of resources, based on propensity to buy. The formula should be customized to your organization and fine-tuned through actual experience and sales force feedback, yielding a powerful tool in helping you maximize return on investment through Consensual Marketing.

Case History: Golden Rule Insurance

Investing According to Propensity to Buy

Golden Rule Insurance Company (GRI), founded in 1940, is one of the nation's leading providers of health insurance for individuals and families.

They are pioneers in the development of the Consensual Marketing Opt-In Process, and you'll see the company name several times in this book. They have tested and built a direct sales channel that now accounts for an estimated 10 percent of their entire individual health insurance business. While we will delve deeper into this case history in a later chapter, one aspect is particularly important now.

Golden Rule has found that one of the main sources for qualified prospects is the Internet. GRI has contracted with many reputable health- or insurance-oriented Web sites to generate inquiries. People who are researching the individual health insurance marketplace come to these Web sites for information.

In the early testing period, all these inquiries came straight through to GRI's Call Center, which is staffed with skilled, licensed insurance professionals. And this created a trap, says Greg Kohne, Assistant Vice President of GRI: "We were attempting to apply an equal amount of energy and effort to all leads. We were at a point where we had to hire more people or decide to begin filtering the leads based on a set of data points that was meaningful."

Analyzing the lead flow, Greg found a wide diversity of leads—from highly qualified individuals who desperately needed advice and insurance now to barely qualified "tire kickers." He also discovered distinct characteristics—including source, timing, and demographic profile—that separated the wheat from the chaff. This was the basis of the filtering or screening for propensity to buy.

Now, with the new process in place, individuals who wish to speak to one of GRI's licensed brokers are first asked to complete a brief questionnaire via e-mail. All the information is transmitted to GRI, where the database screens and qualifies all inquirers.

The first screen is for those who do not qualify, and they are informed electronically. The next screen looks at source. Not surprisingly, individuals who were referred by an existing customer or who inquire via the Golden Rule Web site are the best candidates.

"Referrals outperform the best prospecting lists by 200 percent," Greg adds.

Prospects are then filtered according to their answers to the questionnaire and then scored. Those who are closest to GRI's ideal customer receive the highest scores, since they have the highest propensity to buy.

The result was a 57 percent increase in conversion with no increase in staff. It was achieved by prioritizing prospects using the point scoring propensity-to-buy formula, and allocating resources and investment according to the prospects' propensity to buy.

Building the Consensual Database

Within direct marketing, the quality of the database is the single greatest lever for success. Consensual Marketing takes database functionality to the next level: The database drives the most efficient allocation of resources to achieve the objectives of CMO—to increase near-term revenue and Customer Lifetime Value. Thus, the effectiveness of the Consensual Database is dependent upon its ability to store and sort critical customer information, and the accuracy and recency of this information.

Yvonne Brandon, a former Direct Marketing Manager at IBM, says:

Consensual Marketing provides a powerful competitive advantage, because through profiling, the customer tells you exactly what they want you to sell to them, eliminating those marketing costs associated with creating and sending unwanted correspondence. The Consensual Database is the "engine" that drives this precision deployment of media.

The accuracy and immediacy of the Consensual Database represents a huge competitive advantage. There are four critical success factors associated with creating it:

- The organization of the database
- Database linkages
- The key information to be collected from customers
- Maintaining data hygiene

Andy Grim, Vice President of Sales and Marketing for Golden Rule Insurance Company, offers an anecdote that combines both database development and propensity scoring:

The Consensual process has proven itself on the broker side of our business. Here's how it works: When a broker decides to get licensed with us and becomes eligible to sell our insurance products, they have opted in at the first level. Then we try to profile them—

to get them to respond and answer some key questions about who they are and what their business is. We keep it to no more than five key questions, because, from our experience, if you ask 10, your response goes way down. If you ask 20, it's not going to work at all. Our goal is to get 80 percent of the brokers to answer those five questions. And for us, that's unbelievably valuable.

Brokers who have gotten licensed and have not completed the profile—we're wasting our time trying to do anything with them. If they will not complete that profile, they don't really have any interest in doing business with Golden Rule.

So, the completed profile brings the broker to level two. Level three is when we are able to get them to participate in our online broker service system, which means they can get supplies or access information through our Web site. They can track their customers as they send in applications. It's a free service but it's something they have to do a little work to get involved in.

These three levels of opt-in tell us the broker's propensity to write business with us. Brokers who have the lowest potential don't get anything except for e-mail and direct mail. Brokers who are at the highest rating are assigned to sales representatives, and they're getting e-mail, direct mail, and direct sales contact.

But you've got to cross-reference this with a market model because it's all about being there at the right time with the right message and the right product.

We overlay a market model to identify areas of opportunity. Let's find the best market conditions. That means we're there at the right time, our rates are competitive, we've got the right product, or maybe one of our competitors is experiencing a significant change. All of our big victories come when we capitalize on opportunities.

Now we know the high potential broker and we know the areas of opportunity. If we match those two, we get our foot in the door at the right time—we have something of value to talk about.

Really, the gain is in efficiency. We're faced with continuous cost pressure—get the cost of marketing down. Over the last five years spent developing the Consensual Database for brokers, internal sales and marketing costs have been cut almost in half. At the same time, revenue has more than doubled.

Organization of the Database

The organization of the database must be driven by our ability to respond to customers' needs and requirements. We suggest the following simplified organization to get you started:

- Product purchased/installed
- Industry/application or use
- Geography
- Business driver(s)

The first level of organization is the product or service the customer has purchased from you—what is installed at their location or home. This is the basis of your business relationship. Any inquiry or call for service must first address the product or service they use.

Next is industry or application, because *how* the product or service is used can make a big difference. For instance, CRM software that enables online chat may be based on the same code no matter what the industry, but the specific application or use of that software may differ from airlines to a catalog to a financial institution.

Geography enables you to respond quickly if you must dispatch a field sales or service rep, refer customers to a repair depot or retail store, determine shipping and handling charges, and so on.

Business driver(s) will help you understand the issues that the customer is wrestling with. For instance, if sagging customer satisfaction is a stated business driver, problems with the chat software affect a mission-critical application. This knowledge can help you respond with the proper service in the proper time frame, and the possibility of a value-add by proposing temporary work-arounds or solutions while troubleshooting is in progress.

One small horror story: One manufacturer was entranced by the notion of a Consensual Database and decided his organization had to be complex. The desire was to collect every bit of information the company ever wanted to know, all the time, from customers and salespeople (field and inside sales) as well. And a great many customers and salespeople complied. After approximately three months of shoehorning data into the system, it completely fell apart. It was too heavy and too complex to respond to marketing requirements!

And an insight from IBM's testing of CMO: while it was imperative to keep the database as simple as possible, additional coding was required to:

- Enable IBM to understand what communications had been or would be sent to a customer
- Ensure that customers received only the correct information and did not receive duplicate information

Database Linkages

Let us share a real-life story to illustrate the importance of database linkages.

The Roman family has been a longtime customer of one of New York's most beautiful department stores, Bloomingdale's. While reading the *New York Times* one morning, my wife, Sheri, saw an ad for a white sale at Bloomingdale's. The ad featured the exact sheets and towels she wanted. So she dialed the featured 800 number.

"Welcome to Bloomingdale's, how can I help?"

Sheri said she was responding to the white sale ad and would like to place her order.

"Great," the rep said, "May I please have the source code."

Sheri looked, but there was no source code anywhere on the page. She asked if the rep had a copy of the ad.

The rep responded, "I'm sorry, but without the source code I cannot verify that this is a legitimate call."

Sheri asked for the supervisor. She explained to this individual that we had been customers of Bloomingdale's for over 20 years and were very insulted at the rude way we were being treated, but wanted to place the order and get on with the day. The supervisor asked for the source code.

Sheri explained that she knew about source codes and was surprised herself to see that one was not on the ad. Clearly the agency had made a mistake. Please look at the ad yourself she told the supervisor.

"I'm sorry," the supervisor replied, "but this is obviously a fraudulent call," and hung up.

The outcome was anathema to the goals of Consensual Marketing. Therefore, database linkages (and we define a linkage as real-time access to key data) should include:

- Telemarketing/telesales
- Marketing
- Field sales
- Customer service
- Technical assistance
- Fulfillment

Key Information to Collect from Customers

We are not by any means advocating that the database become synonymous with "Big Brother" of *1984* fame. Rather, we are urging a focus on key data, enabling you to maintain both responsiveness and agility. *Simple* is the watchword.

Basic information may include:

- Name, title, functional role (A functional role is the same from company to company. Titles vary widely.)
- Reach information (e.g., address, phone, fax, e-mail)
- Business drivers (why they are interested in your product or service)
- Media preference/aversion
- Contact frequency
- Household names, per Decision-Making Unit (DMU) (*Authors' aside:* VOC Research indicates and experience confirms that in B2B no decision is made in a vacuum. Per the subject and nature of the decision, different functional roles interact as decision makers and influencers. These functional roles may or may not be in geographic proximity. We call the interaction of these functional roles a Decision-Making Unit, or DMU. Identifying and

associating these functional roles helps both marketing and sales influence decisions.)

And one important caveat: customer data is an enabler, not a commodity to be sold. Can you partner with other marketers to bring additional information to customers, given their profile and expressed consent? Of course. Will renting your list, no matter what sheep's clothing we put over it, cut it? Absolutely not. At the core of Consensual Marketing is a bond of trust. And as all bonds of trust, it can break very easily.

Doug Rose, Vice President Merchandising Brand Development, QVC:

I often joke how I may be satisfied with my laptop computer but I'm never going to trust it. What matters more than satisfaction is trust. And trust is an emotional connection. Many companies make the mistake of saying, "Gee our satisfaction scores are up 3 percent this year. We must be doing great." Meanwhile, they haven't built any trust. And so, the next guy to come around the corner with a better offer is going to get all their business. I think satisfaction is a relatively easy thing to affect through efficiency. But trust is something that can only come through people.

Maintaining Data Hygiene

Customer data is extremely perishable. Industry averages tell us that B2C data appears to deteriorate by about 1 to 2 percent per month. Business-to-business data, especially volatile sectors like technology, may deteriorate by 1 to 2 percent per week.

Your ability to respond to customers varies directly with the completeness and recency of the information. It is critical that you refresh key data with every interactive contact: "Mr. Smith, thank you for calling in today. Have I answered your question to your satisfaction? Before we say good-bye, let me just make sure we have your last name spelled correctly and have your correct address."

Title and reach information, such as mail stop, phone, e-mail, and fax, are among the most perishable. Incorrect information here can prove devastating. It will block the message from ever arriving. Deployment of a database scrub is an effective tactic in maintaining database hygiene.

The following case history will describe the methodology and the potential benefits.

Case History: Applied Biosystems

Applied Biosystems is an innovative biotech company just south of San Francisco. They develop and manufacture the scientific instruments used in the detection, separation, duplication, identification, and measurement of DNA and RNA through the process of PCR (polymerase chain reaction). In fact, Applied Biosystems created and manufactured much of the instrumentation used in decoding the human genome.

The introduction of their PRISM 7700 Sequence Detection System marked a significant scientific development. This technology pushed the envelope, enabling the process of DNA detection, separation, duplication, identification, and measurement to be faster and more accurate. Accordingly, Applied Biosystems wanted to tell their scientist customers about it in a highly interactive environment. It was decided to invite these scientists to a conveniently located regional workshop.

But no one was confident that they had absolutely accurate database and reach information for these scientists. So it was decided to conduct a database scrub via outbound telemarketing. This would be the fastest and most thorough means. The first objective was to try to verify contact information for the scientists through the company's switchboard. But because they would inevitably end up speaking with some scientist who happened to pick up the phone, grad students and experienced technicians made the calls from carefully structured scripts.

The objectives:

- Select one contact per department.
- State the purpose of the call and ask permission to verify their information.
- Verify the spelling of the scientist's name, title, and all other contact information.
- Ask permission to verify the contact information for other scientists in the department who were on the database.
- Ask for referrals: "Are there other scientists or colleagues involved in this type of research who would benefit from attending?"

These phone reps were trained to generate the information as well as talk the scientific talk and answer questions. The results were dramatic:

- 35 percent of the records were inaccurate
- 2 percent of the records were undeliverable and were deleted
- 10 percent of the contacts asked to preregister (during the scrub!)
- 18 percent of contacts provided referrals

These referrals were gold. They represented 15 percent of the invitations sent, 58 percent of the registrants, and 61 percent of the attendees.

As previously stated, data building and verification are a critical objective of every interactive conversation. Database scrubs should be deployed once a quarter, as new sources are added, and as markets are prioritized.

To give you an idea of the mechanics of the process, and the cost, let's assume you have 10,000 names in the database. Expectations are to reach 80 percent—8,000—via outbound records. Given industry averages, assume that reps will average 10 completed calls per hour. Stated differently, the project will require 800 hours to complete.

One communicator calling for 6.5 hours a day would require 123 days to complete this list. More realistically, six communicators would require 20 days. If the cost were $30 an hour for 800 hours, the final bill would be $24,000. This is an investment in building a proprietary corporate asset—with names competitors don't have!

John B. Kahan, General Manager, Corporate CRM, Microsoft Corporation, is responsible for driving Microsoft's worldwide implementation of CRM. He shares these important insights:

Companies can distinguish themselves in one-to-one relationships through the quality of customer data they accumulate. This data improves their ability to provide value per customer's stated and implied needs.

We serve many millions of customers worldwide. Our challenge is to show our customers that we truly value their relationships. An effective way of doing this is by establishing two-way communications that provide value to the customer across all touch points.

The key measures that companies use to judge the effectiveness of CRM/Consensual Marketing efforts are customer satisfaction, loyalty (lifetime value), and shareholder return.

The difference between Consensual Marketing and business as usual is significant. First, the focus is on the customer needs. By continually focusing on the customer, companies can minimize internal disagreements. Second, companies can now leverage technology to establish and nurture relationships well beyond what was possible only a few short years ago. Now marketers and business managers can take charge of the customer relationship. It is not technology for technology sake, it is technology for the customer's sake.

Points to Remember

- Focus on building and maintaining the relationship.
- Understand and market to each stage of the Customer Life Cycle.
- Objective: increase immediate sales *and* Customer Lifetime Value.
- Invest in the highest potential for return: you may not be spending enough on your best customers.
- Construct a simple point-scoring model to determine a prospect's "propensity to buy," as of the first conversation.
- Build the Consensual Database:
  o Function of the database is to drive the most efficient allocation of resources.
  o Organize it simply—stay agile and responsive.
  o Collect and analyze key customer information.
  o Information is the enabler—not a commodity to be sold.
  o Link the database to key areas of the organization.
  o Invest in the accuracy and recency of customer information.

Step Two: Voice of Customer Research

Learning Customer Messaging and Communication Needs and Preferences

THE SECOND STEP in the Consensual Marketing Opt-In Process is implementing Voice of Customer (VOC) Messaging and Communication Research. We will discuss this specialized research technique, explaining how it differs from other forms of research, its value to you, and its contribution to the Consensual Marketing Opt-In Process. We'll cover the following concepts:

- Rationale for the VOC technique, and its benefits
- Validating critical marketing issues through VOC
- Setting research goals
- Establishing the Research Matrix
- Important questions you should consider asking your customers
- Significant lessons from past VOC efforts

And we'll include a comprehensive case study with details and results to show you how VOC Messaging and Communication Research both guides and enriches the Consensual Marketing process.

The Rationale for VOC Research

Voice of Customer Messaging and Communication Research is a specialized methodology whose goal is to bring customer messaging and communication needs and preferences to the marketing planning table. The lessons learned are powerful and will help you avoid making significant mistakes.

Bringing Customer Needs to the Planning Table

Of the many research vehicles available, focus groups, telephone surveys, and e-surveys are three of the most common. We recognize their strengths and also see that each has significant weaknesses. For example, focus group findings are frequently influenced by the presence of a dominant personality on the panel. And traditional telephone surveys and e-surveys can only go so deep in uncovering information. There's no probing. It's in the survey or it's not.

Through one-on-one in-depth customer conversations, VOC Messaging and Communication Research generates powerful, directional, qualitative marketing intelligence regarding:

- Awareness/perception of your company
- Business issues/drivers
- Decision-making process, roles, and responsibilities
- Barriers to purchasing/switching to your company
- Media mix and sequence
- Optimal contact preference and timing

VOC Messaging and Communication Research also allows you to pretest critical parts of your strategy; in particular:

- Positioning
- Messaging
- Creative
- Offers

Joanna Sinnwell of Hewlett-Packard makes an important observation. "With all the tools available to us today," she says, "we often forget that it is the human interaction that makes or breaks an account relationship."

Setting Messaging and Communication Research Goals

The VOC goals must be clearly articulated and actionable. This is business research—your company deserves the maximum return on its investment. Some key questions to ask when setting your goals:

- Why are we doing this research?
- What important issues do we want this research to shed light on?
- What action or tactic will be more effective with these insights?

Consider how the following sample companies have defined their goals:

Company 1

- How do customers and prospects see the key benefits of our products?
- How do customers and prospects see the key benefits of the competition's products?
- How do customers and prospects prefer to receive information about our products?
- How do customers and prospects define their unique messaging and information requirements?
- How long does the decision-making process take, and who are the decision makers and influencers?
- What information is required at each step and via what media?
- What are customers' and prospects' reactions to messages, tactics, and offers?

Company 2

- Understand the messaging and communication requirements of decision makers as they consider our product.
- Generate the requirements for constructing a Contact Management process to identify and nurture decision-maker leads who are interested in our product until they are ready for rep/reseller contact.
- Identify offers and tactics that decision makers interested in our product find compelling and *competitively differentiating*.

- Define the customer-driven information required to identify prime candidates for equipment upgrades within our installed base.

Company 3

- Understand how our company can reposition itself as a relevant, trusted, and value-added adviser versus a commodity provider.
- Define the most compelling value statement per customer needs.
- Test the language and relevancy of current and proposed messaging.

Company 4

- How to gain the account.
- How to retain the account.
- How to grow the account.

"Involve the reps, sales management, product management, and research in the creation and setup of the research; this establishes the necessary connections and buy-in, up front."—Joanna Sinnwell, Imaging and Printing Commercial Program Manager, Hewlett-Packard

Establishing the Research Matrix

The Research Matrix defines our research target market: Whom are we going to talk to, and, thus, how are we going to analyze these results? For example, if our goal is to gain, retain, and expand the account, which is the concerns of Company 4, above, that might yield the Research Matrix that follows. The columns represent types of companies, as defined by the customers' sales volume, and the rows represent stages in the Customer Life Cycle. All these variables pertain to Company 4.

	Large Company	Small Company
Prospect	Cell 1	Cell 2
New sale	Cell 3	Cell 4
Lost account	Cell 5	Cell 6
Existing customer	Cell 7	Cell 8
Past customer	Cell 9	Cell 10

This Research Matrix has 10 unique research cells and is in line with the stated goals: we will be able to analyze the responses of each cell, compare them to other cells, and learn how to gain, retain, and expand the account.

Now we have to populate each cell with the appropriate number of interviews. Our experience suggests that you will need between three and five interviews per cell. Two interviews in a cell are too few, and more than five interviews yield outcomes that are repetitious. The total number of interviews should be between 30 and 50. Given the need to generate results as quickly as possible, we recommend 30.

The Research Matrix with three interviews per cell looks like this:

	Large Company	Small Company
Prospect	3	3
New sale	3	3
Lost account	3	3
Existing customer	3	3
Past customer	3	3

This Research Matrix calls for 30 in-depth interviews.

Here's another Research Matrix that would address the stated goals of Company 4:

	Industry A	Industry B	Industry C
Technical specifier	3	3	3
Financial buyer	3	3	3
End user	3	3	3

This matrix has nine cells for a total of 27 interviews. The difference is that for this company:

- There are significant differences in the needs and requirements of their customers as defined by vertical industry.
- Influencing the complex decision-making process, which involves three job functions, is seen as key to achieving the research goals.

Given the same goals, how would you construct your Research Matrix?

Frequently Asked Questions about the Process

Here are the most frequently asked questions about the VOC Messaging and Communication Research process:

What is the duration of a VOC interview? A 30-question interview averages 45 minutes to an hour, although many go longer, based upon the willingness of the interviewee and the richness of the input.

Who conducts these interviews? The interviewer should be a senior member of your team. Prior experience conducting VOC Interviews is a big plus.

What about the projectability of results? VOC Messaging and Communication Research yields solid, qualitative, directional results. When companies have conducted subsequent quantitative studies, results have validated the VOC findings.

Questions to Ask Your Customers

- How do customers view your company, and what attributes or values do they think of regarding your company?
- How do customers view your competition, and what attributes or values do they think of regarding the competition?
- What are the critical issues or business drivers facing decision makers that would attract them to your product or service?
- How do they express their hierarchy of needs regarding your product or service?
- How long does the decision-making process take?
- Who are the decision makers and influencers?
- What information is required at each step of the decision-making process and via what media?
- Are there barriers to purchasing or switching to your company, product, or service?
- How can your company gain competitive differentiation?
- How do decision makers and influencers prefer to get information about advances and innovation?

- How do they define their unique messaging and information requirements?
- What are their reactions to your planned:
  - Positioning
  - Offers
  - Creative
- What is the optimal media mix?
- What is their contact preference?
- What is the optimal value-added role for sales channels?

The last question in the interview should go something like this:

Given the goals of this research and the interview process we have just completed together, what advice would you have for (the company) as they seek to (restate goals emphasizing the customer benefit, such as "to provide superior service to our valued customers")?

This truly brings the customers to the planning table, and you might be surprised to see how much some enjoy this question. Customers stop and think before replying. Their thoughts are always enlightening—they are giving you their unedited viewpoint both as a businessperson and as a customer.

Eric Borchers, Imaging and Printing Enterprise Marketing Manager, Hewlett-Packard, reveals what VOC showed his group:

We were able to hear honest and often intense reactions and beliefs that were later validated in quantitative research. Although many account reps have shared customers' latest issues and reactions, marketing was able to hear, firsthand, their real feelings about our products and directions.

Significant Findings from Past VOC Efforts

Below, we will review several case histories. The first five are actually snippets of case histories and focus on VOC Messaging and Communication Research findings and implications. The last, from Applied Biosystems, is a complete case history. It begins with the goals of the marketing program, goes through VOC Research lessons, and ends with the specific results of implementation.

We have now conducted over 55 VOC Messaging and Communication Research efforts representing almost 1,600 hours of research interviews on behalf of clients such as IBM, Agilent Technologies, Hewlett-Packard, Applied Biosystems, AT&T, Golden Rule Insurance, and Franklin Covey. With every implementation of VOC Research there is an epiphany: Some nugget of truth emerges that makes all the difference.

Eric Borchers adds:

> **Listening to customers is an important first step in executing a marketing or sales program. No one is ever "close enough" to the customer, and this anchors us in their world and provides the kind of reality check that is useful to come back to, again and again, in marketing and sales planning and measuring.**

Is It Price or Is It Quality?

In the last chapter we mentioned a small manufacturing concern. For simplicity, let's refer to them here as Company A. As this case history unfolds, it's important to note that Company A has been around for almost 20 years, which means they have weathered many storms. And a new storm engulfed them without any warning: When the president opened up the monthly trade journals, he found that his company was in the middle of a price war. Competitors were advertising loudly and boldly that they now had the absolute lowest prices. Account managers began raising the flag that they were hearing price pushback on the phone from new inquirers.

Company A was worried. If they met these competitively advertised prices, it would seriously cut into their profitability. If they fought back and exceeded these discounts, there was no end in sight. The ones who lose in a price war are the companies duking it out. And once the price has been devalued, there's no going back. What would this do to their installed base and retention? Company A always recognized that there was price sensitivity. They never were the cheapest guy on the block. They had always prided themselves on their continuing investments in new technology—to continually produce a better product—and their dedication to customer satisfaction. Had the whole world changed overnight? Would customers switch manufacturers at the drop of a hat to save a dollar?

Before responding to the competition, Company A deployed VOC Messaging and Communication Research for quick turnaround customer feedback. What did their large, long-term customers think? What did prospects looking for a manufacturing partner think? But not wanting to skew the research toward discounting alone, the goals of the research were drawn broadly:

- How to gain the account
- How to retain the account
- How to expand the account

The Research Matrix included each major customer and prospect group:

- High volume/long- and short-term customers
- Low volume/long- and short-term customers
- Decreasing volume customers
- Recent wins
- Recent losses
- Prospects

VOC Research results stated clearly that customers—those with a long-term relationship with Company A, or who matched the profile of these long-term customers—said price is important, but quality is more important. Customer quotes included:

- "Of course I look at price, but if the quality and delivery aren't there, the price means nothing."
- "We pay for quality."
- "Quality is number one. I would not sacrifice quality for price."
- "Service is at the top of my list. Responsiveness, get me answers quick."

The Benefit Hierarchy that emerged said that customers were looking for: (1) quality, (2) price, and (3) delivery.

In fact, their most valued customers stated that they would *pay between 5 and 15 percent more* to do business with Company A. Here's a typical comment: "I would pay more for consistently high quality and on-time delivery."

Price sensitivity, however, was detected at the low end of the customer spectrum: smaller companies and those interested in lower technology manufacturing.

Clearly, given the VOC Messaging and Communication Research results, it would have been disastrous if Company A had changed its marketing strategy from quality to price competition, from a value-added supplier to a commodity that competes on the basis of price alone.

If It's Such a Good Deal, How Come I Don't Know About It?

In Chapter 2 you were introduced to Golden Rule Insurance. In addition to being brilliant marketers, the company knows a good idea for an insurance product when they hear it. The idea was the Medical Savings Account (MSA), and Golden Rule was a vocal supporter as the legislation passed Congress. By combining a high-deductible health insurance policy and a savings account, MSAs offer the self-employed an opportunity to save on health insurance and taxes. And Golden Rule was surprised that the self-employed did not turn out in large numbers to purchase MSAs once they became available.

Through VOC Messaging and Communication Research, Golden Rule gained practical insights regarding how to speak so these customers could listen.

The subject of insurance, particularly health insurance, was uncomfortable to the customers interviewed. Unless there was a significant life event, like a huge jump in premiums or being newly self-employed, the subject was avoided. The language of insurance was viewed as foreign and impenetrable. While MSAs, and Golden Rule Insurance as champion of this legislation, had gained some degree of mass market coverage, it fell on deaf ears.

Customers' advice was to "personalize the message to the self-employed segment and to the individual" via media and message. The communications backbone should be PR, but in targeted, vertical publications and through industry associations. The message should be in plain English and include clear illustrations:

- "Tell us how you have satisfied customers like me."
- "Show us that Golden Rule is the authority. Show me how an MSA works."

Would they buy direct? Initially, most of the customers interviewed preferred purchasing through an insurance broker. Then Golden Rule asked them to detail what they would require to buy direct. Input included:

- Concise, meaningful information about the background and stability of Golden Rule Insurance.

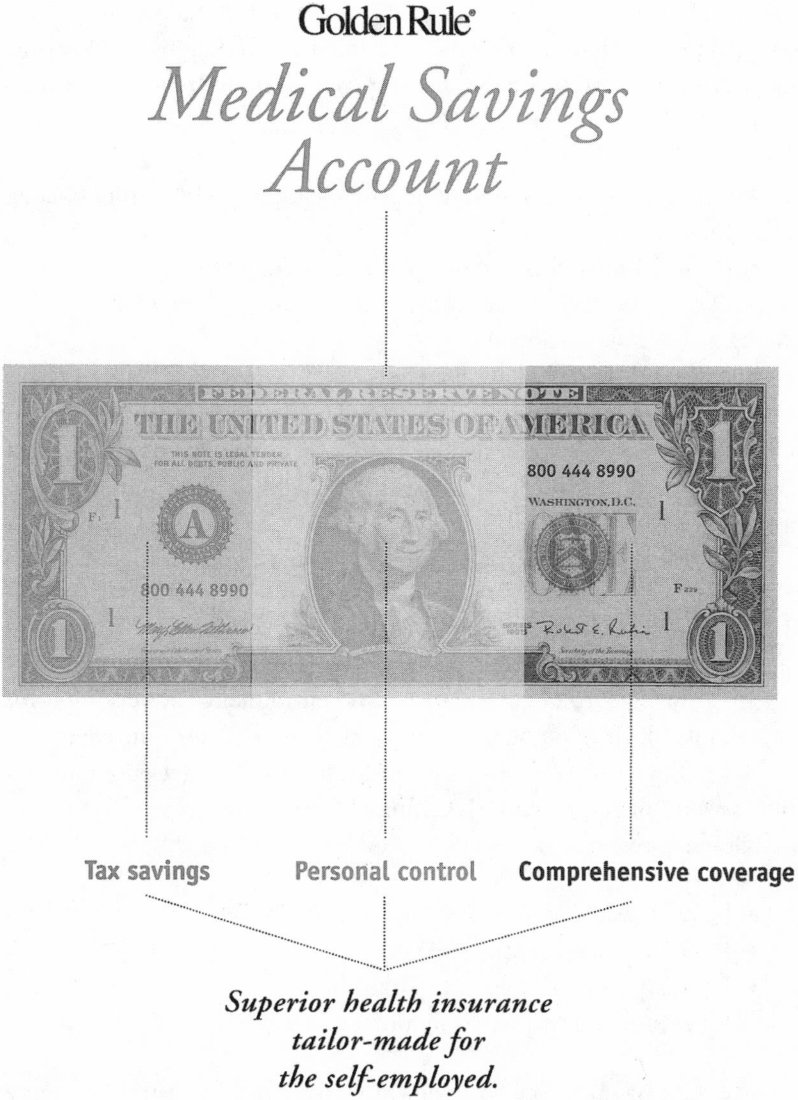

Figure 3.1 Golden Rule Insurance Brochure on Medical Savings Accounts

- Licensed, trained telephone reps who provide caring, one-on-one consultation and advice.
- "It really depends on who is on the other end of the phone. Don't talk jargon. Help, but don't push—allow time for thinking."

Figure 3.1 shows the cover of the MSA brochure developed after VOC input.

If Golden Rule Insurance met these and other conditions, most of the customers interviewed said they would buy direct. But the customers must *opt in* to the communications process. Subsequent testing by Golden Rule Insurance has shown that to produce the most desirable return on marketing investment, customers must:

- Opt in to receiving communications regarding MSAs from Golden Rule Insurance
- Receive only information on the topic(s) requested
- Determine media selection by taking into account their preference(s) and aversion(s)
- Dictate the timeline for contact
- Be assured that their privacy would be respected—that opting in to this database did not also benefit Golden Rule Insurance through list rental and subject them to an onslaught of spam

Most Decisions Are Made in November

ACE Computer Camp was entering its fourth year of meteoric growth and was smug about its ability to attain and surpass the previous year's target for camper enrollment. They set the enrollment bar very high for Year 4, introducing computer camps to many new areas of the country.

Started by two college buddies and self-described geeks (Figure 3.2 shows their fun graphics), ACE's culture had traditionally viewed the year as follows:

- September through November: take it easy
- December and January: party
- February through May: work like crazy
- June, July, and August: camp time

Feeling pressure from their new investors to achieve the aggressive enrollment goals for Year 4, partying was relegated to weekends and "go

Figure 3.2   ACE Graphic

crazy" began in December. They turned to VOC Messaging and Communication Research to fine-tune their positioning, pretest several potential offers, and sharpen their messaging. Research was conducted at the end of December and the beginning of January so marketing and media plans could be drawn up and creative could begin. The first communications were to go out in middle to late February.

The Research Matrix addressed the different ages (8 to 16) and segments of their database, beginning with inquirers and going to multiyear campers. One of the early questions, intended both to elicit information and to warm up the interviewee (the camper's parent), was: "When during the year do you usually make a decision about summer camp?" Given that ACE's enrollment campaigns began in February, the answers were eye openers:

- "We usually make a decision by November."
- "Our child knows right away if he wants to go back. If he wants to, we'll sign for the next summer as we're picking him up in August."
- "Why don't we ever hear from ACE until well after the new year?"

Understanding that camp selection decisions were made earlier gave ACE two big opportunities to increase the bottom line. The first was to capture more market share by beginning recruitment efforts significantly earlier in the year. The second was to leverage the camp experience into increased reregistration rates through early enrollment at the end of camp (which would also drive down marketing costs).

However, they had already missed the opportunity for their fourth season. They were simply too late, proving the old adage that if you snooze you lose.

Bathing Suits in Winter

The following story is related by Charles A. Prescott, Vice President, International Business Development & Government Affairs, Direct Marketing Association, regarding a company that should have done its VOC homework:

> **There's a wonderful anecdote about the department store Marks and Spencer which shows the extraordinary power of listening to your customers. The Grand Dame of retailing in London, England, had been having a tough time for quite a few years. So they hired some consultants, and the consultants put surveyors in about a dozen stores in different cities. For a few weeks in the winter, as customers were leaving the stores empty-handed, the surveyors asked these customers what they were looking for that they did not find. And Marks and Spencer discovered a couple of really interesting things which it did not know:**
>
> **1. Women bought bathing suits in the wintertime.**
> **2. An increasing number of women were employed and needed appropriate business apparel.**
>
> **Marks and Spencer didn't carry any of those things. That led them to another amazing conclusion: All of their buyers and merchandisers were middle-aged men who had no clue what women wanted to buy—because they never asked them.**

If all you're doing is looking at the statistics of what you manage to sell, and you don't bother to talk to people who don't find what they want, you're not going to change. You'll continue to get the exact same results. This is a wonderful example of having your business guided by the people who make you rich or don't make you rich. And now, Marks and Spencer does carry business-appropriate female attire and bathing suits in the winter.

No Value!

IBM has been at the forefront of deploying VOC Messaging and Communication Research as "standard operating procedure" prior to launching significant projects. Here's a synopsis of VOC findings from several different implementations:

One initiative focused on introducing IBM's comprehensive new hardware/software solutions to private medical practices ranging from 3 to 49 physicians. The solution, when compared to the competition, appeared to be robust with important benefits for the practice. Yet the sales force had characterized this marketplace as: "Hard to see the decision maker."

Ramona Anton, former Health Segment Manager at IBM, sheds some light on the issue: "The main issue from our point of view was how do we get the customer to understand that we have a knowledgeable, experienced team in place with responsibility for the customer's well-being?" [1]

VOC Messaging and Communication Research results gave important direction to the effort:

- Contrary to sales force assumptions, all interviews (which included the doctors) identified the office or practice manager as the decision maker versus the traditional contact—the doctor. Physicians, especially in the larger more lucrative practices, had decided to hand off office and technology responsibilities in order to concentrate on the practice of medicine.
- There was confusion and some irritation regarding the roles of IBM reps and IBM's third-party sales partners—the VARS, or value-added resellers.

- "I don't know who all these people are or what their roles are, but I do know I'm paying their salary. No value."
- "Too confusing, too many layers. The division of responsibility is not clear and is not satisfying my needs."
- "Flatten the organization—get closer, increase your knowledge of the marketplace. Manage your business partners better, more closely."

Customer responses also helped IBM prioritize its sales efforts. Analysis indicated that practices focusing solely on the software solutions viewed IBM as a commodity vendor. However, practices that recognized the importance of the hardware viewed IBM as a partner.

Curt Gillespie, former IBM Business Unit Executive, reports that the response was tremendous. [2] "For the first phase," he says, "we saw an 841 percent improvement in response over previous programs. We received more qualified inquiries for this initial phase than we had projected for the entire pilot, with an increase in leads of more that 442 percent."

You Are Arrogant and Out of Touch

Here's another case study, as related by Yvonne Brandon, former Direct Marketing Manager for IBM's Worldwide e-Business on Demand Operating Environment Initiatives:

As IBM was preparing to bring its new solution for manufacturers to market (called Business and Production Planning), VOC Research was deployed to learn more about how to position the sales force (both IBM reps and VARS) to bring the greatest value to decision makers. The Research Matrix included both large and medium-sized customers. The responses from the medium-sized businesses were like a cold shower:

- "IBM is not responsive. IBM needs to spend more time listening to customer needs."
- "You are arrogant and out-of-touch."
- "Sell and run. Ask if what you've sold is working. Follow-through on after-sale satisfaction."
- "Reps are focused on selling hardware, not solving my problems. My daddy said, when you go to the eye doctor, expect to come home with glasses."

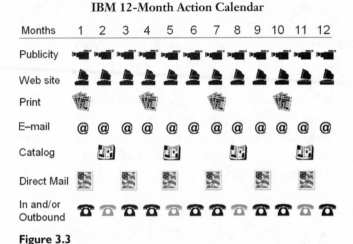

Figure 3.3

IBM's response—a complete recalibration of their commitment to and coverage of the mid-market, beginning with the implementation of a special event to bring the benefits of the manufacturing solution directly to mid-market decision makers. Per IBM's analysis, 25 percent of attendees were projected as qualified inquiries.

VOC input gave IBM the information they needed to put together a 12-Month Action Calendar detailing the media and sales force deployment, encompassing 49 focused contacts with the customer over the next year (Figure 3.3).

Is This Boring to You? It's Important to Us!

This case study summarizes several of Hewlett-Packard's VOC Messaging and Communication Research efforts over different product groups, and it focuses on core findings that can be applied to all their marketing programs.

Eric Borchers explains:

We gained several key insights into our customers' current problems and attitudes during the VOC Messaging and Communication Research. These insights helped clarify urgent issues and the future direction of marketing and sales programs and tools.

One of the insights concerned the communication of HP's strengths amid the noise of the Compaq merger. Customers were concerned that the basic HP values were getting lost in what they perceived as hype or marketing spin:

- "HP has good account teams and a good technical heritage. This should be your focus. Is this boring to you? It's important to us!"
- "The benefit to us is not just hardware—it's people and service. Keep the people partnership in your messages. HP is there for you."
- "Breadth of quality products—robust, good support—it's why HP is the standard."
- "HP has the largest market share, which makes life easier for us. The drivers are accepted on the network. And, end users are comfortable with the brand. This allows us to focus on other areas."
- "Steer clear of competitor bashing. Play to your strengths. Tired of bashing. Don't be negative."

Joanna Sinnwell, Hewlett-Packard's Imaging and Printing Commercial Program Manager, adds that "we learned that these current HP strengths and our product reliability are critical in establishing and sustaining credibility."

HP also learned that the decision-making process might be significantly more complex than previously thought, prompting HP to communicate higher and wider within an organization. This has both promotional and database implications. The database should link each of the appropriate decision makers involved in a project, without regard to location (e.g., the Decision Making Unit, or DMU). Titles may include:

- IT Manager
- Facilities Manager
- Corporate Level Executive
- Line of Business Manager
- Networking
- Purchasing
- Potentially other departments as well

A case in point: "I manage copiers. IT manages printers. Procurement manages fax. Scanners are managed by the Scanning Department."

Hewlett-Packard
Pro-forma Contact Management Plan
(media and message will vary by functional responsibility
— this chart addresses one title)

Potential Touch-point	Potential Value / Competitive Differentiation	Potential Media	Potential Timing
Awareness	• Innovation • HP heritage • Future vision • Range/ dependability • TCO • People • Service / support • Offer • Call to Action	Publicity • Reprints used in fulfillment D.R. Print Ads Targeted Direct Mail Web Inbound Outbound Fulfillment Rep / VAR	Year-round

Preference	• HP heritage
	• Future vision
	• Proof points
	• Innovation
	• TCO
	• Range/ dependability
	• Service / support
	• Offer
	• Call to Action
		Publicity
		• Reprints used in
		  fulfillment
		D.R. Print Ads
		Targeted Direct Mail
		Inbound
		Outbound follow-up to
		  targeted customers
		Fulfillment
		Web
		Rep / VAR
			Year-round

Trial	• Future vision • Proof points • TCO • HP heritage • Innovation • Range/ dependability • Service / support • People • Offer • Call to Action	Inbound Web E-mail Outbound follow-up Fulfillment Rep / VAR	On demand
Purchase	• Thank you • Future vision • HP heritage • Reliability / dependability • Service / support • People • Offer • Call to Action	Direct mail E-mail Rep / VAR	On demand
Support	• Service / support • People • Reliability / dependability • HP heritage • Future vision • Offer • Call to Action	Publicity Direct mail E-mail Fulfillment Inbound Outbound Web Rep / VAR	Quarterly
Repurchase	• Future vision • Innovation • HP heritage • Proof points • TCO • Range / reliability • People • Offer • Call to Action	Publicity Direct mail E-mail Fulfillment Inbound Outbound Web Rep / VAR	Monthly

Figure 3.4 Hewlett-Packard Contact Management Plan

Customers also reminded HP that to effectively communicate (and sell) wider and higher requires the *consistent delivery of value to each of these decision makers over time*. And each of the decision makers may define value differently. HP must respond to the individual's unique messaging and timing needs, as well as their media preferences and aversions. Figure 3.4 illustrates the Contact Management Plan for one of the titles who was part of the Decision Making Unit.

Case History: Applied Biosystems

Applied Biosystems (formerly a division of PerkinElmer) is an innovative company. We met them in the last chapter. If you recall, they develop and manufacture the scientific instrumentation used by DNA researchers. In fact, they're responsible for many of the instruments used by Celera in decoding the human genome.

The GeneAmp PCR System 2400 is one of their products.[3] It's a small thermal cycler primarily used in university labs (larger ones are used in commercial enterprises, such as pharmaceutical companies). A thermal cycler is used to prepare DNA for detection and analysis. Very basically, a thermal cycler heats and cools DNA samples through the PCR (polymerase chain reaction) cycle. PCR is the reagent-induced process for isolating and replicating strands of DNA.

Applied Biosystems (AB) had a problem because its sales and market share for the 2400 thermal cycler was declining due to increased competition. In addition, its sales efforts had relied primarily on a highly technical and expensive field sales force.

A new strategy was developed to address these challenges: create a new sales channel to sell the 2400 directly to universities and thus free the sales force to concentrate on higher ticket, more technically complex products. This was potentially a win-win strategy for AB: reduce the cost of sale for the 2400 while increasing the field's concentration on higherend products. But before investing its precious resources, AB deployed Voice of Customer Messaging and Communication Research to understand customers' reactions and input.

The research had the following goals:

- Identify the VOC-driven requirements for a direct channel: what media should be deployed so prospects and customers would feel comfortable buying direct?

- Identify the features of the 2400 that were most important to researchers and scientists.
- Pretest offers that researchers and scientists would find appropriate.

The VOC lessons in reference to the first two goals were straightforward:

- Print advertising would not influence a purchase decision.
- Direct mail was preferred for technical communications (see Figure 3.5).

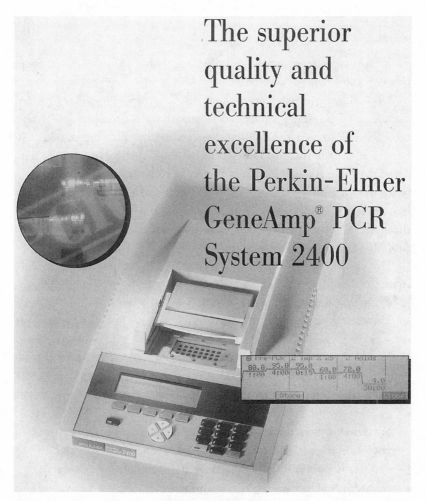

The superior quality and technical excellence of the Perkin-Elmer GeneAmp® PCR System 2400

Figure 3.5 Direct Mail Package for the PCR System 2400

- E-mail was acceptable for short, promotional messages, but only if the scientists opted in.
- High-quality, knowledgeable telemarketing, both inbound and outbound, would be acceptable, but both must feature scientifically educated, empowered communicators.
- Messaging should highlight the features of the 2400 most important to scientists:
  - Graphical user interface that makes programming fast and easy.
  - Heated cover that maintains a temperature-controlled environment around the sample and eliminates the need for an oil overlay (all DNA scientist-speak).
  - Superior quality—Applied Biosystems is the industry leader—at a low price.

Scientists also requested a tight linkage with Field Sales in the event that rep follow-up was requested.

VOC Research input toward the third goal (compelling offers) proved surprising. Field and Product Management were certain that the best offer was: "Purchase the 2400 at your university discount and AB will bundle in a generous sample supply of AB's top-of-the-line reagent, Amplitaq Gold (Please note: It is the reagent that causes the PCR chain reaction that isolates and replicates strands of DNA). Why not use the best reagent with the best thermal cycler, especially if it's free!" Clearly, the hope was that many would convert from competitive reagents to Amplitaq Gold once they tried it.

During VOC, customers were up in arms over the offer! How dare Applied Biosystems dictate which reagent they should use! AB was impinging on their scientific judgment. Not only wouldn't they respond to this offer, they would be offended if they received it. They viewed the offer as "arm-twisting"!

So, the question Applied Biosystems asked was: "If this offer doesn't work, what would you, our customers and prospects, find compelling?" Here's a summation of the responses:

We trust and respect AB. The 2400 is their thermal cycler of choice. However, the cost of the 2400, even with university discounts, is significantly higher than the competition. University research budgets are tight and shrinking. If Applied Biosystems could pass along some of the savings from moving to a direct

channel versus field sales, it would make the 2400 affordable (and they would regain market share).

With these results, Applied Biosystems decided to pilot the program in two of eight sales districts. The offer: For a three-month period, university-affiliated laboratories could order the GeneAmp PCR System 2400 thermal cycler for 33 percent below list price from AB's new direct unit. The results:

- Doubled forecasted sales in one district*
- Tripled forecasted sales in the second district*
- Conversion rate: 20 percent
- Average order: $2,995
- Cost per order: $345
- Expense to Revenue: 12 percent

Based on the success of the pilot, a national rollout was implemented. As many as 60 percent of 2400 purchasers were expected to buy reagents and consumables (such as tubes) from AB. This now generates an expected ongoing revenue stream of $5,000 per customer per year, significantly reducing Expense to Revenue.

Points to Remember

Voice of Customer Messaging and Communication Research is a specialized methodology whose goal is to bring customer needs and preferences to the marketing planning table. The lessons learned are powerful and will help you avoid making significant mistakes.

Through one-on-one, in-depth customer or prospect interviews, VOC Research generates unique, directional, qualitative marketing intelligence regarding:

- Awareness and perception of your company
- Business issues and drivers

---

* These results are for the 2400 only. Each district also experienced a dramatic increase in revenue from higher priced, more complex instrumentation, because the field was now free to focus on selling these products.

- The decision-making process, roles, and responsibilities
- Barriers to purchasing and/or switching to your company
- Media mix and sequence
- Contact preference

In addition, VOC Research allows you to pretest critical parts of your strategy:

- Positioning
- Messaging
- Creative
- Offers

Garry Dawson, Manager, Marketing Communications Strategy, Hewlett-Packard, says that Voice of Customer Research is a critical contributor to program results:

HP uses VOC to uncover customer needs in the following areas:

1. **Understand the stages of the Enterprise IT buying process.**
2. **Know who is involved in each stage.**
3. **Develop offers for each buyer at every stage.**

Dissecting the many stages of the complex Enterprise product and solution buying process is critical. This includes who is involved at each stage and what information each buyer needs during the process. Previous quantitative research identified decision makers, buying stages, and types of offers. However, quantitative research does not get to the fine points which differentiate HP nor issues which peak customers' interests. VOC is the tool to tackle this need.

Offers can make or break a program. HP uses VOC to find the details of successful offers. It's not good enough to produce a "white paper" or "case study." The content must be informative and show the value of HP . . . all as defined by the customer or prospect. VOC digs into the real content customers/prospects want in offers.

VOC also brings together the program team around a common set of needs. Once the customer needs are identified, the various "opinions" of internal people become secondary to drive decisions. Customer needs take priority over internal assumptions.

In short, VOC Messaging and Communication Research is a specialized and vital contributor to the Consensual Marketing Opt-In Process. In Chapter 4 we will address the next step: integrating media and message with precision and relevance.

Step Three: How to Integrate Media and Message

THE THIRD STEP in the Consensual Marketing Opt-In Process is understanding and applying the Integrated Direct Marketing (IDM) methodology. This chapter provides insights and findings from over 20 years of testing and rolling out IDM implementations to help you reduce waste and dramatically increase response. Our focus will be on how to select, sequence, and integrate your media mix and message in order to generate double-digit response every time.

In this chapter we will discuss:

- The rationale for and definition of IDM
- Dangers of the "two percent solution"
- Organizational silos
- Surrounding the customer with an effective mix of media and response options
- The art and science of integrating and synchronizing media and message

And throughout, we will include comprehensive case studies that illustrate the step-by-step process and results with hard numbers, to show you how and why Integrated Direct Marketing is vital to the Consensual Marketing process.

The Rationale for IDM

Let's start with a statement by William Zengel, Vice President, Association of National Advertisers:

> **With corporate marketing communications expenditures representing almost 3 percent of National GDP, CEOs across America are demanding demonstrable return on investment from their marketers. Yet few marketers have found the way to deliver this Holy Grail—across an integrated platform with a scalable, effective, and efficient solution.**

The Integrated Direct Marketing methodology was created more than 20 years ago. It was devised to significantly improve marketing efficiency, yield, and return on investment. It was born out of our observations that marketers were focusing on primarily single media deployments and were unhappy with the results.

The first test of IDM in the early 1980s was, in fact, the launch of our consulting practice. Rather than send out letters full of fantastic promises regarding the IDM methodology and then hope for the best, we began a four-pronged approach:

- Publicity in direct marketing and advertising publications to bring the concept of IDM to light (thus also leveraging the implied endorsement of the publisher)
- Direct mail to personalize the benefits of IDM to each company
- Outbound telecontact to reach decision makers and probe for their needs and areas of pain—so we could position IDM as an effective solution
- Inbound telecontact to identify those with the greatest interest and needs

Painting by the Numbers

IDM produced dramatic, measurable results for our clients. Its success has been quantified over and over, and we will share the most relevant

case histories with you. But before we go further, to illustrate the importance of IDM today we'd like you to keep four numbers in mind: 10, 65,
176, and 30 million.

Here's a hint: You've seen these before in Chapter 1, and they do not
represent good news. These numbers are plastered to the rear bumper
of your customer's car as it's leaving your parking lot. Customers are
telling marketers to "paint by the numbers," and these are the numbers
for one year:

- The DMA's Mail Preference List increased 10 percent. These are
  people who no longer want to receive direct mail from any marketer. The trend has been steady, 10 percent per year, for several
  years.
- The DMA's Telephone Preference List increased by 65 percent.
  These are people who no longer want to receive phone calls from
  any marketer. The year before, it increased 25 percent.
- The DMA's E-mail Preference (Opt-Out) List increased by 176
  percent. These are individuals who no longer want to receive promotional e-mails from any marketer!
- Thirty million consumers registered for the National Do Not Call
  List in just five weeks. That's an average of 6 million people per
  week—almost a million per day. It's half what the FTC expected to
  register in the first year. It represents 18 percent of all the residential phone numbers in the United States! In just 12 weeks, over 50
  million consumers registered.

Why Is This Happening?

It's not just enough for marketers to know these numbers: we've got to dig
deeper and ask why this is happening. More than 55 VOC Messaging and
Communication Research efforts we have conducted on behalf of clients
confirm that customers are becoming increasingly alienated and angry due to
untargeted, unfocused, unsolicited mail, e-mail, and phone calls. Customers
are responding to marketers' messages with strong words of their own:

- "The fastest way to be forgotten is to buy."
- "You flood me with mail instead of taking the time to understand
  my needs."

- "What's the value of your communications? I get about one garbage can a day of unsolicited, irrelevant information."

All the numbers add up to a mandate for marketers to change the way they're doing business and to redefine the role of marketing communications and database deployment. This means refocusing on the customer, on his or her satisfaction and lifetime value, and it means eliminating marketing waste.

Professor Philip Kotler of the J. L. Kellogg School of Management provides perspective:

We are assaulted with pitches from every part of the world via every medium. And we want to shut them off. I believe in opt-in relationships with targeted consumers who want us to reach them with relevant information at the right time and the right way. I don't like the opt-out burden. I'd rather be in a society where everything is automatically opted out and the only things I get are when I personally decide to opt in.

Direct marketing is in a sense a marketer's dream. It should also be a consumer's dream when it works right because it means that the marketers know enough about me not to bother me when I don't want to be bothered and to help me when I have an interest. And that is so much better than mass marketing blasting away at everyone and getting a 1 to 2 percent response rate, if that, and 98 to 99 percent waste. Direct marketing is a dream but is becoming a nightmare because it's being done with carelessness. Direct marketing has a long way to go to work the way the public wants it to work.

The bottom line is that the entire communications mix has to be reevaluated. There is too much inertia in budgets where marketers feel safe doing what they have always done. Nobody wants to take a risk or take a chance of sales going down by switching to what really might be a more promising, more effective deployment of media.

Marketers today are risk averse, and this is counterintuitive. When they're under pressure, they should be more experimental

because what was working before isn't, and they should search for something that will work.

The Two Percent Solution

Professor Kotler brings up a seminal point: ours may be the only industry that has been able to turn a profit when 2 percent of its customers say yes and 98 percent say no (see Figure 4.1). What incredible waste! What shortsightedness! Out of every 100 messages, 98 customers throw us in the trash (see Figure 4.2). It's a waste of time, effort, materials, and relationships. Marketers can whistle a customer-focused tune all day long, but if a 2 percent response is acceptable, then the real message is that the marketer is interested in the quick sale, not the relationship.

Vincent Amen, former Vice President of Public Programs for Franklin Covey, and President of Growth Coach, says:

Humans don't change when they walk into their offices, they bring all their B2C likes and dislikes with them into the B2B marketplace. They don't want their valuable time wasted by

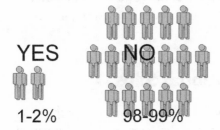

Figure 4.1 Depiction of Inefficient Marketing

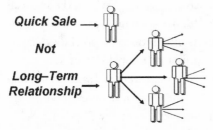

Figure 4.2 The Goal of Traditional Direct Marketing

unwanted, impersonal, poorly targeted marketing messages. These messages don't bring value—they reflect incompetence on the marketer and his organization.

Please put on your customer hat for a moment. The deployment of media and message is not only generating awareness and response for the marketer, it's shaping the customer's experience of the company. If you, with your customer hat on, were to receive consistently irrelevant and intrusive messages from a company, would you be impressed . . . buy from them . . . recommend them to your friends?

John Hunter, Senior Vice President of Customer Services, QVC, sheds some light on the issue:

Marketers are too happy with the 2 percent response rate. They have no idea what's happening with the other 98 percent. Go find out what's happening to the 98 percent who don't want to buy. Don't get so enamored with the 2 percent. Find out how many people you're alienating, that will never come back, or will tell 10 of their friends about the negative experience.

We have to believe that some portion of the 98 percent who didn't respond weren't just neutral about the offer. They were, in fact, annoyed.

Organizational Silos

A major cause of the current marketing *dis*-integration is the way organizations have grown up. The evolution of business has caused organizations to become a series of silos of information—each silo representing a specific area of expertise. Within many corporations, each of the following is a separate department that behaves as a silo: Web marketing, call centers, advertising, direct response, PR. Measurement criteria and agendas vary from silo to silo, which inhibits integration and precludes a companywide focus on the customer. It promotes "intersilo" warfare.

The most typical is the friction between marketing and sales. Marketing is measured by the amount and cost of the gross leads they produce. So Marketing manufactures leads and throws them over the wall to Sales. Sales, however, is measured by net revenue. They catch the leads and pronounce them dead on arrival—competitors, students, idle requests, and folks who are no longer there. No one is playing nicely in the sandbox.

This organizational structure also feeds the notion of every silo for itself. So if one silo is in charge of vanilla ice cream and another is in charge of strawberry, both feel an equal right to attack the customer database. Who cares what the customers said they like? They'll change. These silos, and funding by product versus customer set, perpetuate the notion that marketers are in control and that if we just pound on the customers long enough, they'll buy.

Integrating and Synchronizing Media and Message

Garry Dawson, Manager of Marketing Communications Strategy for Hewlett-Packard's Americas Enterprise Systems Group, is an IDM veteran:

> **Historically, HP, like many tech companies, organized and measured communications in a "silo" fashion. Each discipline . . . was asked to perform to the best of their abilities. Functions were optimized to stand alone. There were no mandates to create an integrated team or plan.**
>
> **Today, HP recognizes the only way to remain competitive and exceed business goals is to integrate marcom [marketing communications]. Each "campaign" must contain one voice (customer relevant message) across all functions. The principles of IDM apply to every communications challenge.**
>
> **IDM has improved response rates and the number of leads generated per program by two times or more. In very controlled programs response rates have been 30 percent!**

The Definition of IDM

Integrated Direct Marketing integrates and sequences media and message through an understanding of the *customer's time dimension*. Where is the customer within his or her life cycle? Where is the customer within the decision-making process? Different messages and different media are deployed in accordance with customer preferences to provide them with the information they require to move to the next stage, and to create an interactive dialogue where both parties listen and learn. This enables marketers to better meet the customer's ongoing and future needs.

IDM concentrates on surrounding customers with an effective mix of media and informed choices to create the most relevant, compelling, and competitively differentiating customer experience. This means deploying our palette of media and message to present the right information to the right person at the right time.

Don Schultz, Professor Emeritus, Northwestern University, Medill School of Journalism, and founder of Agora, Inc., consultants, says about this approach:

> **How do people touch you—how do they touch your brand, how do they touch your organization? And how can you be where they want you to be, not where you want to be? Here are two concepts. One is relevance and the other is receptivity. When is my product or my service or my offer relevant to you, and when do you want to receive information about it? It's their choice. A little while ago, Dow Chemical was investigating customer touch points. They went out and asked customers, how do you want to get information about us? What customers told them is, the stuff we want is stuff that's relevant to us, not stuff that's relevant to you. And that's the big difference.**

The IDM process helps you manage the precision sequencing of media and message—even managing the time interval between touches to *hours*. IDM provides the proven guidelines for media synchronization. A key example, which will be discussed in Chapter 6, is "Response Compression," where the optimal timing between receipt of mail and receipt of an outbound touch is 24 to 72 hours.

IDM is sensitive to frequency of touches and deploys media through a *regulated touch process*. The frequency of touches is driven by the customer's self-declared interest and self-indicated propensity to buy. Media preference also drives interactive contact but only at appropriate points. This is a far cry from many corporations that suggest self-imposed frequency limits on each medium but do not enforce them.

This process of precision media deployment enables IDM to consistently generate double-digit response. It allows the marketer to do more with less—generating more revenue with less waste, with the same or less budget. Which is especially important in times of decreasing budgets.

IDM not only drives higher response, but also promotes increased spending. Here's some interesting input from Jupiter Research: [1]

Customers who purchase from multiple channels are increasing their spending. Customers overwhelmingly move from Web to store, from store to Web, and from catalog to Web in the process of researching and completing purchases. Customers who purchase in multiple channels appear to spend up to 30 percent more than their single-channel counterparts.

Spray and Pray

By implementing the IDM process, you will consistently achieve double-digit qualified response. This is a far cry from the "Spray and Pray" marketing (Figure 4.3), which unfortunately is the norm.

Traditionally, marketers load the marketing budget into the old "blunderbuss" and fill the sky with scattershot. Our mental image is of Elmer Fudd going duck hunting. Our hope is that one, two, or maybe three of these will hit the target. And miraculously, we've put dinner on the table again. Is there a level of skill involved? Sure. Is there more than a fair share of luck involved? Absolutely.

Marketing Budget

SALE!

Figure 4.3 "Spray and Pray" Marketing

Al Ries, Chairman, Ries & Ries, Atlanta, Georgia: [2]

Too much advertising, too much mail, too many phone calls, too much e-mail. There is a direct relationship between the volume of advertising and the effectiveness of each single advertisement. We have known for years, for example, that a print advertisement in a "thin" issue of a publication will be far more effective than the same advertisement in a "thick" issue of the same publication. For the most part marketers are aware of the problem, but hate to switch from their existing systems which were successful in the past.

The Customer Life Cycle

IDM responds to the stages of the Customer Life Cycle (Figure 4.4), which we've seen depicted before, and thus it increases your relevance, response, and revenue.

In the presale period, customers are researching their needs and separating the wheat from the chaff. Marketers respond with integrated media and sales strategies to surround the customer with information and informed choices.

The sale stage brings the opportunity for "thank you" marketing, which is always productive but rarely done. At one large technology company, branch managers were asked to place calls to mid-market customers who had just made a significant purchase. The customers were dumbfounded. They never knew this person really existed—and they were tickled to know their business was appreciated. One telecommunications company engaged in thank you marketing by calling purchasers of business telephone systems. In the first few calls they uncovered a major flaw. The installation instructions said to place one unit at least 36 inches from the other unit. The cord supplied was only 18 inches long.

The growth and retention phase is most often disregarded. And yet it provides significant opportunity to engage the customer in interactive ongoing communications. The opportunities are:

- Consultative needs assessment
- Problem identification and resolution
- Increase market penetration and repeat sales

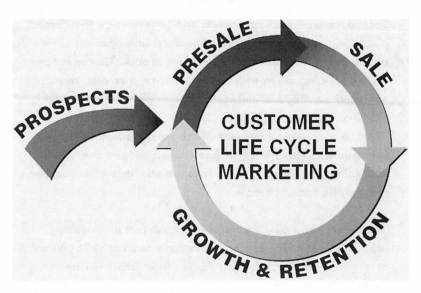

Figure 4.4   Customer Life Cycle

A Media Mix with Unprecedented Power

The IDM Media Mix includes a palette of at least seven brilliant colors:

- PR
- Direct response print advertising
- Internet
- E-mail
- Direct mail
- Inbound and outbound telecontact
- Field sales channels

How many of these seven components are you using? How many are you integrating with precision and relevance?

Garry Dawson of Hewlett-Packard puts it all together, step-by-step:

First, we must change the paradigm of "finding" prospects to "knowing where prospects and customers go for information." If you are where customers are already searching for information, your cost per response and lead will decline (assuming the offer is relevant).

Second, recognize that prospects and customers go to different places (e.g., trade publications, Webcasts, white papers) at various stages of the decision and purchase process. Customers use their own information networks to become aware of, consider, and purchase products and solutions.

Third, at each stage a relevant offer is needed to deliver value to your audience. It's no longer just enough to have one offer for your campaign. You may need a separate offer by audience and by stage of the decision process.

The net results should dramatically cut the cost of marketing . . . especially waste. HP has seen marketing waste cut by 50 percent or more. Moreover, program results have improved by three times or more.

PR

The terms *publicity* and *public relations* have become synonymous and are now referred to as simply PR. The value of PR has increased dramatically. It is no longer a passive medium and a "nice to have" addition to the media mix. It has proved itself to be a powerful driver of highly qualified response and a necessary element of the media mix.

PR is increasingly replacing print advertising in its ability to create an umbrella of awareness for a product or service at an affordable ROI. Too often, customers see an advertising blitz as the self-serving work of a company with a lot of money. PR enjoys the benefit of the implied third-party endorsement. No company paid for this. "This magazine," the thinking goes, "researched the information, found value, and wrote a story about the product or company." And if it appears in a periodical, "it must be true." This is the aura of verisimilitude—the appearance or semblance of truth—that surrounds stories that are published.

Al Ries on PR:

The best way to launch a new brand, in our opinion, is with PR. After the brand has achieved credibility, then a company can switch to advertising to maintain the brand. The strength of PR is its ability to generate credibility for a brand. The weakness of PR

is the fact that after a brand has become strongly established, it is no longer "new" and further publicity is difficult to obtain.

We have found that PR consistently generates the highest quality of responses and leads, which also convert at a higher percentage than any other medium. But PR is most often overlooked by direct marketers. The reason might be because it is a nontraditional direct response medium, or perhaps because it is not the easiest or most predictable medium to use.

"There is not enough focus by marketers on the value of Publicity/PR to gain new customers and support current customers in the buying decision that they have already made."—Vincent J. Amen

The first step in harnessing the direct response power of PR is to identify the periodicals or online magazines (or "zines") that the target audience trusts and turns to for information and advice. The more vertical and specific the publication is to the target audience, the more effective PR will be in generating awareness and response. Mass market publications won't do the trick for most marketers. That's because there is too much spill, given that the target market is too small a percentage of total readership.

Read these publications and become familiar with their content and style. Request the materials they make available to advertisers. This will usually contain their editorial calendar, which will help you with planning and timing. It will tell you what topics they want to cover in upcoming issues. Identify the editors who specialize in stories that are consistent with your product or service. These vertical or affinity publications are always looking for content.

Develop several story ideas (and be prepared to take the idea and bring it to a completed manuscript, should the editor request it). These ideas must be newsworthy. Editors will rarely publish a puff piece on your product or service. Every editor will be looking for the value to the publication's readership. And, because the objective is awareness and response, you must work into the story a substantial value that readers can only get by contacting your company. This is the critical "call to action" that makes PR so effective as a direct response medium. It turns the story from passive to active—inviting the reader to take action to receive value. The case history in the next section is a good example.

Now comes the hard part. We can leverage but we cannot control whether the story gets picked up. And lead times are frequently three to six months. Two strong leverage points:

- The newsworthiness of the story idea and its applicability to the readership of the publication.
- Creating a relationship with the editor by consistently providing value. In fact, create a mini-IDM program for each editor you target!

"We use PR to create an awareness of QVC's programming. And hopefully encourage people to watch our channel. And we also try to use PR to convey the messages of trust and respect for the customer."—Doug Rose, Vice President Merchandising Brand Development, QVC

"PR is the most underutilized asset in the marcom portfolio. PR has a huge potential to drive business. I'm making the integration of PR into the marcom mix my most important initiative."—Garry Dawson

Case History: Catalog Development

The following case history illustrates the power of PR within the IDM Media Mix.

There's a very popular catalog that features a wide selection of specialty papers—blank, patterned, designed, etc.—catering to the desktop publishing world. This catalog was originated in a warehouse in New Jersey, the brainstorm of two brothers and their dad. One of the brothers, the younger, was a very successful paper merchant who serviced businesses throughout the New York City metropolitan area the old-fashioned way—delivering cartons of paper by truck. The older brother had the idea of expanding this business into mail order. He was willing to leave his job in real estate to spearhead the endeavor, and his dad, recently retired, was looking for something to do.

It was a great idea, but there was very little start-up money. Investors wanted to see the idea generate some early results before they would fully back it. But that put the fledgling organization in a "Catch 22"—

since they lacked the funds to place ads and buy lists, which would generate the early results. Their limited working capital was spent on catalog development.

PR was identified as a key leverage point. If they could get magazines to pick up a story, the word would be out. Consumers and businesses would know of the catalog and interest would be generated. Investors would see the coverage and hear the buzz. Articles would be proof-positive that the idea of the catalog had merit. And PR was basically free. The big investment was time.

The family went to local magazine stands and bought every publication that catered to the desktop publishing market. They took them home, read them, and prioritized the publications that addressed the target market most directly. Within each of these publications they identified the editor(s) who specialized in technology and technology consumables.

Next, they developed several newsworthy stories. One of the best was: Considering the proliferation of technology, printing methods, and devices, which paper works best for each application, given the wide variety of paper contents, manufacturing processes, and finishes?

And within each story they embedded a call to action: "We offer free paper consultation. If you have a problem or a question, call us and speak to our resident expert. Even the call is free."

The list of publications and editors was divided up among the principals. The story ideas were sent out in small batches of mail. Each story idea had to be followed up with a call, and they didn't want to outstrip their ability to follow up within 24 to 72 hours of the editor's receipt of the letter. Each phone call was scripted to ensure that value was imparted, whether by voice mail, the actual conversation, or actual contact. Each editor was contacted once a week for six weeks (six story ideas sent over a six-week period). In PR, persistence counts.

The result: The story, reflecting the story lines mentioned above, was picked up by several key publications, which generated an impressive response. These were not just folks interested in the free service; these were buyers. A comparison to subsequent baselines of response and conversion shows that these inquirers generated the highest conversion and the highest average order of any subsequent medium or promotional effort.

Direct Response Print Advertising

"Advertising should work hand-in-glove with the PR plan. Stand-alone ads or an ad campaign separate from PR yields low results. Customer relevant messaging and offer content should be consistent across PR, advertising, and all other media."—Garry Dawson

There are five keys to successfully integrating Direct Response Print Advertising into the IDM Media Mix:

Message

- The message should capture the essential customer benefits (the most important benefits communicated as simply as possible).
- It should be consistent with the results of VOC Messaging and Communication Research.
- Subsequent communications in the media mix should expand upon these net customer benefits.

Timing

- In the best of all worlds, advertising should be in the same issue as the PR placement (story).
- At the very least, print advertising should begin one week following the PR placement and continue for two to three insertions, contingent upon the frequency of the publication and its relevance to the target market.

Placement (the List of Periodicals)

- The initial media plan should be based on the results of Voice of Customer Messaging and Communication Research and independent investigation.
- Prioritize the publications your decision makers and influencers are truly influenced by.

Don't Overspend

- Each medium must sing for its supper. Budget allocations should be based upon actual and potential response and conversion rates.

Direct Response Orientation

- Make no mistake—these ads are direct response executions. The desired outcome is action as measured by response.
- Traditionally, advertising has been measured by "impressions" and building awareness. We agree. We definitely want to impress the target market. But the only way we know to truly quantify the effectiveness of the advertising budget is to measure results: How many responded, how many bought, what was the revenue, what was the ROI?

Al Ries has some things to say on this subject:

The strength of print is its ability to target specific markets. You can use magazines to target specific industries, occupations, interests, etc. For example, you can reach automobile enthusiasts in such publications as *Road & Track, Car & Driver*. You can use magazines to target specific cities or regions. Print advertising works best for products or services with a high degree of consumer appeal. With such products, a reader is likely to tear out an ad for further reference. The weakness of print advertising is that it is expensive.

E-mail and Direct Mail

The Internet and e-mail will be discussed in depth in Chapter 5. For now, we offer these words of wisdom:

- "For most companies, having a Web site is just as important as having a postal address. Most companies today cannot remain in business without having a web address." Al Ries.
- "E-mail . . . because it is cheap and easy to deploy . . . has become an abused medium. Astonishingly, the tried-and-true lessons of direct mail have had to be relearned by the proponents of this medium." Vincent J. Amen.

Concerning direct mail, Charles A. Prescott, Vice President, International Business Development & Government Affairs, Direct Marketing Association, has this to say:

Direct mail is the major direct response vehicle that we measure throughout the world. It has shown to be the major vehicle everywhere except the United States.

At some point following the early introduction of the Internet and the widespread acceptance of e-mail, marketers began turning away from direct mail. This coincided with the economic slump in the United States, which focused companies more on expense than revenue. Certainly, in an expense-focused economy, direct mail looked like a dinosaur. Marketers wondered: "Why should we spend money on printing and postage when e-mail costs nothing to deliver?"

"Direct mail is exactly like print advertising except that its strengths are magnified (the targeting factor) and so are its weaknesses (the cost factor)."—Al Ries

But to focus solely on expense is a fatal flaw. Expense should be viewed in light of the revenue it drives. So we have to ask: Did customers also turn away from direct mail?

Here's some interesting information reported in eMarketer,[3] "the source for Internet and e-business research and analysis": A Vertis study asked U.S. adults 18 and over what type of marketing they would like to receive instead of phone calls. The results:

- 31 percent, direct mail
- 24 percent, newspaper inserts
- 18 percent, catalog
- 11 percent, newspaper ads
- 10 percent, e-mail

Reinforcing the view that consumers' views regarding media have not changed all that much, the same issue of eMarketer contrasts a study done by the Auriemma Consulting Group, which asked consumers their most and least preferred marketing channels. The most preferred was direct mail (32 percent), which was followed by TV, radio, and print ads (30 percent). The least preferred channel was telecontact—59 percent did not want it.

It does not appear that customers have turned away from direct mail. In fact, they seem to value it. This is echoed in results from our own

Voice of Customer Messaging and Communication Research: "If it's important, send it to me by mail."

The Internet magazine eMarketer[4] also reports on another Vertis Consumer Focus study, this one indicating that the number of U.S. adults who respond to direct mail grew from 34 percent in 2001 to 46 percent in 2003—a 35 percent increase. The study also indicated that the number of "young baby boomers" who are responsive to direct mail was similar, growing from 36 percent in 2001 to 49 percent in 2003—a 36 percent increase.

The conclusion and our recommendation: Direct mail is a very productive medium widely overlooked by marketers. It should be part of your IDM Media Mix, with deployment subject to the results of Voice of Customer Messaging and Communication Research and Consensual profiling.

The following leverage points, which we will go into, will make your direct mail more effective:

- Strategy
- List
- Format/creative
- Offer
- Postage

Strategy

Within IDM and CMO, direct mail should be used in accordance with the VOC quote: "If it's something important, send it by mail." When content plus audience warrant the investment in this medium, do it right, with the leverage points as a guide. That means, in most cases, you do not want to use an expensive direct mail piece for cold prospecting.

List

List or database is the most important leverage point—the same as is true for any other direct response medium. The old saying goes, "I could have a terrific product and a lousy list and go broke. I could have a mediocre product and a terrific list and make a bundle."

If you're using your database to communicate with your customers, please reread Chapter 2, especially the section on the Consensual Database. You should be selecting prequalified names—individuals whose interest is consistent with the information you are sending and who have stated that direct mail is a preferred medium.

If you're prospecting and/or using rental lists, here are some hints:

Choose a List Broker Carefully

Our suggestion is to source List Brokers by referral. Who are colleagues using that they can recommend? Try to come up with a short list of two or three. The reputation and resources of the list brokerage are important. Of equal importance is your specific contact. This individual List Broker controls your customer experience.

A good List Broker is more than just a salesperson or a shipping clerk. They have knowledge, experience, and insight that can be brought to bear on your project. Ask about their background.

Then test! Testing is the foundation of continuous improvement. If your search process has identified two List Brokers, give them both the same assignment. In both cases, start from the beginning. Bring them into strategy, target market, competitive issues, offer, previous results, etc. The more they understand, the better job they can do. Then compare their recommendations. If there is no clear winner and each provided value, consider using both.

No One List Will Satisfy All Your Needs!

Each list has its own strengths. You need to combine the strengths of several different lists to give you the best shot at success. Here's an example: An insurance company is looking to speak to small-business owners. Some of the types of lists they should consider:

- **A compiled list based on the phone book.** This list will provide coverage, i.e., every small business has a phone.
- **A compiled list that contains reliable demographic information,** i.e., small businesses (based upon the number of employees, annual sales, SIC, etc.).
- **An association list,** i.e., individuals who belong to respected affinity or industry-specific associations.
- **A responder list,** i.e., business owners who have recently inquired about insurance products.

These lists should be deduped (remove duplication) and combined through merge/purge. The resulting file will give you "tiered" results. For example, the top tier will be businesses where we know the demographics, know that the owner belongs to a respected association and has recently inquired about insurance products via direct response. Not a bad list to have. These folks may have the highest propensity to buy. Marketers should consider investing the most against this tier or segment of the file. Subsequent tiers will contain records with less information.

Accurate source coding (by each list and/or test cell), source code capture, and timely response reporting will tell you which tier worked best.

Testing Should Become Standard Operating Procedure

Recommend that every campaign should contain at least one projectable test of the leverage points discussed in this section. Tips for successful testing:

- Test only one variable at a time.
- Make sure you have a control cell (no test).
- Watch your quantity per test cell. Statistical logarithmic charts may indicate that for a 99 percent confidence level you need to have several tens of thousands per test cell. Few of us mail in those kinds of quantities. And few things in life are 99 percent sure. Practically speaking, we feel that 5,000 pieces per test cell is about the minimum quantity for a meaningful test. Below that, the percentage of response is likely to swing on only one or two responses. (For instance, if you mailed 1,000 pieces, 1 response = 0.1%, 2 responses = 0.2%, etc.) And that makes judgments difficult.

Format/Creative

Drawing upon testing that clients have done, we can say that the following works:

- A closed-face package with a personalized address. No labels or windows.
- A personalized letter. We mean logical personalization, not seeing how many times their first name can appear in copy. And to that

point—unless we've earned the right to be on a first-name basis, the salutation should be formal (Dear Mr., Ms., Mrs., Dr., etc.). The personalization should also extend to copy, i.e., version it to respond to a specific customer concern or area of interest. The purpose of the cover letter is directional: tell the customer what's in the mail package and what's in it for them.

- A brochure that contains the details of the product and offer. It should be attractive and invite pass-along.
- A response device that reiterates the offer and encourages inbound phone response while presenting all other response options—phone, fax, mail, e-mail, Web. As we recommended previously, inbound responders are self-motivated and thus convert at a higher rate. Also, inbound is interactive—you have the ability to probe and demonstrate how your product or service addresses customer needs. Upsell and cross-sell are also possible via inbound.
- A return envelope. Should the customer wish to respond by mail, testing has shown that they are reluctant to put sensitive information, such as a phone number and e-mail address, on a postcard/business reply card where anyone can see it.

Many creative treatments we have seen strive to be different for the sake of being different. Use caution and test first. We have found that even the most gorgeous self-mailers still pull like self-mailers, i.e., eliciting a low level of marginally qualified response.

Offer

Consider an offer strategy that includes a series of offers you will send to prospects over time, given the different stages in their decision-making process. The following offers, for example, escalate in commitment and complexity:

- Offer 1: A "white paper" (response to this offer indicates a lower level of qualification/propensity to buy)
- Offer 2: An invitation to a seminar or event (response to this offer indicates a more qualified/more likely-to-buy customer)
- Offer 3: Schedule an appointment to see a rep (response is highly qualified/has a high propensity to buy)

Postage

In an expense-focused culture, there is never a question about what postage to use: Bulk Third. In a return-on-investment-focused culture, we should ask what level of investment will drive the greatest revenue. In our experience First Class mail with a live stamp (not a presort stamp) generates the highest level of qualified response. The additional cost is offset by the increased:

- Deliverability
- Openability
- Response
- Revenue

Think about how you sort your mail, whether at the office or at home. Voice of Customer Messaging and Communication Research tells us that when mail is delivered, people often stand over the wastebasket and try to eliminate as much as possible. The first things that go are those pieces sent as bulk mail. Next are presorted pieces where we don't know the company (the logo on the outer envelope is very important—in fact, if we recognize the logo and have a relationship with the company, it may make the cut) or where there is a teaser that smacks of another credit card offer. Self-mailers get chucked. "Resident" mailings are history. The mailers people seem to open, other than the regular monthly bills, are the personalized envelopes with a live stamp.

Many of our clients have tested the levels of postage to satisfy the questions: Should we send direct mail via Bulk Third to save money? Does First Class postage really generate more business? Can we get the results of First Class but still save money through presorting and preprinting an indicia? Why not just use a meter?

Recommendation: Conduct your own test and measure it by the bottom line—which test cell/postage variation generates the most money.

Case Study: The Phoenician

The Phoenician is one of the truly over-the-top resorts in the United States. During Voice of Customer Research a repeat guest commented that upon first arrival, he knew it was the holiest place on earth. You walk into the lobby, look around, and say, "Holy cow." You go to the restaurant and read the menu and say, "Holy moley." And so on.

Marketing management at the Phoenician was intrigued by the IDM methodology and decided to test IDM versus their traditional mix of image advertising. Traditionally, they invested in television because "television makes the phones ring" and the logical extension is that if the phones are ringing, they must be booking reservations.

Debbie Kellam, Marketing Manager for the Phoenician, explains:

We conducted Voice of Customer Messaging and Communication Research and found that guests would welcome communications directly from the Phoenician and suggested direct mail. We tested the IDM combination of direct mail and well-trained and scripted proactive reservation agents handling inbound telecontact versus our television, newspaper, and magazine advertising. We adhered to IDM's strict process of metrics to bring this to the bottom line and understand which vehicles generated what revenue. The question we were looking to answer was, can we drive qualified response in conjunction with our traditional image-advertising approach? Test results were eye-opening.

The Phoenician traditionally allocated its marketing budget as follows:

- Television = 36 percent
- Newspaper = 32 percent
- Magazine = 26 percent
- Direct mail = 6 percent

The budget was redeployed for the IDM test cell as follows:

- Television = 32 percent
- Newspaper = 31 percent
- Magazine = 21 percent
- Direct mail plus inbound = 15 percent

Figure 4.5 illustrates both traditional budget and the redeployment. Within this test, there are only two metrics that really matter. The rest

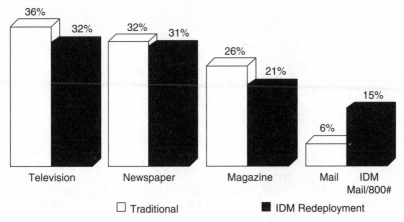

Figure 4.5   Traditional and Redeployment Budgets for the Phoenician

are just milestones along the way: the conversion rate and the revenue generated. The first is a leverage point, the second is the bottom line.

To have a valid point of comparison for conversion rate, the Phoenician developed a historical baseline, which to the best of their ability was neutral to variables such as seasonality. The baseline included response from referrals, repeat guests, travel agents, and media. The conversion rate from the test cells was, however, pure. That is, it did not include response from referrals, repeat guests, etc. The conversion rate for television only considered response from television broadcast advertising, for IDM was just from mail/phone, etc.

The IDM combination of integrated direct mail and inbound tele-contact resulted in a 21 percent conversion versus the baseline of 13 percent —a 62 percent increase over traditional conversion (see Figures 4.6 and 4.7).

The IDM test results:

- Television generated 5 percent of revenue (with 32 percent of the budget)
- Newspaper generated 21 percent of revenue (with 31 percent of the budget)
- Magazine generated 10 percent of revenue (with 21 percent of the budget)
- The IDM combination of direct mail and inbound generated 64 percent of revenue (with 15 percent of the budget)

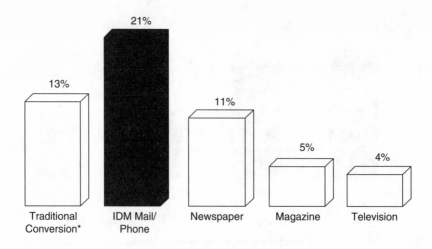

*Includes response from referrals, repeat guests, travel agents, and media

Figure 4.6 Conversion

The lesson for the Phoenician was that image advertising and IDM could comfortably coexist. No amount of IDM testing would completely wean them from image advertising and cause them to shift all of their budget into direct response marketing. This test did show, however, that the selective and strategic implementation of IDM can bring two benefits: a way of extending the Phoenician experience into the homes of valued guests via very targeted and personalized vehicles; and IDM-generated incremental revenue at a very attractive ratio of expense to revenue.

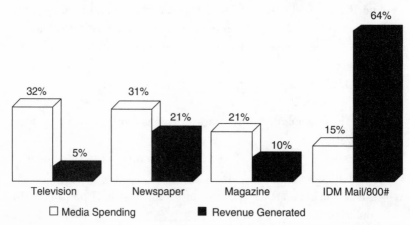

Figure 4.7 Final Results of IDM versus the Traditional Mix Study

Inbound and Outbound Telecontact

Inbound and outbound telecontact will be discussed in depth in Chapter 6. For now, we offer these words of wisdom from Al Ries:

> **The "phone spam" factor has seriously eroded the value of outbound telecontact. Companies that use telecontact in the future will have to figure out ways to generate credibility with each consumer before they approach the consumer by phone.**

Field Sales Channels

This may not be news to you, but Field Sales and Marketing continue to represent a dysfunctional relationship. Relationship may be too strong a word—at times they barely speak. The main reason (other than Field Sales people are "aloof and uncooperative" and Marketing folks are "elitist and snippy") is very basic: Each area of expertise enjoys a different measurement of success. Field Sales is measured by the bottom line: Did they make the sale or didn't they? Did they bring in the net revenue?

Marketing, on the other hand, is traditionally measured by the gross number of leads or inquiries produced. More is better because that drives down the cost per lead. Quality may be seen as an inhibitor to driving quantity. Conversion of these leads or inquiries to sales is interesting, but largely anecdotal. To add insult to injury, in many companies the marketing team determines the criteria for a lead (what are the data points that a response must have to be considered a lead and thus worthy of Field's time?) as well as the Lead Management System, or a process for Field Sales to let Marketing know what happened with those leads.

So Marketing takes these leads and throws them over the silo wall to Field Sales.

The reality of field sales is that time is money. Sales quotas are demanding. Lead quality is essential to driving their success. Having been burnt before, Field Sales frequently sees leads coming from Marketing and makes little effort to work them.

As for feedback to Marketing, the phrase we often hear is: "Administrivia is not my job."

It's uncanny, but for all the years we have worked with American sales forces, we've found one point of consistency: those in the field normally follow up only 30 to 34 percent of leads. Why? No confidence! A typical response would be: "Why should I follow up low-quality stuff from Marketing when I have my own opportunities to work?"

The only reasonable answer is to integrate Field Sales into the marketing process—to treat the Field as Marketing's internal customer. When implemented consistently, the we find that the following IDM eight-step process for field integration generates a 100 percent or more increase in lead follow-up. We find that post-IDM, lead follow-up averages 60 to 85 percent.

Eight Steps for Integration

Step One: Field Sales Must Be a Key Member of the IDM Cross-Functional Team.

We'll go into greater detail regarding the IDM Cross-Functional Team in Chapter 8, but for now we'll note that the rationale for initiating the IDM marketing planning process with all stakeholders present is twofold:

- They have broad experience and expertise that would otherwise be unavailable.
- If they participate in the planning, they have "skin in the game" and will be held co-responsible for results.

And one of the prime stakeholders is Field Sales. A strong, respected representative of Field (selected by Field) must be involved from day one in the IDM marketing planning process. This includes their contribution to analyzing the results of previous efforts and bringing findings to the table. It includes their contribution to strategy development, setting goals and objectives, and the co-responsibility for achieving those goals and objectives.

Step Two: Field Sales Contributes to IDM Voice of Customer Messaging and Communication Research.

VOC Research helps you take the key strategy, positioning, and offer ideas that the cross-functional team developed and pretest them. It's critical that Field Sales be involved in determining: the research goals and objectives; selection of interviewees; the specific areas of questioning within the Interview Guide; and, of course, potential offers and/or events to be pretested. Which leads us to Step Three.

Step Three: Field Sales Contributes to Offer Development.

After all, Field Sales is talking to customers all day long about their needs, your products and services, and the competitive environment. This gives them unique perspective when it comes to offer development. Their unique insight should be put to good use. Plus, it is very important that Field support the final offer that is rolled out. They must support it internally and in their day-to-day contact with the customer base. Most of all, they don't want any surprises when they visit a customer!

Step Four: Field Sales Reviews Creative.

We are not advocating that Field assume the responsibilities of creative director, graphic designer, or copywriter. We are, however, asking for their street-smart input and feedback. Sharpening our creative focus due to Field input will result in more sales.

Step Five: Field Sales Contributes to Database Development.

Field Sales has unique access to the most current customer information. Their own database, whether in the computer, a PDA, three-by-five cards or in their heads, is likely to be deeper, more up-to-date, and accurate than anything Marketing can access. In a recent VOC research program we conducted, Field's database was 10 times deeper than the corporate database (e.g., for every customer name that Marketing was able to access through the database, Field Sales had 10 additional decision-maker names).

Additionally, Field will have the most recent information on "moves, changes, and rearranges"—e.g., executives who have relocated, retired, or have new responsibilities.

Last, and this is gospel, if Field Sales does not have confidence in the list you're using, they will not have confidence in the results of the campaign.

Step Six: Field Sales Defines Lead Criteria.

Within IDM, everyone gets a vote on the information that comprises a lead. However, the most important votes come from Field Sales. They must determine the criteria for a lead because it is their time that must be expended in follow-up. It is their ability to meet quota that is on the line. And the funny thing is, when lead quality meets Field's expectations, follow-up increases.

Step Seven: Field Sales Designs Lead Management Tracking Systems.

It is amazing! The lead management systems we have seen within highly respected corporations are usually so far removed from reality that first the clients explain the system to us, and then explain how they work around it to get the real leads out to the Field. Getting information back from the Field on the results of lead follow-up—it just doesn't happen. Not surprisingly, lead management is where most companies fail. The system must be designed by the Field or it will never work. The system must be true to the demands of the Field and lead criteria.

And if you are to get the Field to send back the results of lead follow-up, the lead management system cannot be perceived as a "police action." This feedback is essential for marketing to continuously improve. It answers important sales and marketing questions, such as:

- Was the lead sufficiently qualified?
- What were the results of the first conversation?
- When is follow-up?
- Did they purchase?
- What? When? How much?
- If not, why?

Step Eight: Shared Metrics for Marketing and Field Sales.

Both Marketing and Field Sales must be measured by the bottom line. There is no other way. Both camps are in the same leaky canoe. Unless

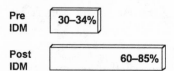

Successful integration of Field Sales equals:

- **Higher quality leads**
- **Increased lead follow–up**

Pre IDM — 30–34%

Post IDM — 60–85%

Figure 4.8   Field Integration Summary Chart

they both work together and bail, the canoe sinks. Leads that don't convert are worthless.

Instead of working at odds, Marketing and Field Sales must work in tandem (see Figure 4.8).

Optimal Sequencing of Media and Message

Figure 4.9 is based on the analysis of hundreds of marketing campaigns over many industries. It provides a proven guideline for the precision timing of your media deployment.

1. Begin with Publicity/PR to generate the umbrella of awareness. Print advertising should begin its three insertion flight one week after PR appears—with one exception: If possible, always begin print advertising in the issue carrying the PR story.
2. Print advertising directs the awareness created by PR and channels it into response. Ideally, we entice customers with print and drive them to direct mail and/or e-mail, which is deployed one week after the initial print advertising insertion.
3. Direct mail/e-mail provides more in-depth information than the print ad. Therefore, responses generated by these media will be better qualified.
4. Outbound telecontact is deployed with the principle of Response Compression in mind. Testing and analyses have proved that customer-focused outbound is most effective when reaching the decision maker within 24 to 72 hours after mail or e-mail receipt.

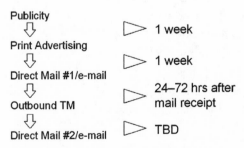

Figure 4.9 Precision Timing of Your Media

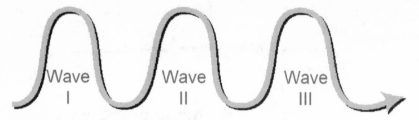

Figure 4.10   Wave Mailing Pattern

To enable Response Compression, mail is released in waves (Figure 4.10) of predetermined quantities based on the capacity of outbound to reach these customers. (We will discuss this in depth in Chapter 6.)

Investing Based on Return on Investment

"We very carefully test and evaluate each medium. Only when a particular medium generates sufficient ROI do we expand our investment in that medium. This helps to ensure that we operate our business on a profitable basis."—Greg Kohne, Assistant Vice President, Direct Sales, Golden Rule Insurance

Throughout both Consensual Marketing and IDM, our belief is that you should invest with an eye toward the expected return—that expense should be justified by revenue. Figure 4.11 was developed from analyzing the relative media contribution and media return on investment (ROI) from hundreds of campaigns. The chart indicates the percentage of the marketing budget that you should consider allocating to each medium. This is dramatically different from traditional marketing budget allocation, which is skewed toward advertising. Take this as a guideline and refine it through testing and your own unique experience. You'll see how this approach works in the AT&T case study that follows.

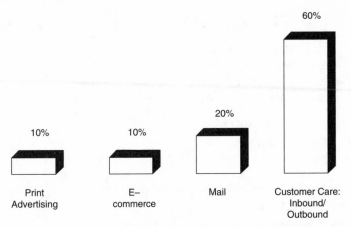

Figure 4.11 Media Investment Based upon Potential Return

Case History: AT&T

This case history is one of our favorites because it clearly quantifies the benefits of implementing the IDM process. It's based on an AT&T product introduction, and compares the actual results of traditional media and budget allocation versus results achieved from IDM media and budget deployment. It is a pure A/B test:

- Same product
- Same budget
- Same target market profile
- Same time frame
- Very different go-to-market processes

Overview

The target market was small- to medium-sized businesses throughout the United States. The average sale was $10,000. The objective: generate high-quality leads for sales force follow-up.

Traditionally, AT&T's marketing budget was heavily skewed toward advertising (primarily broadcast) and direct mail. This allocation of 70 percent advertising and 30 percent mail was followed for the "A version" of the test. The A test group was the traditional AT&T media allocation. Budget for IDM was redeployed as follows in the B or IDM test group:

	TRADITIONAL		IDM	
	Budget	Leads	Budget	Leads
•Advertising	70%	35%	10%	10%
•Mail	30%	65%	25%	20%
•Telemarketing	–	–	65%	70%
Leads per	1,000	50		150

300% increase

Figure 4.12   AT&T Media Allocation

- 10 percent advertising, primarily vertical print advertising
- 25 percent direct mail
- 65 percent inbound and outbound telecontact

The majority of the IDM budget went for inbound and outbound telecontact because of its ability to generate significant incremental response and revenue. We don't mean the valueless inbound experience of speaking with disinterested "robots" or the people calling us during dinner. We mean the high-value integration of these high-powered media components with an emphasis on customer service. The interactivity of these channels allows you to listen to customer needs, position the benefits of the product, and qualify the sales opportunity.

As seen in Figure 4.12, on the traditional side, advertising, at 70 percent of the budget, generated 35 percent of the leads. Mail, at 30 percent of budget, generated 65 percent of the leads. For the IDM cell, the budget allocation and lead generation percentages are more in line. Advertising received 10 percent of the budget and generated 10 percent of the leads. Direct mail represented 25 percent and generated 20 percent of leads. Inbound and outbound telecontact received 65 percent of the budget and produced 70 percent of the leads.

In terms of leads per 1,000, IDM produced a 300 percent increase.

But that's only half the story. Let's follow the leads through to conversion (Figure 4.13).

The traditional allocation of media generated 50 leads per 1,000. The IDM allocation generated 150 per 1,000. Field Sales followed up 32 percent of the leads from the traditional cell and converted 10 percent, generating 1.6 sales per 1,000. For the IDM cell, Sales followed up 60

	TRADITIONAL	IDM
•Leads per 1,000	50	150
•Sales Force Lead Follow–Up	32%	60%
•Conversion	10%	25%
Sales per 1,000	1.6	22.5

1,400% increase

Figure 4.13   AT&T Lead Conversion

percent of the leads and converted 25 percent, yielding 22.5 sales per 1,000. That's a 1,400 percent increase.

Bottom-Line Results

Let's review some additional details (see Figure 4.14).

The marketing budget for each test cell was $250,000. The traditional cell allocated $175,000 to broadcast advertising. AT&T Marketing executives felt more comfortable seeing their product on television, regardless of the amount of "spill" (put differently, the target market is a small portion of the viewing public, so a large part of budget is "spilled" on generating impressions among an audience that is not qualified for the product). Advertising, at $175,000, generated 438 leads. Mail, at $75,000, generated 812 leads. The total for the traditional cell was 1,250 leads at a cost per lead of $200.

Within the IDM cell, direct response print advertising was placed only in vertical publications. The $25,000 investment generated 375 leads. The

	TRADITIONAL		IDM	
	Budget	Leads	Budget	Leads
•Advertising	$175K	438	$25K	375
•Mail	75K	812	63K	750
•Telemarketing	–	–	162K	2,625
•Leads		1,250		3,750
Cost per Lead		$200		$66

Figure 4.14   AT&T Budget and Media Allocation, Chart 1

	TRADITIONAL	IDM
•Leads	1,250	3,750
•Cost per Lead	$200	$66
•Sales Force Lead Follow–Up	400	2,250
•Conversion	40	563
Marketing Cost per Sale	$6,250	$444

Figure 4.15   AT&T Budget and Media Allocation, Chart 2

combination of direct mail and inbound and outbound telecontact represented the lion's share of investment at $225,000 and generated the majority of leads: 750 and 2,625, in Figure 4.14, for a combined total of 3,375. Total leads from the IDM cell were 3,750 at a cost per lead of $66.

Let's look at lead conversion.

The traditional budget allocation (see Figure 4.15) produced 1,250 leads at a cost per lead of $200. The sales force followed up 32 percent, or 400 leads. Why so low? No confidence. It's the same story we discussed before. Field Sales was not involved in the planning or execution of the campaign. Yet they were expected to tenaciously pursue the resulting "leads." Conversion rate was 10 percent, which yielded 40 sales. If Field has no confidence in the leads, you wouldn't expect a high closing ratio, and they didn't get one. Marketing cost per sale was $6,250.

The IDM cell began with 3,750 leads at a cost per lead of $66. Field Sales, having been involved in the entire IDM process since day one and having set the criteria for leads, followed up on 60 percent of the opportunities, or 2,250. They converted 25 percent—generating 563 sales, at a marketing cost per sale of $444.

Remember that the average sale was $10,000. So gross margin for the traditional cell was $3,750, or 38 percent of the selling price. Tough to make a profit since there's a whole lot of expense not yet accounted for. Gross margin for the IDM cell, however, was $9,556, or 96 percent of the selling price. Substantially more profitable on a per sale basis.

Finally, let's look at the bottom line. AT&T invested $250,000 in each cell: What did they get for their investment?

- The traditional cell generated 40 sales, or $400,000 in gross revenue. That's a marketing E:R (expense to revenue ratio) of 62.5 percent.

- IDM generated 563 sales, or $5,630,000 in gross revenue, for a marketing E:R of 4 percent.

The numbers speak for themselves.

Points to Remember

Integrated Direct Marketing (IDM) integrates and sequences media and message with an understanding of the customer's time dimension. Where is the customer within his or her life cycle? Where is the customer within the decision-making process?

IDM concentrates on surrounding customers with a powerful and relevant mix of stimuli and choices to create the most relevant, compelling, competitively differentiating customer experience.

IDM focuses on the precision sequencing of media and message.

IDM is sensitive to frequency and deploys media in accordance with a regulated touch process. The frequency of touches is driven by the customer's self-declared interest and indicated propensity to buy.

IDM consistently generates double-digit response, and because of these efficiencies, allows the marketer to do more with less—generating more revenue with less waste, with the same or lower budget.

The IDM Media Mix includes at least these seven media:

- PR
- Direct response print advertising
- Internet
- E-mail
- Direct mail
- Inbound and outbound telecontact
- Field sales channels

IDM is the tactical framework for implementing the Consensual Marketing Opt-In Process.

"IDM can be used to meet most, if not all, marcom objectives. The principles of IDM apply to every communications challenge."—Garry Dawson

Step Four: Let's Get Real about E-marketing

THE FOURTH STEP in the Consensual Marketing Opt-In Process concerns the effective and profitable deployment of the Internet—Web sites and e-mail—as part of the IDM Media Mix. While "e" has certainly changed the marketing landscape, many marketers have gone down the wrong path. This chapter will provide the "how to" information to help you leverage this important medium to its greatest effect and return on investment.

Concepts we will cover to help you increase the effectiveness of e-mail include:

- Getting real about e-mail
- E-mail is primarily a retention tool
- Prospect by affinity
- Substitute trust for permission
- Develop and deploy e-mail in accordance with CMO best practices

Concepts we will address to help you increase the value of the Internet include:

- Integrating the Internet
- Maximizing the Internet's customer experience
- The primary uses of the Internet

- Generating and updating the Consensual profile via the Web
- Retail and the Web
- Search Engine Marketing (SEM)

And throughout, we will include comprehensive case studies that illustrate the step-by-step process and results with hard numbers to show you how and why the Consensual Marketing process can significantly improve your e-marketing.

Let's Get Real about E-mail

Let's face it: We have seen the Promised Land. We held the golden eggs in our hand, and then our greed got in the way.

"E-mail would be an ideal medium because it allows a company to target its messages at a very low cost, except that its usefulness has been seriously compromised by the spam factor. Too many consumers delete e-mail without giving a message a second thought."—Al Ries, Chairman, Ries & Ries

Spam (and to a smaller extent, worms, viruses, etc.) has successfully polluted the well. Customers, whether business or consumer, are conditioned to view all e-mails with distrust. If in doubt—throw it out. According to research from RoperASW for Bigfoot Interactive:[1]

- 57.7 percent of U.S. Internet users delete newsletters or other *requested* e-mail.
- 62.8 percent delete marketing or promotional messages that they *asked for.*

The cost of spam is astounding. The Radicati Group projects that spam will cost corporations around the world $198 billion by 2007.[2] Let's look at a small subset of the cost: Internet Service Providers.

[Chris] Shivers, systems administrator for Aristotle, Inc., a small Internet service provider, told a panel at the FTC forum . . . "spam costs me $5 per customer per year." That's significant

> since . . . the firm's average customer spends about $6 per month. Out of 4 million messages, Aristotle found that 2.5 million are spam. His annual cost to pay for the technology and manpower to cope is $112,000. But he added, "I'll have to spend that again in the next six months."[3]

Research from Quris actually points out areas of opportunity. This research was focused on determining the factors that drive U.S. consumers away from e-mail programs. The primary factor was the frequency of e-mails: too many, too fast, and the customer is gone. Over half said that once they've lost interest in the product or service, they drop out of the program. Thirty-five percent are turned off once the e-mails get boring, and 34 percent said they are history if the e-mails *offer no significant value*. We recommend that you consider everything on this list[4] a potential leverage point:

- 68 percent of e-mails come too frequently
- 51 percent lost interest in product/service/topic
- 35 percent said their e-mails were generally boring
- 34 percent said e-mails offered no significant value
- 30 percent suspected the company of "sharing my address"

To achieve the potential of e-mail as an effective part of the IDM Media Mix, marketers should recognize and act upon the following:

- E-mail is primarily a retention tool.
- Prospect by affinity.
- Substitute trust for permission.
- Develop and deploy e-mail with the customers' needs and requirements in mind, not yours.

And to know what the results are, and what you might be doing wrong, test!

E-mail Is Primarily a Retention Tool

The majority of your e-mail efforts should be directed to your customer base. This gives you the greatest opportunity to bring messages of value that respond to each customer's stated information needs, increase Customer Lifetime Value, and achieve a very attractive ROI. Customers are significantly more likely to open, read, and respond to e-mail received within the parameters of a consensual relationship. Retention messages are read almost twice as frequently as acquisition messages.[5]

The speed of electronic delivery can, in itself, be an important benefit for customers. For one, the ability to impart cutting-edge information in minutes or hours versus days or weeks can add substantial benefit to a relationship. Yvonne Brandon, former Direct Marketing Manager for IBM's Worldwide e-Business on Demand Operating Environment Initiatives, gives us insight into the importance of electronic delivery for IBM's Premier Club members (who are their top software customers worldwide):

> **Previously, executives would receive information on technological advances via our hardcopy publication, *Trend News*. Lead times, however, could be as long as six weeks. Solutions in the information systems industry change rapidly and the information we were sending customers was frequently obsolete by the time it reached the customers. An important benefit to IBM Software Premier Club customers was the ability to receive this essential information immediately and conveniently.**

E-mail should only be deployed as an integrated part of the IDM Media Mix. Single medium deployments can only perpetuate the dismal response rates direct marketers currently experience. It appears that e-mail response rates underachieve the 2 percent norm. According to the DMA's 2003 "Response Rate Study: Direct & Interactive Marketing Campaigns," the average response rate for an e-mail campaign is 1 percent. *Response*, in the study, is defined as orders divided by quantity.[6]

The study noted the average e-mail response rates by industry:

- Retail = 1.8 percent
- Travel = 1.5 percent
- Financial products and services = 1.1 percent
- Catalog = 0.8 percent
- Publishing = 0.8 percent
- Computers and electronic products = 0.4 percent

These response rates are awful. Just because e-mail appears to cost less going out the door doesn't mean we should significantly lower our expectations for response. Look at it this way: if used irresponsibly, e-mail becomes a cheap, easy way to tick off far more individuals than ever before. Deployed responsibly—as a retention tool, as part of the IDM Media Mix, in accordance with the principles of the Consensual Marketing Opt-In Process—e-mail can bring relevant, timely messages of value that enhance and extend the consensual relationship and thus increase Customer Lifetime Value. Double-digit response must become the norm.

Prospect by Affinity

Every marketer has to prospect. However, if you're marketing value-added products or services, cold prospecting by e-mail is not the way to go: The damage to your reputation and customer goodwill are very costly, near term and especially long term. And in the event of antispam legislation, you may have the opportunity to quantify the potential loss in dollars and cents.

> *"Spam is forcing down response rates and pushing up consumer angst, thus jeopardizing relationships."*—Mickey Alam Khan, Senior Editor, *DM News*

You might say, "Sure, but it costs just about nothing to reach so many people. So what if only one or two buy? I'm still making a profit." We suggest, however, that while there may be low-hanging fruit along the path, the land mines underfoot can ruin your day. Consider the following story from ACE Computer Camp, which readers were introduced to in Chapter 3.

Prior to the camping season, ACE decided to test prospecting by e-mail. It made sense: they were looking for families interested in computer camps, so why not try to reach them via computer? It would be great, they thought, if they could make this medium work. So ACE rented a list, put together an HTML message about all the fun and learning kids could get by attending ACE summer camp, and sent it out. There were pictures of kids with braces concentrating in front of screens, and smiling kids jumping in the pool. Hardly a pernicious message.

Within moments they received a handful of return e-mails accusing them of spamming. Remember, this is a kid's summer camp, not ads for a porn site. These same irate consumers then contacted ACE's ISP, which proceeded to take down ACE's Web site—no investigation, no notice, no warning. These same irate e-vigilantes took the liberty of also contacting ACE's sponsors—a list of the sponsors, prominent industry names, was an element in the e-mail promotion—who immediately communicated their displeasure, several of whom withdrew their financial support. Again, no investigation, no notice, no warning.

The results: The promotion was relatively inexpensive to launch. A few families responded and a couple of campers registered. After several days, they were able to change ISPs and get their Web site back up. After several weeks, they were able to repair relations with almost all sponsors and were able to replace the one sponsor who refused to be mollified.

The conclusion: the ends were not worth the means.

Using the Consensual model, we recommend the deployment of e-mail for prospecting by affinity. There are two types of affinity: external and internal. Here's an illustration of external affinity.

Company X is a manufacturer of the widget. The company has established a Consensual relationship with its customer base and succeeded in using that ongoing relationship to increase Customer Lifetime Value. Company X has been successful and wants to grow. Additionally, there is some customer attrition. Thus, there is a need for prospecting.

From experience, and given the results of VOC Messaging and Communication Research, Company X knows that customers belong to and respect the Widget Users Group of America (WUGA). The company approaches WUGA with the following proposition:

We (Company X) are a respected manufacturer of the widget. We know that our customers belong to and respect your organization. We'd like to form a strategic partnership. Company X will contribute market and industry intelligence to WUGA and will host a quarterly workshop during which we will discuss the practical application of the new widget technology. In return, we'd like the opportunity to invite your members who are not our customers to learn more about our capabilities and services. We would like to have a link on your Web site—a link that very clearly explains that Company X has a presence on the WUGA Web site because we are a respected manufacturer and we contribute to the benefits WUGA extends to members. We'd also like to send an e-mail to your members who are not our customers. The text of the e-mail would reference our support and contribution to the benefits WUGA extends to members and invite them to learn more about us.

That's using e-mail to prospect by external affinity. Internal affinity is when prospects have relationships with you but have yet to become customers. An example would be inquiries.

Substitute Trust for Permission

"By building our business model on a 100 percent opt-in basis, our prospects have in one way, shape, or form raised their hand, requesting our assistance in their search for health insurance."—Greg Kohne, Assistant Vice President, Direct Sales, Golden Rule Insurance

The Consensual Marketing Opt-In Process goes beyond the concept of permission. Permission, within e-marketing, is viewed as a single-medium tactic; for instance, I give you permission to send me stuff via e-mail. The goal of Consensual Marketing is a long-term relationship based on the exchange of value over multiple media, with respect to the customer's stated information needs and media preferences.

The goal of Consensual Marketing is to create permission and trust. Trust over time. Trust that marketers are living up to their side of the Consensual bargain. Trust that marketers are listening and learning. The burden of maintaining that trust is with the marketer. The more potentially irritating a medium can be—such as e-mail or outbound calls—the more sensitive marketers must be to the concept of trust.

Here are some important thoughts on trust from two gurus at QVC. We'll revisit these concepts again in Chapter 6.

Doug Rose, Vice President, Merchandising Brand Development:

If you ask people "Are you satisfied?" they may very well be satisfied. I often joke how I may be satisfied with my laptop computer but I'm never going to trust it. What matters more than satisfaction is trust. And trust is an emotional connection. Many companies make the mistake of saying "Gee, our satisfaction scores are up 3 percent this year, we must be doing great." Meanwhile, they haven't built any trust. And so, the next guy to come around the corner is going to get all their business. I think satisfaction is a rel-

atively easy thing to affect through efficiency. But trust is something that can only come through people.

John Hunter, Senior Vice President of Customer Services:

You can build up some chips in your emotional bank account with trust, but it's very easy to lose when you don't have a consistent strategy that you're executing day in and day out. You have to earn the customer's trust every day. I don't think there's a company that can stay in business without addressing the issue of trust.

In practical terms, the application and maintenance of trust to e-mail involves the following:

- **Set a privacy policy, publish it and live by it.** Specific to e-mail, your customer names and e-mail addresses are your family jewels. They are not commodities to be sold on the open market. You shouldn't be trading small dollars today for the big dollars tomorrow that can come from loyal, trusting customers.
- **Give customers plenty of opportunity to provide feedback, or to change their mind.** This is consistent with some good advice from research results. A Quris/Executive Summary Consulting survey[7] identified the following e-mail marketing privacy and customer support practices preferred by U.S. e-mail users (on a scale of 1 to 5, where 5 is "very positive"):
  - o Unsubscribe option in all e-mails: 4.7
  - o Explicit no-share-address policy: 4.6
  - o 48-hour e-mail support answers: 4.5
  - o Personal preferences page that can be edited: 4.4
  - o Provide phone number in e-mails: 4.4
  - o Explicit privacy policy: 4.3
  - o Double opt-in confirmation: 4.2

  The practices least preferred by customers are companies making assumptions about permission (1.5) or the right to share their e-mail address (1.4).
- **Messaging in accordance with customer preferences.** Even if sales are down, blasting out irrelevant messages isn't the answer.

- **Be responsive.** Currently, marketers are not e-mail responsive. It's not just a few customers who are sending in e-messages—virtually all customers use e-mail to contact companies. This trend should be reversed: Marketers need to be responsive to the messages their customers send.

According to a recent survey of customers worldwide conducted by Genesys Telecommunications Laboratories,[8] nearly 90 percent of consumers have sent an e-mail to a company regarding some sort of customer service or product issue.

According to the article "A Failing Grade for E-mail Replies" published in *Target Marketing* magazine:[9]

Many companies continually fail to promptly respond to e-mail inquiries. In its recent Customer Service Webtrack report, Jupiter Research reveals that 88 percent of consumers surveyed expect a response to e-mail inquiries within 24 hours; only 54 percent of companies sampled met these expectations.

A lack of e-mail response to inquiries in a timely manner drives up the number of customer service telephone calls. This will result in higher customer service costs and lost revenues, which will be compounded as customer service e-mail inquiries are projected to jump . . . to 3.3 billion in 2008.

ERDM also conducted e-mail responsiveness research. The three-year e-mail survey consisted of 38 respected companies, including IBM, Compaq, Dell, Apple, Amazon.com, DoubleClick.com, Barnes&Noble.com, American Airlines, Continental Airlines, Delta Airlines, L.L. Bean, the American Marketing Association, the Direct Marketing Association, and the Phoenician.

Each year, these and the other companies were sent the following one-sentence e-mail: What is your corporate policy regarding the turnaround time for e-mails addressed to customer service?

ERDM doesn't measure what they say, we measure what they do—when and if we get a reply, and the quality of that reply. We measure this against customer expectations of receiving a reply within 24 hours. (The Voice of Customer Messaging and Communication results indicated that

	Year 1		Year 2		Year 3	
Total e-mails	37		38		38	
Within 4 hours	13	**35%**	20	**52%**	13	**35%**
Within 8 hours	2	6%			4	11%
Within 24 hours	2	6%	4	11%	5	13%
25 – 72 hours	2	6%	5	13%	5	13%
Longer	5	13%				
No response	13	**34%**	9	**24%**	11	**28%**

Figure 5.1 Results of E-mail Responsiveness Survey

the bar for e-mail responsiveness is lower than the Quris/Executive Summary Consulting survey reports.)

What we found (depicted in Figure 5.1):

More companies responded within 24 hours from year 1 to year 2. However, that trend is going down from year 2 to year 3:

- Year 1: 47 percent
- Year 2: 63 percent
- Year 3: 59 percent

Another 13 percent responded within 25 to 72 hours:

- Year 1: 6 percent, and an additional 13 percent responded in 73 or more hours
- Year 2: 13 percent
- Year 3: 13 percent

Twenty-eight percent did not respond at all, and the trend appears to be going up:

- Year 1: 34 percent
- Year 2: 24 percent
- Year 3: 28 percent

Based upon the results, we can make the following observations:

- The e-mail responsiveness of these respected companies clearly does not match customer's expectations (response within 24 hours).

- There is an overall lack of quality. The most frequent error was inexcusable: In every case we provided a contact name. In many cases the contact name was misspelled in the return e-mail. In some cases, the gender was incorrect (for instance, the e-mail we sent was from Paula Lepanto, the reply we received was addressed to Paul Lepanto).

- One company, a packaged goods giant, got back to us and requested birth date as a prerequisite to a reply. This left us with the impression that "no one is watching the store." Ridiculous replies clearly convey the message that both the customer and the medium are not sufficiently valued (bringing to mind the old catchphrase: "This would be a wonderful business if it weren't for all those annoying customers").

- Two companies decided to respond by phone versus e-mail, each a full two days after the e-mail was sent. Clearly, this was inappropriate to the request.

There isn't any other way to say this: marketers must meet customers' expectations for e-mail responsiveness. It's difficult—but not impossible. Respond within 24 hours, even if it's to say you're delayed. And, of course, respect the customer's name and spell it correctly. Substitute trust for permission.

Develop and Deploy E-mail with the Customer in Mind

"Astonishingly, the tried and true lessons of Direct Mail have had to be relearned by the proponents of e-mail."—Vincent J. Amen, former Vice President of Public Programs, Franklin Covey; President, Growth Coach

According to a study called The Merchant Speaks conducted by the e-tailing group research firm:[10]

Personalization and customer preferences are the least important components of the respondent's strategies. Only 33 percent . . . take advantage of personalized messaging in their e-mail

interactions with customers, and only 6 percent consider their messages to be very personalized. . . . Only 7 percent of companies empower customers to choose the frequency of e-mail communications. . . . Only 37 percent use the customer opt-in model.

These must be *direct response executions*, according to the following criteria:

- **If you have a benefit, put it in the subject line and say it quickly.** If you don't have a benefit to put in the subject line, reconsider sending the e-mail. For instance, which e-mail would you open:

    Subject: New technical advance for (your computer) from
    (your computer manufacturer)
    Subject: Buy this now

- **Personalization works.** Address customers appropriately, and spell their names correctly. Ask yourself: have we earned the right to call them by their first name? Probably not, so stay formal. Vary paragraphs based upon customer needs and interests. For example:

Mr./s.   :

Thank you for your interest. Attached is all the information you will need to become a distributor of our world-famous homemade ice cream.

Enclosed is a brochure that will tell you more about our range of flavors. In response to your question, page 17 details the special care we take in the preparation of our chocolate.

- **Your first sentence, or headline, should answer some basic customer questions.** They are:

    What are you selling?
    Why should I care?
    What do you want me to do?

- **Body copy should be crisp and benefit-rich.** It should answer the customer question, "What's in it for me?" Lay the copy out so it's open and inviting. Make sure people who need reading glasses don't have to squint at the type size you've selected. Use subheads to help people who skim.

- **There should be a compelling, competitively differentiating offer.**
- **Emphasize the benefit of calling the 800 number.** Inbound is your opportunity to learn about the customer's needs, and to upsell and cross-sell as appropriate.
- **Pay attention to your landing page.** It's part of the e-mail promotion, the customer's response chain. The page must reinforce the same positioning, benefits, and offer. Don't send folks to your home page and expect them to figure it out.
- **Test.** Testing drives continuous improvement. The most important e-mail tests are list and offer. For other test ideas, here's some good advice concerning research, from Marketing Sherpa. These are the most worthwhile e-mail tests after list and offer testing (in order of importance):

  Landing page

  Subject line

  HTML versus text (It is interesting to note that according to *Catalog Age*, 85 to 90 percent of marketing or promotional e-mails are HTML. Text is easier and faster to download, faster to deploy, and may be differentiating.)

  Personalization

  Long copy versus short copy

Integrating the Internet

"For most companies, having a Web site is just as important as having a postal address. Most companies today cannot remain in business without having a Web address."—Al Ries

The Internet is a tough place. It promises low-cost transactions, but the investment is like that of a bricks-and-mortar company, and frequently it's in addition to the existing bricks and mortar. There is a virtual mandate from customers to have a Web presence, but that presence is not always contributing proportionately to the bottom line.

A big problem is that the playing field is absolutely flat. It's hard to differentiate yourself, especially for those in the high-end or luxury category. The "wow" factor is elusive. To complicate matters, your ability to "wow" is dependent upon each individual's available technology and their patience in waiting for stuff to download.

So the questions become: Where is the real payback? How do you invest and deploy resources to generate the greatest return on investment? The answer lies in maximizing the customer experience while investing and deploying resources that reflect the three important uses of the Internet (the three Rs):

- Research (and lead generation)
- Retention (and entry into the Consensual process)
- Retail

The following subsections will provide more detail on the customer experience, research, retention, and retail.

Maximizing the Internet's Customer Experience

The Internet was built around the concept of "help yourself": it puts the information, and thus the power, into the consumer's hands. No matter where you are or who you are, you can easily go anywhere in the world to find any person, place, or thing.

Greg Kohne, of Golden Rule Insurance:

> **I believe that our lives are more hectic today than ever. Therefore people are more resistant to perceived intrusions into their lives. The Internet is changing everything about how we learn about products and services. Prior to the Internet, people needed to receive information about products and services. Due to the Internet, the evolving mindset is, "If I need something I'll do a search." This search can be done at the consumer's convenience. The more they get used to this convenience, the less they will tolerate a perceived intrusion.**

The Internet was not built around the concept of "go help yourself." But this is the message we hear when we call a company for some specific information and the rep says, "That's on our Web site, here's the address, good-bye." What we heard is "go help yourself." What we heard is a blow-off. And, by extension, so is the benign neglect we all experience when we go to a Web site, can't find what we want and can't get any help. This jeopardizes customer relationships.

Recognize that competitive differentiation on the Web is built around the concept of "how may we help you?" The compelling message is: "Come to our site because it is the easiest and the friendliest. Let us be your resource and your guide. We'll ask what's important to you and then show you where the information is, via *your* medium of choice." Which is really what Consensual Marketing is all about.

For perspective on the customer experience, we spoke to Don Vultaggio, Chairman of Hormel Brewing. Don is the genius behind AriZona Iced Tea. The AriZona brand is a creation of New York–based Ferolito Vultaggio & Sons. From its introduction in 1992, AriZona has grown to become one of the leading players in ready-to-drink beverages. The AriZona product portfolio has grown to include flavored teas, juices, and coffee.

Admittedly, Don is not in direct response. But his comments all apply:

First and foremost, it's a people business. I have to like you or like doing business with you. Companies get bogged down by all the high-tech stuff. It often distracts them from the primary requirement of paying attention to the customer.

A solid relationship with a customer must be based on:

- **How easy I consciously make it to do business with us, in your terms.**
- **The quality of my products.**
- **Competitive pricing—price is rarely the number one factor. We must help our customer see our price in light of all other value-adds.**

Ease of doing business is often undervalued. It is a major competitive advantage. You have to consciously work to make your organization and processes easy for that customer to do business with.

We must constantly work to:

- Add value to the customer experience. Remember that competitive differentiation on the Web is built around the concept of "how may we help you?"
- Retain and improve our credibility.

Stanford University and Consumer WebWatch conducted a study[11] to determine the factors that affect the credibility of a Web site. They are, in descending order:

- Design/appearance = 46.1 percent
- Information design/structure = 28.5 percent
- Information focus = 25.1 percent
- Company motive = 15.5 percent
- Information usefulness = 14.8 percent
- Information accuracy = 14.3 percent
- Name recognition and reputation = 14.1 percent

Some of these are very broad and difficult to control and may require companywide efforts to change, such as company motive and reputation. Others, like design, can be improved relatively easily. You need continual testing to evaluate the direction—positive or negative—and the size of a change's impact.

Customers Speak Out

The results of ERDM's Voice of Customer Messaging and Communication Research indicate the following customer requirements:

- "Keep it easy, interactive, and visual."
- "When I go to a Web site I ask three questions: (1) Who are you? (2) Why should I care/why are you any different from the rest? (3) What's in it for me? Construct your site to help me find good answers to those questions."
- "Make it easy to speak with a live person."

In short, personalize the customer experience. Provide an experience that is meaningful to the customer. Tailor your Web site to match your customers' needs. Generic information won't provide differentiation. Provide value as your customer defines value.

If the customer raises a hand, they are looking for a way out of information overload. They're lost. Provide caring customer service and they'll be back. And when they do come back, you can provide increasingly specific information to further improve their experience, and their opinion of you.

Real-time personalized response is the price of admission to competitive differentiation. Even if you lose an order, you were there, on the spot, with a quality answer. That will buy you respect in the world of information clutter, and respect buys a return visit.

Customers have taught us that value must be both compelling and competitively differentiating. We were road testing a positioning statement and asked customers if they found it compelling. They said yes. We asked if competitors could make the same claim. They said yes!

And one small digression: if you're a high Lifetime Value client engaged in an online e-chat with a customer service rep, what's the quality of your experience if that rep is conducting six conversations at the same time? You must maintain the high quality of the customer experience, especially for your best customers. As Consensual Marketing points out, vary your marketing investment per potential return, increase the investment in your best customers. They are not conducting six conversations while they're online with you. Concentrate on their needs. Speak to them directly and with value.

Research and Lead Generation

Given the results of ERDM's Voice of Customer Messaging and Communication Research, one of the primary uses of the Web, in both B2B and B2C, is for research—the electronic ferreting out of information and comparison. And this is tough because the customer may use your site for research, then purchase the same item elsewhere. Thus, the presentation of the information becomes crucial to the customer experience: Can they find what they need? And if they find it, can they understand it? A case in point comes from Golden Rule Insurance.

Researching health insurance is something we'd all rather avoid. So when the time comes and circumstances force you to gather the information on what's available, the worst possible case is when all the information is in insurance-speak. Golden Rule has found that the presentation of health insurance information in plain, no-nonsense English is what customers need and appreciate.

Successful research can be funneled into lead generation. In the case of Golden Rule, customers come to consider them an adviser, versus a vendor, because of the straightforward presentation of information. As they move through the decision cycle from research and evaluation to consideration and then purchase, Golden Rule becomes a major contender.

Presenting the information so your audience can understand it is as important for B2B as the above B2C example. A customer quote from VOC Research sums it up: "Remember, the Web is very friendly for IT personnel. It can be less friendly and even scary for Marketing and Sales."

If you can satisfy the customer's research needs and they ask for more, you've earned the right to ask the basic customer questions. Don't be afraid to ask for profiling information—this is a fair exchange of information between you and the customer. Here's another customer quote: "If we request in-depth information, it's okay to ask us for information in return."

This does not mean that at this stage it's okay to ask them their birthday, their weight, or the color of their eyes. It does mean that it's okay to begin a dialogue. Ask them for:

- Name
- Contact information
- Preferred method of contact
- What question or challenge they are researching

And then respond quickly, taking into account their media preference, and with value.

Retention and Entry into Consensual Marketing

As with e-mail, customer retention is a primary use of the Internet. It is this goal that will generate the greatest return on investment. Which flies in the face of the arrogance that the Internet has created among some marketers: "So what if this customer goes away? There's millions more on the Internet. Look at how many hits we got today!"

Don Schultz, Professor Emeritus, Northwestern University, Medill School of Journalism:

A couple of years ago we had a group of students who were asked to work on developing a retention program for AOL. AOL had never had a retention program. They'd always focused on acquisition. If you went away, they didn't care. They'd send you another disk with a bunch of free hours and assume they could churn you back into the fold.

Hits are not customers. Unnamed prospects-to-be are nowhere near as valuable as the "bird in hand." There is no concept that can be leveraged, like Lifetime Value for prospects.

Two important uses of Web sites for retention are:

- Generating and updating Consensual profiles
- Customer-specific Web sites

Generating and Updating Consensual Profiles

The Web is the right place for most customers to enter their Consensual information and to update their profile. VOC Research and experience confirms that a specific page for a customer to use to enter or revise personal information works. Customers appreciate the opportunity to view what they have selected as their preferences and requirements, and to change their mind as their focus and responsibilities change.

Also use this page to communicate important information, such as a calendar of upcoming events. Let the customer know what's planned. It may be outside of their current profiled interests today, but it might correspond to a new company initiative or other impending development.

Also, restate your commitment to the Consensual model and your privacy policy. We would also recommend having a mechanism to request and capture referrals. In our experience, referrals convert to customers at a higher rate than any other list. Satisfied customers have few qualms about generating appropriate referrals.

Customer Specific Web Sites

One of the highest payback deployments of Web sites is creating a B2B Web site specific to your customer. A terrific example comes from Marianne Gaige, President and Chief Operating Officer of the Cathedral Corporation. Cathedral is a leader in data management, printing, personalization, and high volume mailing. They provide a wide range of marketing and financial communication services, including invoice and statement presentment, check and remittance rendering, direct mail marketing services, customer care correspondence, and Internet billing and payment.

Founded in 1907, this privately held company has grown at an annual rate of approximately 25 percent over the last 10 years as they diversified from providing data processing and printing services solely to churches to providing critical document printing and mailing services (such as financial statements sent to customers) to companies in the financial services, health care, and utility industries.

Marianne Gaige:

> Our narrow focus on a few industries has allowed us to realize that there are real differences in the way customers in various industries view their relationship with us. By designing a different customer service center Web site for each individual customer, we are able to tailor not only the look of the customer service center but also the functionality of it. For example, customers who make regular changes to the marketing messages on their monthly statements may want the online customization and proofing module to be the first section that pops up.

> Since we are already providing online billing and payment for utilities as well as online statement archival for financial services organizations, there were not a lot of technical difficulties in developing the customer service sites. The real difficulty was in working with the customer to develop the site to reflect their needs. The sites were all developed with extensive feedback from our customers to truly make them useful.

> We continually reference the information in the online customer service center in our other communications with customers. We also e-mail the customer on a regular basis to let them know when information on the Web has been updated. The only potential weakness is that our employees could (if we let them) think that this presentment on the Web qualifies as communicating with the customer. We are very careful to make sure that this does not replace regular, meaningful personal contact with our customers.

> I think that online presentment of all of the facets of our relationship has increased our knowledge of our customers and allows us to manage the relationship in a more organized manner. Our customers are universally pleased with their sites. Customers feel that our ability to communicate with them has been improved.

Retail and the Web

"Retailers especially are at the forefront of integrating the Internet with other channels. A retail company without a Web strategy is one without a future."—Mickey Alam Khan

A report from the e-tailing group[12] provides the following information about conversion rates among online retailers in the United States. Conversion is defined as the number of orders divided by the number of visits:

- zero to 3 percent = 39 percent
- 4 to 10 percent = 37 percent
- 11 or more percent = 9 percent
- Do not know conversion rate = 14 percent

It is disturbing that conversion rates are so low, to the point where it's unlikely that marketers would tolerate them from any other medium. The response rates are especially low considering these people self-selected by going on the Web. Just because the perception is that "e" is cheap does not mean we should lower our expectations for profitability. It is more disturbing, however, that 14 percent of marketers surveyed do not even know the conversion rate.

In short, there is significant opportunity to improve retail on the Web, with the conversion rate being the bottom-line target for the improvement. Let's take a detailed look at two areas:

- Customers' frustrations
- Abandoning the shopping cart

Customers' Frustrations

Frustrations cause customers to leave. They artificially block the sale. Think of your own experiences: attention span on the Web is reduced to nanoseconds, and if something doesn't go right or annoys you, it's click and on to the next. Reducing customers' frustrations will increase the ease of doing business. This will leverage the conversion rate.

A survey from Retail Forward[13] indicates that 64 percent of Internet users are satisfied with their online shopping experience and that shoppers between the ages of 45 and 54 are more likely than younger shoppers to be extremely satisfied. But only 2 percent of those surveyed say their Internet shopping experience is free of frustration. The survey then goes on to identify U.S. consumers' top five frustrations with online shopping:

1. Pop-up boxes while visiting/shopping a site = 52 percent
2. Banner advertisements = 50 percent
3. Congested Web pages = 35 percent
4. Slow load times = 26 percent
5. Difficult to find a specific topic = 20 percent

On reviewing this list, it certainly seems that we've taken our eyes off our customer. All these consumer frustrations are within our power to amend, and quickly. In our opinion, the revenue you receive from pop-ups and banners is a short-term hit that would be more than offset by the increase in conversion and Customer Lifetime Value if they weren't there.

Abandoning the Shopping Cart

The e-tailing group surveyed 200 executives in charge of e-commerce to determine their shopping cart abandonment rates, or the rate that folks who have selected a product and entered into the purchase process drop out before completion. Here's what the executives said[14] regarding the abandon rate they experience:

- zero to 20 percent = 12 percent
- 21 to 50 percent = 28 percent
- 51 to 80 percent = 14 percent
- 80 or more percent = 2 percent
- Do not know abandon rate = 43 percent

Look at that: 43 percent of marketers do not know their shopping cart abandon rate. That's unbelievable. And it leads us to believe that they have abandoned bottom-line responsibility. What are they thinking about if it's not sales?

A report from Vividence[15] has worse news, finding that 75 percent of U.S. Internet shoppers abandon or drop out of the shopping cart before they have completed their transaction. The reasons:

- 72 percent because of high shipping prices
- 61 percent were comparison shopping or browsing
- 56 percent changed their mind
- 51 percent planned a later purchase
- 43 percent found the total cost of items too high
- 41 percent thought the checkout process too long
- 35 percent decided the checkout process required too much personal information
- 34 percent discovered that the site required registration before purchase
- 31 percent found the site unstable or unreliable
- 27 percent found the checkout process confusing

Many of these roadblocks can be corrected, resulting in substantial increases in top line revenue.

We'd like to pass along this tip to retailers: we find that one of the strongest Internet offers is waiving shipping and handling for a specific, limited period of time.

When Franklin Covey's Public Seminar Division began its Internet operation, its goals were to generate monthly revenue of $100,000 from their Time and Life Management Seminars. This addition to the media mix would satisfy the percentage of customers who preferred Web to catalog or retail, and would generate incremental registrations and income because of its ability to reach more potential customers. The Web site began to generate $70,000 a month almost immediately, which quickly grew to $120,000 a month gross contribution.

However, metrics showed that 50 percent of all purchasers were dropping out of the shopping cart before completing the registration.

Vince Amen, then Vice President of Public Programs for Franklin Covey, decided to test a deployment of customer-service-oriented outbound telephone follow-up—with certain restrictions. Only business phones were eligible for the call list; there was no calling folks at home. And first, before any calls were placed, the record of transactions was researched to make sure these customers hadn't already registered through other media.

The results were eye-opening. Franklin Covey found that there were two primary reasons for customers not completing the purchase:

- They had questions, and pricing was chief among them. They needed answers and couldn't find them.
- They did not have the authority to make the purchase—they needed to take the information about the seminar to their boss or training coordinator to get approval before they booked.

Outbound reps were able to provide the information requested. They also agreed to place follow-up calls to facilitate registrations once customers had received the approvals they needed. This resulted in a 60 percent conversion rate and a 20 percent increase in monthly revenue!

There are two powerful findings here:

- Although these were e-channel buyers, they appreciated Franklin Covey reaching out with a relevant human touch. There was positive customer feedback to this deployment of outbound telemarketing.
- There's gold in the people who abandon the shopping cart and don't complete the transaction.

Search Engine Marketing

When folks want something on the Web but don't know exactly where it is, they rely on search engines. They go to Google or Yahoo! or any of the other popular search engines, type in a query, and start at the top of the results of the search. Search Engine Marketing, or SEM, is the science of understanding and leveraging how the individual search engines transform the query into results and how they rank the search results.

According to a survey from WebTrends and iProspect,[16] 41 percent of U.S. marketers are currently running paid SEM efforts. Twenty-three percent of these feel that SEM is a significant contributor to their marketing mix. (However, only 11 percent are evaluating their SEM efforts using a detailed ROI analysis.)

Web Site Promotion and Search Engine Optimization

Site traffic building allows you to bring your prospective customers to your site without a costly marketing campaign. Using search engines and directories as virtual conduits connecting your customers to your offering gives you the ability to stretch your marketing dollar. Site promotion allows you to:

- Increase Web site recognition
- Inform current and potential customers of your offerings
- Fill the sales pipeline with new visitors and potential buyers

Here's how to drive additional traffic to your Web site via search engines and directories:

- **Assess your Web site.** Before you can attempt to drive additional traffic to your Web site, you must evaluate your situation. What are your Web site's strengths and weaknesses?
- **Site design.** Before you begin the optimization process, there are some key factors that need to be addressed in a site's design that can be problematic for search engines if not eliminated:

    Eliminate frames. Frames hinder a search engine's ability to index content on each page of your Web site.

    Eliminate problematic symbols in URLs. Some Web sites that are delivered dynamically (ASP) contain problematic symbols in their URLs.

    Use text links. As effective marketers, we must make it as easy as possible for the search engine spider to index each page of your Web site. Most spiders have trouble navigating through links contained in graphics. That's why text links are so important. Search engine spiders can easily navigate through links contained in text.

    Avoid intro pages. An introduction page with no text links and no content is similar to handing out blank business cards. Start your Web site with your home page.

    Be wary of flash. Flash intro pages often cause problems in the site traffic building process because search engine spiders can only index HTML content on a Web page. Flash can be used in sites, but in small portions, such as a small part of a page. Major problems will occur if the entire site is designed in flash.

- **Determine your top keyword phrases.** What phrases are your prospective customers using to find your type of company on the Internet? Target phrases high in popularity and low in competition.

Also, select phrases that are at least two to three words in length. Realize that you can target phrases that are within phrases (e.g., "Southern California Shopping Malls" contains "Southern California Shopping," "California Shopping Malls," and "California Shopping"). A good start is to select 10 of your favorite keyword phrases. Remember, every phrase you select will have to be used in your Web content. So don't select phrases that fall outside of your scope of business.

- **Incorporate top keyword phrases in your site.** After you have avoided each design hurdle, you're ready to optimize your site:

  Target one keyword phrase per Web page of your Web site.
  Write keyword-rich titles and metadata for each page.
  You must use the keyword phrase in a repetitive manner in the content.

- **Submit your Web site to the top search engines and directories.** A high percentage of submissions are free of charge. Submit once, and if your pages have not been indexed after one month, submit again until your pages are included. You can expect drastic improvement in three months and great results in six.[17]

Case History: Golden Rule Insurance

The market emphasis for Golden Rule Insurance is to provide individual health insurance, and GRI markets through many distribution channels: brokerage, sponsored, Internet, general agents, and direct sales.

The Direct Sales Unit, established in 1998, is the subject of this case history. This was GRI's first operating unit devoted to business-to-consumer (B2C) marketing, and has since its inception been highly profitable, generating a significant revenue stream.

GRI's hallmark has been an unwavering Consensual focus on the customer versus any medium or channel of distribution. This was embraced by the Direct Sales Unit. The unit was founded in the belief that:

- According to VOC Research findings, "self-serve" is painful, especially for individual health insurance.
- Health insurance is complex, and plans from different companies can vary widely.

- Health insurance, as we all know, is expensive.
- Choosing the right company, and the right plan, is critical for customers' well-being and peace of mind.

Thus, the Direct Sales Unit began by building a top-flight Call Center versus a Web site. Their goal was to drive prospects to the Call Center to manage the customer experience and to deliver the highest quality service and advice. The Internet was viewed as a way to attract potential customers. GRI's first goal was to establish conversion and profitability, and then to increase volume.

In offering individual health insurance direct to consumers, GRI's Direct Sales Unit used many customer channels (see Figure 5.2). The criteria for the selection of customer channels was that they had to be highly targeted. Additionally, GRI had to have the ability to control and regulate lead volume. The cost had to be in line with GRI's overall ROI criteria.

Greg Kohne, Assistant Vice President for Direct Sales, and the executive directly in charge of P&L, says: "The big challenge was how to generate significantly higher sales volumes without crashing our financial model."

GRI realized many things—the first being the importance of the Internet. Andy Grim, Vice President of Sales and Marketing, the senior executive overseeing the Direct Sales Unit says:

We found in most cases that Web advertising is ineffective. Advertising generates too many unqualified browsers. What we found to be effective is investing our lead generation dollars in building mutually beneficial partnerships with other Web sites where we pay for qualified leads—not clicks.

Figure 5.2   GRI Direct Sales, Customer Channels Chart

It's important to note that this entire program is based on 100 percent opt-in. Prospects contact GRI. Prospects request that GRI contact them. Andy Grim continues:

Once we receive a lead, we then:
- **Use e-mail to acknowledge the inquiry and ask prequalifying questions**
- **Use direct mail to send them complete information and an application**
- **Follow with an outbound call from a licensed rep in our Call Center**

All prospect names were filtered beforehand. Qualified names passed, nonqualified names did not. All leads were scored by their propensity to buy and were then sorted: "A" leads received priority treatment from the reps, each of whom was fully licensed and an expert in individual health insurance. The resulting health insurance "consultation" began with a needs analysis to truly understand the client's situation, to determine and clarify their goals. Once customer needs were established and discussed, a product recommendation was made:

- Based upon what was best for the client.
- With integrity: If the GRI product was not a good fit, GRI told the client. If the insurance plan the client had currently was better, GRI told them.

The development and deployment of a Consensual Database was the foundation of this entire program. By asking for 100 percent opt-in at the first contact, GRI consciously asked customers to give their consent to the detailed dialogue.

The information provided by consumers was profiled and point-scored to determine propensity to buy. Thus, the database actually *drove the allocation of marketing touches and resources* in accordance with the individual's propensity to buy. More money was spent in multitouch contacts with higher potential leads.

Greg Kohne adds:

Our database is what gives us the ability to drive incredibly high ROI. For example, we've used it to build profiles of those

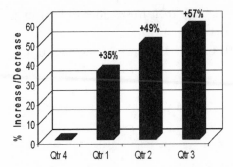

Figure 5.3   GRI Sale Conversion Results Chart

prospects that are most likely to be interested in the products we offer. As customers move through our sales process, we collect information in our database that is used to determine each customer's propensity to buy. We also have a database mining program in place to keep in touch with potential customers who for whatever reason did not purchase from us. These things ensure that we are allocating our resources properly and getting the most out of our marketing dollars.

The results: a 57 percent increase in conversion (Figure 5.3).

Points to Remember

Both e-mail and Web sites should be deployed as part of the IDM Media Mix.

Whether it's e-mail or Web sites, the goal of customer retention will generate the most attractive ROI.

Work at establishing a bond of trust between you and your e-customers. Permission is just a stop along the way.

The best practices of Consensual Marketing apply to the development and deployment of both e-mail and Web sites. Learn from direct marketing's successes and failures.

The customer experience is central to Consensual Marketing and the effective deployment of all e-media. An excellent customer experience provides compelling competitive differentiation.

In addition to retention, customers also look to Web sites for research and retail sales. Marketers should optimize their Web sites given the needs of their customers—understanding their frustrations and reaching out to them when they abandon the shopping cart.

Consider Search Engine Marketing (SEM) to drive customers to your Web site.

Step Five: Rethinking Customer Care

THE FIFTH STEP in the Consensual Marketing Opt-In Process focuses on proactive customer service as a powerful competitive differentiator. Additionally, this chapter will discuss the customer care center and how the highest quality of inbound and outbound telecontact can deliver exceptional customer value and service.

Concepts we will cover include:

- Customer care as a powerful competitive differentiator
- The Call Center as the face of the company
- Implementing a customer care process
- The importance of the customer care reps
- Creating the inside/outside partnership with Field Sales
- The value of inbound calls
- Requirements for value-added inbound
- Outbound customer care
- Guidelines for achieving quality telesales
- Leveraging the synergy between mail and outbound

Throughout, we will include comprehensive case studies that illustrate the step-by-step process and measurable results as a "how to" template for implementing proactive customer service and the highest quality inbound and outbound telecontact—critical elements of the Consensual Marketing process.

Customer Care as a Competitive Differentiator

Let's face it: expectations regarding customer service are often low. We pump our own gas. We check the oil and squeegee the windshield. Customer service reps are increasingly distant: there used to be a person on the other side of the counter; then there was a voice on the phone; and now we are pushed to an impersonal e-mail address for any customer service issue. The quality of customer service suffers.

Don Schultz, Professor Emeritus, Northwestern University, Medill School of Journalism and founder of consultancy Agora, Inc., shares the following anecdote:

> I was talking to some people about research they had done regarding shoppers at Wal-Mart. They found that when people talked about shopping there they would say, "I'm going to put on my suit of armor and I'm going to Wal-Mart." At some point Wal-Mart's price and supply chain is not going to overcome the fact that those people feel like they have to put on armor to go shopping.

> The supply chain model always says squeeze the waste out of the system. But then no one ever looks at what the result of squeezing the waste out of the system is—it's the customer experience. People are too mobile today. They are not captives like they used to be. I can shop anywhere. I can get online and I can find any product in the world. Why wouldn't I consider doing that rather than putting myself into a retail shopping experience that I know is going to be awful?

Poor customer service is like driving customers away with a cattle prod. The cost savings today will not equate to the lost revenue opportunity tomorrow. Marketers must remember, as we saw in Chapter 1, that the key to creating a successful customer relationship and to enhancing and lengthening that relationship is the delivery of value over time. And it is an indisputable truth that the only arbiter of "value" is the customer.

Marketers must remember these three indisputable truths:

- We need customers more than they need us.
- They have many choices besides us.
- Loyalty and trust cannot be taken for granted; they must be earned every day.

Call Centers as the Face of the Company

A recent global consumer survey[1] by Genesys Telecommunications Laboratories finds that consumers identify Call Center agents as the "face" of a company and largely base their purchasing and loyalty decisions on the quality of service they receive.

The survey finds that more than half of the 2,367 respondents report having ceased doing business with a company because of a negative Call Center experience. Conversely, 76 percent of respondents indicated that they would buy from a company based on a positive Call Center experience.

Thus, the ability of the Call Center to provide proactive customer service is very visible to customers. In the course of live, interactive contact, reps can probe, understand, empathize, offer potential solutions, and ensure satisfaction.

But the dedication to customer service must be evident throughout the organization. As long as companies fund and compensate by product, and manage money versus valuing customers or leveraging Customer Lifetime Value, marketers will struggle to provide the level of customer care that will be a competitive differentiator. For example, we can tell Field Sales to be customer-oriented and we can give them training and tools. But if we then give them a quota for the number of widgets sold, they will run over customers in an effort to meet the quota and keep their jobs. If companies don't invest, train, empower, and measure reps in relation to specific customer care goals, they will not achieve a differentiating level of customer care.

The Moment of Contact

The essence of our commitment to a customer is experienced in that fleeting moment of contact with our representative. We may call it a touch, but how do customers experience it? As a caress? An indifferent shrug of the shoulders? As a slap? As a roundhouse to the jaw? If we direct or mandate that customers touch us only via the Web, what's their experience? How do we reach out? If they use chat and our operator is conducting six conversations at the same time, what's their experience? Does this further the relationship?

Whether we call it trust or a relationship, the onus is on the marketer to nurture the customer to achieve increased retention and Customer Lifetime Value. Creating the efficient transactional framework only brings you up to zero. Customers expect that: it's nothing special. But providing the value-add, the caring customer service, is the true competitive differentiator.

Horst H. Schulze is former CEO of Ritz Carlton Hotels, and President and CEO of the West Paces Hotel Group, LLC. He is an expert on proactive customer service as a competitive differentiator. His thoughts help us to make the connection between proactive customer service and increased Customer Lifetime Value:

> **Proactive customer service, simply, is the anticipation of your customer's needs and desires. The one word that I could substitute for service is "care."**
>
> **The company and the individual are the variables in consistently providing proactive care to the customer. The company and the individual employee must see proactive customer care as a strategic product.**
>
> **The customer wants three things:**
>
> 1. **They want the item they are buying to be defect-free.**
> 2. **They don't want to wait for it.**
> 3. **They want you to care (which we call service). "Care for me because I spent a lot of money for the car," or "Care for me even though I only bought a bottle of water," or "Care for me if I buy a hotel room."**
>
> **The moment of interaction with the customer is the moment of truth. How do you judge the service? You judge it by the interaction with another human being.**

We find that many companies do not have a process for the consistent delivery of customer care, for managing that moment of customer interaction. The reason seems to be that many companies do not recognize that customer care is a product unto itself, a strategic addition to whatever else they produce, separate and distinct from a car, or the bottle of water mentioned above. Just as there must be a process for the quality manufacturing and delivery of the car or water, companies need a repeatable, measurable process for the quality delivery of customer care.

Implementing a Customer Care Process

In response to our question, "How do you implement a process for the consistent delivery of customer care?" Horst Schulze continues:

In the case of a hotel, I determine what talent is required in each particular job category. For example, the talent of the front desk clerk is, of course, to say hello, to welcome people, to say goodbye, to attend to a client's concern, to be compassionate. Then we hire based upon the talent needed for that job category, and begin the training.

Now the individual hired has to understand the organization, understand who we are and what we think, our philosophy, our heart, our soul. We also teach them the technical aspects of the job. And then the training continues every day.

We have what we call a "lineup"—a 10-minute teaching session every day in every hotel worldwide before every shift. The teaching of the day comes from the corporate office to all hotels worldwide. The messages could be based on customer survey letters. I might see in the customer survey a little bit of a slip in an area and we might make that the key message for the next week, to be timely and responsive to the voice of the customer. This way, the sign on the hotel in Hong Kong means the same thing as the sign on the hotel in Paris.

Long Term versus Short Term

At the heart of the issue is a pitched battle between short- and long-term thinking. Short-term thinking focuses solely on the transaction. How can you get more money today? Can you charge more? What expenses can be eliminated? In the instance of hotels, it drives decisions to cut corners—flowers cost money, so get rid of the flowers. Prices climb and value erodes. Short-term goals may be met, but at the expense of long-term opportunity.

Mr. Schulze concludes:

> **A long-term decision for me is to manage the product to a point that a customer wants to buy it. The easiest way of doing that is to show the customer that I care. If the customer senses that I care, the customer eventually will rely and trust me and is willing to pay more for my product. And so, that's the strategy. It's customer focus.**

The Customer Care Center

Within direct response, and specifically within the Consensual Marketing Opt-In Process, an effective place for the delivery of customer care is the call center—person-to-person. A recent survey[2] from RightNow Technologies and Harris Interactive reveals that 74 percent of U.S. consumers prefer to contact a company about customer service related issues via the phone. Only 26 percent prefer e-mail, and 15 percent prefer submitting their request via Web forms.

It all comes down to the reps, and marketers' investment in these reps. In fact, the focus is on the consistent delivery of quality customer care by the individual rep to the individual customer.

Single, Empowered Point of Contact

Within your organization you should carefully assess who is on the front line for the delivery of customer care. In the case of a hotel, it's the waiter, the busboy, the doorman, the bartender, etc. Each of these individuals must function as a single, empowered point of contact for the delivery of high quality customer care.

They must feel the company's commitment to customer care as a strategic product.

Horst Schulze again provides important perspective:

> **When we open a hotel, I always do the orientation. Here we have all the employees assembled, 100, 200, in the room. I introduce myself. "My name is Horst Schulze. I am the president of this company, Ritz Carlton. We are a worldwide company and I am very important." Of course, there was shock in the room. Some of them thought, "Oh yeah, he is!" but others were shocked and said, "Who the heck is this?" I said, "Yes, I'm very important, I'm the president. But let me tell you something, you are equally important." Let's see how important your job is and how important mine is. I know my job is important. So is yours. In fact, if you don't show up on Monday and the beds are not made or we don't check people in or we don't start the food, we have a disaster. If I don't show up on Monday, nobody will know. It's a fact! So, you have to know just how important you are here. And I feel that very, very strongly. I cannot expect service if I don't create an environment where the employee wants to give service.**

We subscribe to long-term thinking, which embraces customer care as a strategic goal that builds corporate wealth. Immediate profits and market share cannot be ignored. But to succeed long-term in a service economy, we must add customer satisfaction and lifetime value to the list of strategic goals. Customer care leverages customer satisfaction and lifetime value, and these are potentially huge contributors to the bottom line when you consider referrals, repeat purchases, and purchases of related products and services. The consistent delivery of customer care creates the framework for compelling competitive advantage.

Seven Propositions

The *Harvard Business Review* offers seven propositions that will help you drive the process of customer care:[3]

1. **Customer loyalty drives profitability and growth.** A 5 percent increase in customer loyalty can boost profits by 25 to 85 percent.

2. **Customer satisfaction drives customer loyalty.** Xerox found that its very satisfied customers were six times more likely to repurchase company equipment than customers who were merely satisfied.

3. **Value drives customer satisfaction.** An insurer's efforts to deliver maximum value include funding a team that provides special services at the sites of major catastrophes. The company has one of the highest margins in its industry.

4. **Employee productivity drives value.** Southwest Airlines deplanes and reloads two-thirds of its flights in 15 minutes or less; pilots fly an average 20 hours more per month than competitors. Fares stay low while service remains high.

5. **Employee loyalty drives productivity.** One auto dealer's annual cost of replacing a sales rep who had eight years of experience with one who had less than a year was $432,000 in lost sales.

6. **Employee satisfaction drives loyalty.** In one company study, 30 percent of all dissatisfied employees expressed an intention to leave, compared to only 10 percent of all satisfied employees. Moreover, it was found that low employee turnover was closely linked to high customer satisfaction.

7. **Internal quality drives employee satisfaction.** Service workers are happiest when they're empowered to make things right for customers and when they have responsibilities that add depth to their work.

The Tie That Binds

In the face of mediocrity, customer care becomes a differentiator. More than a differentiator, it brings customers back for more. QVC is the perfect example. Over its 17-year history, QVC has answered over 1 billion phone calls and shipped over 600 million packages to over 25 million customers on three continents.

QVC was founded on three customer-focused principles: quality, value, and convenience. QVC's growth formula has not changed from its first day in business: exceeding customer expectations at every opportunity. The following dialogue between John Hunter, Senior Vice President of Customer Services, and Doug Rose, Vice President of Merchandising Brand Development, shows that superb customer care goes straight to the bottom line:

DOUG: I was shocked when we did an analysis of our customer file and found that of our domestic shipping sales volume, 93 percent of those revenues were generated by customers who bought more than once.

JOHN: Shopping at QVC must be a very pleasant experience. "I like that," and you come back and do it again. The number one engine bringing new customers to QVC is word-of-mouth. It's people telling their friends they had such a great experience. "Oh, where'd you get that DVD player?" or "Where'd you get that bracelet?" The positive word-of-mouth is happy customers. Our retention strategy, actually, is a very effective acquisition strategy. The percentage of new customers that come to us as referrals runs around 23 percent.

The Importance of the Customer Care Reps

Specialization

Everyone who puts on a headset is required to deliver customer service every minute of every day. However, some skills and personalities may be more geared to sales than to being a customer service rep and solving problems all day. One suggestion that has worked exceedingly well for many of our clients is to establish a structure based on the specialization of reps. This means dividing the Call Center into perhaps three areas of responsibility:

- **Inquiries/inbound sales.** This is the training ground. Reps handle calls from folks who are kicking tires. They need information. Reps learn to probe for need and then personalize the information. Many of these callers already know what they want, and they need someone to take the order. Success in this group is identifying leads for follow-up, thus producing incremental sales.
- **Outbound sales/follow-up.** Experienced salespeople are here. They take the high potential opportunities generated by the first group and work the leads. This group generates the "above the line" sales—the sales the company would not have otherwise realized.
- **Customer service.** Service-oriented people are here. They must also be absolute experts in the company and its products and services.

The more experienced the rep, the more empowerment and latitude they receive to handle the situation and ensure customer satisfaction.

Elevate the Status of the Rep

Mr. Schulze raised a critical point: employees must want to deliver customer care. They must feel important to the organization and embrace the organization's goals and strategies. They must feel that the organization is behind them, supporting them in their efforts.

Therefore, we recommend that marketers elevate the status of the rep.

Think about the skills you teach, and require excellence in listening, probing, determining need, positioning benefits, and empathizing with the customer. In some cases, a high degree of technical knowledge is required.

So instead of "representative," consider the titles Product Advisor, Sales Advisor, Service Professional, etc. Which title would motivate you to go the extra mile to help a customer: Communicator or Service Professional? Would you rather speak with a rep or a Travel Planner? One word of caution: If you elevate the status of your reps by name, you must also elevate their skill set to deliver on the promise.

Inside/Outside Partnership with the Field

The consistent delivery of high-quality customer care implies a seamless transfer of information from the phone-based rep to the field-based rep. No matter who the customer calls, or when, each individual should have the most current data. This is a significant benefit to both the customer and the company. The customer receives treatment that says: "We value you." This increases customer satisfaction and loyalty. However, this is not the current state of affairs.

Traditionally, the sales rep is the locus of all the account-specific information. They know the people and the issues. And they are always on the road selling, which makes them largely unavailable to customers calling with questions. Customers contact the company and speak with the "inside" rep, who has to start at square one.

The inside/outside partnership model has two requirements for success. The first is a contact management software system that links the customer care center with Field Sales. It becomes the central hub of information, maintaining the most current data on customers. We've looked at many, both off-the-shelf and "home-grown." We recommend you look at off-the-shelf solutions first—you're likely to get 85 percent of the functionality you desire right off the bat, and at a lower cost.

The second prerequisite is a mandate from management to create and nurture the inside/outside partnership, to consistently use the contact management software and populate it with current sales information. We suggest that this mandate be both a carrot and a stick. The carrot: the partnership and exchange of information will increase satisfaction, sales, and commissions. The stick: there isn't a choice.

The inside/outside partnership model we would suggest was implemented by IBM at a time when the company was confronted with a drop in customer satisfaction among their best customers. Understanding how many millions of dollars hinge on each point of customer satisfaction, IBM investigated and found two primary reasons for the dissatisfaction: (1) the ton of irrelevant marketing information dumped on customers, and (2) customers were frustrated that simple requests often meant following a labyrinth of contacts in search of an answer.

In regard to the second point, here's a quote from ERDM's VOC Research (the first point will be discussed in detail in Chapter 8):

> **I can't get my questions answered. I call, but my sales rep is on the road. So I get transferred to another very nice individual who doesn't have the answer. Who transfers me to someone else, to someone else, ending in a voice mailbox. Who is this person I'm leaving a message for? I don't know. Please get me out of voice mail hell.**

Customers were articulate, and IBM took immediate action to set up a care center specifically for this customer set. In IBM's parlance, this was called the SPOE: a Single Point of Entry. No matter what the customer wanted, they could call the SPOE and get immediate satisfaction. Thus, one of the most important products of the SPOE was customer care.

IBM staffed the SPOE with carefully selected and trained individuals. Each had a technical background and broad sales experience so they were intimately aware of the technology used by these customers. It was important that the SPOE agent could "talk the talk." Each agent had been with IBM for a while and knew where to go within the organization to find answers and solve problems. Each received specialized training to meet the needs of their customer set and the requirements of advanced teleskills. And each was empowered to take ownership of whatever issue the customer presented.

If a customer called to make an appointment with his or her sales rep, the SPOE agent had their calendar. If the issue was service, the SPOE agent stayed on the line with the customer as they transferred to the service desk and reported the trouble. The SPOE agent followed up to make sure the problem was fixed. If the issue was information, the SPOE agent took responsibility for gathering the data and, as necessary, the experts to handle highly technical topics. The SPOE agent would also place outbound calls to follow up important technical white papers and product releases to answer questions.

Inbound Calls Are a Gift

Think about this: inbound calls are customer generated. They are calling for one of three reasons: to inquire, make a purchase, or resolve an issue. And, by definition, inbound callers are more qualified and likely to spend.

Callers want to speak to a live person—someone who represents the company well. Callers want immediate gratification.

View each inbound call as a gift. Even the problem calls give you the opportunity to fix what's broken and mend the relationship. With each inbound call you can learn something new about the customer, tell them something about your company they didn't know, show them you care, leverage Customer Lifetime Value. What a fabulous opportunity.

Usually, inbound callers are greeted by autoprompt hell. When we call a company, we make sure there's scratch paper at hand to write down which extension is for what, until we find what we want. This is also helpful if we get disconnected and have to call back. This is hostage marketing. The customer simply has nowhere else to go.

If we manage to work our way through the endless maze, we sit, listening to either an "est" sales pitch (the best, the greatest, the cheapest) or music. Finally, we're rewarded with indifferent human robots who do *not*:

- Communicate value
- Satisfy customers
- Increase revenue (passively handling an inbound order is not selling, it's order taking)
- Contribute to your brand

What do your customers experience when they call your 800 number? Perhaps, on a regular basis, you should put on your customer hat and make a test call.

"The value of the 'human touch' of inbound telecontact has been overwhelmed by technology that is efficient for the organization but adds little value to the customer experience"—Vincent Amen, former Vice President of Public Programs for Franklin Covey, and President of Growth Coach

The Value of an Inbound Call

Inbound calls are also remarkably expensive. At seminars, when we ask participants what they think an inbound call costs, we hear replies such as: $6.43, or $7.57, or $10. This is defining the cost of an inbound call in relation to the productivity of the inbound Call Center. Roughly, here's the logic: The average talk time for an inbound call is x. The cost of salary, benefits, computer, HVAC, etc., is y. Therefore, each inbound call costs z. This is certainly valid but perpetuates the view of the Call Center as an expense.

If, however, we view the Call Center as a customer care center and revenue generator, we find the cost is generally between $50 and $250. This represents the cost of the marketing activity to stimulate those inbound calls.

Of course, Inbound is more than just answering the phone. It is a series of interconnected processes. Think of it as a funnel. Customer-initiated calls come in and are met with proactive, value-added contact. The empowered rep probes for need in order to position the features and benefits of your product or service. The immediate result is either a sale or defined follow-up action. Based on the caller's propensity to buy, callers are scored as an A, B, C, or D lead. Follow-up action often involves personalized fulfillment via fax, e-mail, or direct mail. A and B leads are then routed for targeted outbound calling, and C and D leads are worked via a combination of media, given a predetermined contact management plan. The result: significantly increased sales (Figure 6.1).

Figure 6.2 depicts a simple example of what the successful integration of inbound can achieve. Let's say that base mail response is 2 percent. The careful integration of a toll-free 800 number can provide a 50 to 100 per-

Figure 6.1   The Importance of Inbound Contacts

cent incremental lift in qualified response. This means that the 800 number must be promoted with value: What will you get if you call it? A disinterested reactive robot? Not much value. An educated, empowered expert on the subject who is there to answer questions and guide you? This will increase inbound response. But we have to deliver! The folks answering the phone must be trained and coached to deliver the promised value and the customer care. That's when the response rate has the potential to double.

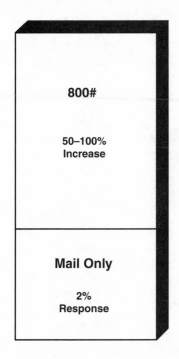

Figure 6.2 Increase of Inbound Response

Requirements for Value-Added Inbound

There are three requirements, which we will discuss, for the successful integration of inbound into the IDM Media Mix:

- Visible integration
- Interactive scripting
- Result-tracking metrics

Visible Integration

The toll-free number should be visibly integrated into all communications: publicity, advertising, mail, and Internet. This does not mean that the 800 number should be as large and bold as possible. It does mean that the 800 number and the value of calling it should play a prominent role in both design and copy. Here are two examples of copy treatments:

My name is _____ and I have been assigned by the ABC Corporation as the project manager on your account, should you accept our proposal. If your needs are immediate, you can reach me anytime at 1-800-123-4567. Or I will give you a call later this week to learn more about your needs.

Call 1-800-123-4567 now and speak with a licensed, experienced representative who will help you to select the individual health insurance that's right for your needs.

Interactive Scripting

Too often scripts are viewed as straitjackets: "Why would I want to stifle the spontaneity of our communicators with a script? They'll sound like robots." What's the last movie you saw where the actors weren't working from a script?

The behaviors reps with scripts will exhibit will be confidence, consistency, and effectiveness. Here's how the process of interactive scripting works.

Whenever a script is written, no matter who wrote it, it is "best guess." It must be put through the crucible of customer interaction. Because you want the script to be the best possible, you should get the best reps to test it live. Listen to their suggestions and incorporate them into the script.

Then distribute the script to the balance of reps, letting them know that the superstars have tested it, modified it, and are endorsing it. Nonjudgmental role-playing will help them get comfortable. Then, when they've been on the phone for a while, hold a feedback session with the best reps in the room and let them talk. Take the best of the comments and incorporate them into the script. Call monitoring will provide additional input. What you will have created with this approach is a system to take the best sales and customer service techniques of the best reps and distribute them to everyone else. This will raise the productivity of the entire Call Center. The resulting consistency will drive the projectability of the results.

Continue to hold regular feedback sessions and to update the script. Two things are important here:

- The reps own the script. It is their tool, their lever for success. They will do a better job and be less likely to view the script as a demon if they feel the empowerment. Let's face it: the idea that reps sound like robots if they have a script is nonsense. Every actor you see on TV, in the movies, or on stage is using a script. Most of them don't sound like robots. Plus, if the reps basically write the script, they'll internalize it faster.
- A script that doesn't change will lose its effectiveness. The marketplace is always changing. Reps are in direct contact with the marketplace every day, all day. If they discover that something isn't working anymore, get rid of it and find a new approach.

Result-Tracking Metrics

Consistent with changing the view of the Call Center from a corporate expense to a customer care center that generates revenue, marketers should also expand their view of result-tracking metrics. The effective management of the Call Center must incorporate both quantitative metrics regarding productivity and sales and qualitative metrics regarding the quality of the customer interaction. (Chapter 7 will provide detail regarding the reports and the critical leverage points for improving the productivity and quality of in- and outbound telecontact.)

One metrics process that deserves mention here is reasons for "Not interested now" analysis. When a rep asks for the sale, one of two things will happen. The customer will say yes or no. Most times, the customer says no. This analysis brings that intelligence back to marketing. Why did they say no? What were the reasons? The data is collected and reported weekly in rank order.

This is powerful feedback. Let's say we're an ice cream manufacturer and we find that the number one reason people aren't buying is they think we don't have pistachio ice cream. But we do have pistachio—why don't people realize that? That means we must immediately adjust our marketing materials and telecontact scripts. Will this have a big impact? The answer is yes—a big cumulative impact, based on the theory of "just one more." What improvements can we make to enable our reps to make just one more sale per day? One more sale multiplied by the number of reps over time results in meaningful dollars.

Learning from QVC

QVC is one of the best examples of fully integrated inbound. We would like to share with you another portion of a conversation we had with John Hunter and Doug Rose:

> JOHN: Our sales proposition is informational. If you watch the show, the host is demonstrating how the product works and its value. It's always soft sell, and often with a content expert. It's the "neighbor across the backyard fence concept"—not too "salesy" or too slick, but comfortable, as if you were talking to your neighbor about a product you bought and you're telling him why you thought it was good, as opposed to a polished salesperson who is really pushing the item.
>
> So we take all of that and say, "What experience do you have to create over the phone with the customer?" The same warm, friendly, "neighbor across the back fence" is what we try to do over the phone.
>
> DOUG: The order entry representative is not allowed to take a call from a customer until they've had 25 hours of training. Half of the training consists of the basic mechanics of how to process an order using our order entry system so that they're efficient. But the other half is the intangible high-touch human aspect of being a representative of QVC. Be a nice person; don't be so efficient that you sound cold. If someone wants to chitchat, you can allow that to some degree. Just remember our business is really about the pleasure of shopping—the social aspect. So humanity is a very important part of our brand.
>
> The call center culture is a friendly, warm environment. Everyone knows we have productivity numbers. But everyone feels it's a pretty good place to work—people build a sense of community. We spend a lot of time creating the right kind of environment. We take care of our employees and we expect them to take care of the customers.

JOHN: Our rep training includes classroom work plus another two weeks under very close surveillance when they take their first calls. We try to create an environment where customers feel good. They can't watch some nice show host that's very pleasant and friendly on TV, and then pick up the phone and have a rep that says, "Hey, what do you want? Hurry up, you know, I got 3.2 seconds to take this order."

Outbound Customer Care

"The 'phone spam' factor has seriously eroded the value of outbound tele-contact. Companies that use telecontact in the future will have to figure out ways to generate credibility with each consumer before they approach the consumer by phone."—Al Ries, Chairman, Ries & Ries

Outbound telecontact is a sharp double-edged sword. It is both the most powerful medium for generating response, leads, and sales and the most powerful medium for creating customer dissatisfaction. Unfortunately, the industry has been very successful in giving itself a terrible reputation. The words *outbound telemarketing* are enough to make many wince.

Customers are outspoken, as you can see from these customer quotes from ERDM's VOC Research:

- "Telemarketing is intrusive. If I'm interested, I'll call you."
- "Irrelevant. Unstructured. Offensive."
- "You're not listening. Cold calling is not appreciated."
- "How much of a relationship do you feel with the folks who call during dinner?"

For perspective, we are also out-of-step with many other countries, as Charles A. Prescott, Vice President, International Business Development & Government Affairs, Direct Marketing Association, reveals:

Germany is the most extreme with respect to telephone marketing. It's reflected in their telecommunications law of the '70s, and that law says that telephone numbers cannot be used to market. You can't call people at their homes or, in some cases, even at their businesses, unless they have previously

expressed an affirmative consent. In some European countries, such as the UK, there is a mandated use of the national Do Not Call List.

I think American companies who use outbound telecontact had a glorious run. I don't know if you could say we are now coming into sync with the rest of the world with respect to personal sensitivity, but I will say that when I would talk about frequency of telecontact in this country with people from Europe, they were absolutely aghast.

Outbound is not for everyone. There are many customers who simply will not be won back, whether at home or at the office. Many applications of outbound, such as cold calling, are inefficient and annoying.

And outbound is just not appropriate for every company's media mix, as Doug Rose of QVC indicates:

Our culture and business practices have kept us loyal to a noninvasive philosophy regarding communications with our customers. There is a cultural bias and rigorous testing has borne out that consumers' buying behaviors are too difficult to forecast—even very sophisticated tools fail. Let's face it, you can't place a general outbound call: "Hi, this is QVC. Would you like to buy something today?" You have to be specific. So if you guess wrong, it's perceived as an outbound telecontact call that is interrupting dinner.

Guidelines for Achieving Quality Telesales

Here are our suggested guidelines for achieving IDM and CMO quality outbound telecontact:

1. **Synchronize outbound with other media,** such as direct mail, fax and e-mail. Outbound should not stand alone. Cold calls equal junk phone. Rather, it should be timed to follow prior contacts (with other media that establish the value proposition and rationale for the call). This requires tight integration of the message among the media, and precision timing (which will be discussed later, in the section "Leverage the Synergy between Mail and Outbound").

2. **Outbound must deliver value, as defined by the customer—** call only high potential names. The first point is messaging. The rationale for the outbound call must be of high value to the recipient. Examples of value:
   o "I'm calling today in response to your request that we keep you up-to-date on technological advances regarding your widget. We just released widget one and sent you a complete technological overview. Specifically, page four addresses the advanced capabilities, which you said was your primary interest. I'd be happy to walk you through the materials and answer any questions, if you have the time."
   o "Our records show that earlier this week you called for onsite repair. The technician was there yesterday. I'm following up to make sure the problem has been corrected to your satisfaction."
   o "Hi. This is Joe from the florist. Valentine's Day is coming fast. We sent you a reminder via e-mail to get your wife flowers, as in years past. I'm calling to help facilitate your order, get it there on time and keep you out of the doghouse."
   o "Mr. Roman, we recently sent you an invitation for the opening of the symphony. As a longtime donor, we would be honored if you would attend. I'm calling this morning to facilitate the reservation for you and your wife and to arrange any transportation or lodging that may be necessary."

   The second point is the list. Once again, the list is the primary lever for success. Outbound is expensive, both in real dollars and in its potential to erode your customer file. It is essential that you select only the high potential names that are not adverse to the medium, and closely monitor results. You'll see this again in the next, but one of the most important metrics is the rate of "Do Not Call" (DNC) requests. If the percentage of DNC rises above 0.5 percent of contacts, stop! Customers are saying "no value"— something is very wrong, and you must find out what it is before continuing.

3. **Engage in thorough precall planning.** Before your reps dial the phone, they must ask themselves the following questions, and have good answers:
   o Why am I calling this person? What are my primary and secondary objectives for the call?

○ What other conversations have taken place with this customer—what does it say in the notes?

○ How do I pronounce this person's name?

And remember, phrases such as "How are you doing?" and "Did you get the information we sent?" bring zero value.

4. **Manage time and energy.** These are finite resources. Reps must manage them effectively. Tips include:

○ Many attempts will result in voice mail. Script effective, compelling voice mail messages to maximize the potential for returned calls.

○ Many contacts will result in callbacks. Set up timed appointments for callbacks. Try to schedule them for times when traditionally it's harder to reach decision makers. And when suggesting the timed appointment, use an either/or approach. For instance: "Which would be better for you, Tuesday at 2 or Thursday at 10?"

5. **Quickly answer the unspoken question: "What's in it for me?"** Assume that the person on the other end of the phone has the attention span of a gnat. Experience says you've got about 12 seconds to show value, to answer that unspoken question, "What's in it for me?" or the call is over.

The following guidelines apply to both inbound and outbound.

6. **Control the call.** There are two sides to control. The first is to be confident in your subject and your professionalism and lead the customer to value. The second is to be courteous. Never forget that the nature of outbound is interruptive. If this isn't a good time for the customer, give them an early, gracious exit.

7. **Probe for clear statements of need.** This is essential for several reasons:

○ To bring the customer further into the conversation.

○ To understand how to position your product or service.

○ To use later on in the conversation as a "gut check." For instance: "We've reviewed all the aspects of this particular individual health policy and from what you've told me, I think it's the right one for you. You said you needed X and the policy provides X. . . . How does this policy sound to you?"

8. **Paraphrase to show understanding.** Paraphrasing is an excellent tactic. It lets the customer know you are actively listening and processing what they said—that you are tracking with them. It will also give you immediate feedback if you got something wrong.

9. **Present the solution with features and benefits.** Folks are interested in the features. But they buy because of the benefits. Features tell you what the thing does. Benefits tell you what it will do for you.

10. **Recognize the types of objections.** There are four basic objections:
    o No need
    o No money
    o No confidence (in your company, product or service)
    o No hurry to purchase

11. **Meet objections with benefit and value.** Embrace questions and objections. They are the customer's way of telling you they do not have enough information to understand the value. They're giving you another shot to persuade them. For it to be your best shot, utilize the principles of interactive scripting. Develop and continuously refine your responses to the most frequent questions and objections.

12. **Go for the sale.** If the rep has followed all the guidelines, he or she has earned the right to ask for the sale. There's no reason to be shy. It's the logical culmination of the conversation.

13. **Upsell/cross-sell whenever appropriate.** The rep's knowledge of the customer's needs, their product expertise, and their positioning as an expert/advisor may reveal opportunities for upsell and/or cross-sell that are beneficial to the customer. If it's not in line with the customer's needs, don't bring it up.

14. **Generate customer referrals.** It's appropriate to ask a satisfied customer if there are friends or colleagues who would also benefit from the value your company provides. This will be a highly responsive list. For many clients, referrals convert at a rate 200 percent higher than prospect names.

15. **Capture the reasons for "Not interested now."** As explained earlier, when we discussed inbound customer care, use customers' reasons for no sale to improve scripts, marketing materials, and overall effectiveness.

16. Implement the tools of quality telecontact. These consist of:
    o Interactive scripting (explained in the section on inbound customer care)
    o Call-quality monitoring (to be addressed in the next chapter)
    o Daily productivity metrics (also to be addressed in the next chapter)

Leverage the Synergy between Mail and Outbound

The time dimension is critical to leveraging qualified leads and sales.

Traditionally, companies wait until mail response peaks and is on the downward slope before deploying outbound telecontact. The rationale for this: Mail is less expensive, so why cannibalize mail response with expensive outbound telecontact?

We recommend a revised view. Use direct mail as a springboard for outbound. Don't let 98 percent of your target audience go stone cold while you wait for 1 to 2 percent mail response. Leverage response with high quality outbound to clearly defined high potential segments of the list. Testing has shown that optimal call timing is 24 to 72 hours after mail receipt. We call this "IDM Response Compression." For e-mail, optimal timing is 12 to 24 hours after receipt. Figure 6.3 depicts the two response times.

With Response Compression, the significant increase in qualified response results in a decreased cost per sale. Direct mail is more produc-

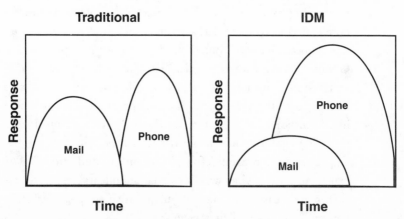

Figure 6.3 IDM Response Compression

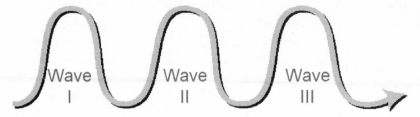

Figure 6.4 Wave Mailing Pattern

tive and telecontact is more profitable. The multiple messages delivered via different channels increase sales.

To achieve Response Compression and have the outbound call arrive within 24 to 72 hours of mail receipt, the quantity mailed must match your capacity to make outbound calls. Thus, we recommend that mail be released in the wave pattern discussed in Chapter 4 and depicted in Figure 6.4, with the size of each wave determined by the outbound capacity.

Wave Mailing Pattern

The mail quantity for each wave of mail should be 130 to 140 percent of outbound capacity, assuming 75 to 80 percent list completion. (*List completion* means we've had a conversation with the decision maker, or we're able to discard the name because it's a bad record, or we've attempted the name four times). Here's how to calculate the quantity for each wave of mail, using a real-life example.

Let's say a rep can complete 50 names a day, and we have four reps available for calling. That would be 200 completed calls per day, or 1,000 completed calls per week.

Understanding that our target is 75 to 80 percent completion, we would have to mail 1,335 names per week.

The wave mail pattern offers an extra benefit. Information from the "Reasons for not interested now" analysis can be used to revise both scripts and copy for personalized, laser-printed direct mail letters for subsequent drops, which will further increase qualified response.

500 Percent Increase in Response

Figure 6.5 will give you an idea of what outbound can do for the bottom line when integrated into the IDM Media Mix and deployed according to

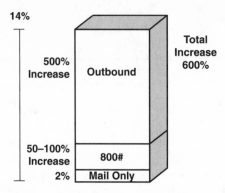

Figure 6.5 Outbound Magnifies Response from 2 to 14 Percent

Consensual Marketing. If we start with a base mail response of 2 percent, the careful integration of inbound can generate a 50 to 100 percent increase in qualified response. Outbound, synchronized with mail or e-mail, will increase response by another 500 percent! So the 2 percent mail response can be magnified to 14 percent or more.

Perspective from the Palms Trading Company

The principles of customer care apply to all companies, both large and small. Palms Trading Company of Albuquerque, New Mexico, is a 70-year-old family-owned Indian trading post. They specialize in American Indian pottery, jewelry, and rugs. Much of their business is done via the phone, in response to collectors throughout the United States who are looking for specific pieces and from existing customers looking for collectibles. One of the company's concerns was creating competitive differentiation over the phone. Company president Guy Berger explains:

> **We decided to change how people experience calling our trading post versus other places they might call. We thought that providing a caring, knowledgeable experience with our reps would set us apart from competitors.**
>
> **So, as part of an overall strategy we call "Personal Shopper," we trained our reps to understand exactly what people are looking**

for, educate the customer as to the best artist or Indian pueblo making the work, and then obtain the piece for the caller.

By providing true personal service, we can deliver the magic of Southwest art to our customers in a way that increases their propensity to buy with each successive conversation.

Since its inception, we feel this program of personal customer service has been a major factor in posting a 21 percent increase in our gross sales over the past four years, notwithstanding a tough economy.

View from the Other Side of the Phone

Here's a view from the other side of the phone, from Ernan's son, Elias Vale Roman, who has been working for his university's Student Calling Center, generating donations:

I try to think of each call as a favor to the contact—a friendly reminder or update. Following are some anecdotes of calls I have made which will hopefully shed some light on the caller-contact relationship:

When I started at the Calling Center, I was given a list of non-donors. One young woman I spoke with, who had also been a telemarketer, kept asking me what her "ask amount" was (the dollar amount we are supposed to aim for, based on collected information about their career, etc.). Since I knew I wasn't supposed to give that information out to the contact, I told her it said $1.6 million, and would cash or credit card be best for her. She laughed and I got my first sale.

After introducing myself to the spouse of a contact, she informed me that I shouldn't bother speaking to her husband because he was not fond of who I was representing. I told her that part of the reason I was calling was to find out the opinions of our contacts and pass them along. She put me on the phone with her husband; he gave me the same line, and I gave him the same response. He seemed surprised, but was willing to share his complaints. After 10 minutes of chatting (during which I listened and responded to what he had to say), he decided that although he still didn't like who I was representing, he was willing to make a donation because he appreciated being heard.

Of course, it is essential that the databases be kept accurately. I don't even want to think about calls I have made with inaccurate records. Suffice it to say that I've called to thank a dead person for their previous donations and to ask if they would be willing to give again.

The four most important aspects of a telecontact call are:

- Avoidance of blatantly prefabricated sentences (the goal is to sound like a human, not a robot)
- Positive tone, reflecting a smile
- Complete and customer-relevant database information (including phonetic pronunciation of names)
- Conveyance of an interest in the contact that extends beyond the sale

Case Study: Franklin Covey Public Programs

The Franklin Covey company offers single- and multiday seminars nationwide based on their bestselling books and best practices, such as *What Matters Most* and *The Seven Habits of Highly Effective People*. Vincent Amen, whom we have quoted previously, was the Vice President of Public Programs, the executive in charge of this division.

The Public Programs Group (PPG) had a strategic issue to test and several corporate objectives to attain. The strategic issue was Vince's—to emphasize the human touch/customer care across all media. "Too often in direct marketing," he told us, "we lose sight of the human side. We are too insulated from customers. We forget the impact of the human touch on satisfaction and conversion."

The corporate objectives were revenue-based and media specific.

1. Direct Mail: reduce promotion expense ratio from 55 to 45 percent, and reduce mail quantities by 25 percent
2. Fax: $100,000 revenue per month at a promotion to expense ratio of 25 percent
3. Web: monthly revenue of $100,000
4. Call Center: leverage the "human touch" to increase revenue

Direct Mail

The objectives were to reduce promotion expense ratio from 55 to 45 percent, and reduce mail quantities by 25 percent. Multimedia tactics were deployed. First, the database was moved to an external database management resource to provide improved segmentation and selectability. To make sure that the organization could take the greatest advantage of the new segmentation and selectability, the Public Programs Group implemented training and strict Call Center performance criteria for source code capture. After all, without the source codes, PPG would never know which of the segments and selections actually worked!

Direct Mail Results

- The promotion expense to revenue ratio was successfully reduced to 45 percent.
- Mail quantities were reduced by 35 percent, a 75 percent improvement over the corporate objective.
- The rate of source code capture increased 133 percent: from 30 to 70 percent of orders.

Key Direct Mail Findings

- The investment of time and effort in the database is essential. The enhancements to the database, especially the list segmentation and selectability, represented at least 65 percent of PPG's success.
- Don't forget the fundamentals, such as source code capture. To increase the capture rate, consider both training and performance goals. Training gives reps the rationale: Why do we need the codes and what do we do with them? In fact, we recommend you share

results reports with the reps. Performance goals should always be three-tiered: conservative (which is what we expect), middle of the road (more aggressive results), and stretch (aggressive). If reps achieve the aggressive goal, we reward them. The "carrot and stick" work well together.

Fax

The objective was $100,000 revenue per month at a promotion to expense ratio of 25 percent. There were several issues PPG had to confront:

- In accordance with Consensual Marketing, we must comply with customers' media preferences. Fortunately, a majority of the file was comfortable with fax communications. Nevertheless, PPG did not want any implementation to be perceived as a "fax blast," since impersonal, generic communications could cause dissatisfaction and increase the "do not fax" rate.
- Any fax implementation had to be carefully balanced with inbound capacity to answer calls. As explained in "Wave Mailing Pattern" earlier, inbound capacity was computed and drove the fax quantities per wave.

Fax Implementation Issues

- The accuracy and updating of fax numbers is a critical success factor. All reps on all programs redoubled their efforts at database building and verification as a component of every conversation.
- The promotion must be designed specifically for the fax medium. The quality of the fax received depends on the state of technology at the recipient. So design also had to take into account the "lowest common denominator." That meant no dark backgrounds or complex charts. Dark backgrounds came over the fax like mud and ate any dropout (white) type. The medium simply wouldn't hold the fine lines of a complex chart. The fax had to be easily readable, necessitating an increase in type size.
- How much copy and how many pages? PPG continually tested these two variables.

Fax Results

- PPG achieved an annual revenue of $1.4 million, versus the goal of $1.2 million, a 17 percent increase over the objective.
- The promotion expense ratio came in under 15 percent, bettering the objective by 40 percent.

Key Fax Findings

- The medium is underutilized—it can be both cost effective and profitable.
- Fax is not "junk" when the message is compelling and targeted.
- The medium is great for rapid ongoing database cleansing.

Web

The objective was to attain monthly Web revenue of $100,000, which would have been an increase of over 40 percent above the current $70,000 a month. After several months of testing, improving, and publicizing the Web site, monthly revenue grew to $120,000. However, research revealed that 50 percent of all customers were dropping out of the shopping cart before they finalized their order.

Web Implementation Issues

- PPG decided to test customer-service-oriented outbound follow-up to the folks who dropped out of the shopping cart.
- It was decided to call business phones only—no calls to homes. PPG did not want to be perceived as a "telemarketer."
- Before any calls were placed, the rep checked customer transactions to make sure the customer had not registered via other media.

Web Results

- PPG discovered two major reasons why people were not completing the registration online: (1) The customer had questions, such as pricing, and could not get them immediately answered, and (2) The customer did not have the authority to make the registration and needed a supervisor's approval.
- PPG managed to achieve a 60 percent conversion rate from those customers who had previously abandoned the shopping cart.

- The incremental revenue generated by these outbound calls increased monthly revenue by an additional 20 percent over objective, putting PPG 40 percent over objective for the year.

Key Web Findings

- Although e-Channel buyers, they appreciated a relevant outbound human touch. Reactions were very positive.
- There is gold in the people who don't complete the transactions.

Call Center

The PPG Call Center was a traditional reactive Call Center, accepting registrations for public seminars. It was viewed internally and throughout the Franklin Covey organization as a cost center. The goals were to move to a proactive, consultative Call Center that provided value and generated revenue.

Call Center Issues

- Call handling was robotic versus personalized. Customers were seen as a "transaction."
- There was insufficient direction, training, or compensation, so reps didn't pursue opportunities for additional revenue, such as identifying additional potential registrants, cross-selling or upselling, and database building.
- There were no processes to measure productivity.

Call Center Implementation Issues

- PPG had to re-create the Call Center and effect a culture change. The Call Center had to embrace: customer focus, accountability, and performance goals.
- PPG immediately began specialized training to help employees see their role as value-added experts, and to teach the necessary skills for consultative selling.
- Daily productivity metrics reporting began as paper-based. Vince knew there would be many changes early on—it's easy to change paper and difficult to change programming. Metrics were not automated until the modifications stabilized.
- Important changes were made to call-quality monitoring, ensuring a rigorous, qualitative, and quantitative process:

○ Increased monitoring frequency from 3 calls per week to 10 calls per rep per week.

○ Sharpened the focus on more consultative and revenue-producing behaviors.

○ Call-quality scoring was weighted to emphasize these key behaviors.

Call Center Results

PPG experienced dramatic improvement in revenue in less than one year after initial implementation:

- $3.8 million in additional revenue due to structured inquiry follow-up and high-quality outbound deployment
- $500,000 in additional revenue from outbound follow-up to e-marketing dropouts
- $100,000 through "Friend Bring a Friend" offers

Key Call Center Findings

The Call Center should not be viewed as a cost center or as a corporate expense, but as an important revenue generator when carefully integrated into the marketing process.

Points to Remember

Customer care is an essential competitive differentiator. Consumers identify Call Center agents as the "face" of a company and largely base their purchasing and loyalty decisions on the quality of service they receive. The solidity of a customer relationship is shaped by the quality of experience in the moment of contact.

Within direct response, and specifically within the Consensual Marketing Opt-In Process, an effective place for the delivery of customer care is the Call Center: person-to-person. A recent survey from RightNow Technologies and Harris Interactive states that 74 percent of U.S. consumers prefer to contact a company about customer service related issues via the phone. Only 26 percent prefer e-mail, and 15 percent prefer the Web.

Within your organization you should carefully assess who is on the front line for the delivery of customer care. In the case of a hotel, it's the waiter, the busboy, the doorman, the bartender, etc. Each of these individuals must function as a single, empowered point of contact for the delivery of high quality customer care.

They must feel the company's commitment to customer care as a strategic product.

Think about the skills you teach, and require excellence in listening, probing, determining need, positioning benefits, and empathizing with the customer. In some cases, a high degree of technical knowledge is required. So instead of "representative," consider the titles Product Advisor, Sales Advisor, Service Professional, etc.

The consistent delivery of high quality customer care implies a seamless transfer of information from the phone-based rep to the field-based rep. No matter who the customer calls, or when, each individual should have the most current data.

Inbound calls are customer generated. They are calling for one of three reasons: to inquire, make a purchase, or resolve an issue. Consider them a gift. The marketing cost of an inbound call is often $50 to $250.

There are three requirements for the successful integration of inbound into the IDM Media Mix: (1) visible integration, (2) interactive scripting, and (3) result-tracking metrics.

Outbound telecontact is a sharp double-edged sword. It is both the most powerful medium for generating response, leads, and sales, and the most powerful medium for creating customer dissatisfaction.

The guidelines for achieving IDM and CMO quality telesales:

1. Synchronize outbound with other media such as direct mail, fax, and e-mail.
2. Outbound must deliver value, as defined by the customer—call only high potential names.
3. Engage in thorough precall planning.
4. Manage time and your energy.
5. Quickly answer the unspoken question, "What's in it for me?"

(The remaining guidelines apply to both inbound and outbound.)

6. Control the call.
7. Probe for clear statements of need.
8. Paraphrase to show understanding.
9. Present the solution with features and benefits.
10. Recognize the types of objections. The four basic types are:

- o No need
- o No money
- o No confidence (in your company, product, or service)
- o No hurry to purchase
11. Meet objections with benefit and value.
12. Go for the sale.
13. Upsell/cross-sell whenever appropriate.
14. Generate customer referrals.
15. Capture the reasons for "Not interested now."
16. Implement the tools of quality telecontact:
    - o Interactive scripting (explained in the section "Requirements for Value-Added Inbound")
    - o Call-quality monitoring (to be addressed in the next chapter)
    - o Daily productivity metrics (also to be addressed in the next chapter)

In conclusion, we recommend that there be a consistent, repeatable process for the delivery of high quality customer care. Companies must recognize that customer care is a unique strategic product. Increasing customer satisfaction and lifetime value are two goals that companies should embrace.

The next chapter will address the metrics and measurement processes that enable continuous improvement of response and sales and are central to increasing customer satisfaction and Lifetime Value.

Step Six: Metrics That Fuel Continuous Improvement

T HE SIXTH STEP in the Consensual Marketing Opt-In Process concerns the metrics that enable the marketer to make real-time improvements to the marketing process. This chapter will provide productivity and quality metrics, and will show you how to identify the key indicators—critical elements that leverage optimal performance. We will also offer recommendations regarding how to analyze this data and what action steps to take based on this analysis.

Concepts we will cover include:

- The rationale for detailed productivity and quality metrics
- Source coding as a prerequisite
- Metrics and key indicators for:
  - PR
  - Direct Response Print Advertising
  - Direct mail
  - Fax
  - Customer care center metrics (including Call Quality Monitoring)
  - E-mail and Internet

- The Marketing Daily Dashboard Report
- Guidelines for constructing a projectable testing matrix
- Constructing a response curve as a forecasting tool
- Expense to revenue (E:R) guidelines

"God Is in the Details"

So said Ludwig Mies van der Rohe in 1959. It's still true.

Think of each marketing campaign as an organic system. Just as with any organism, there are many actions and interactions that take place below the surface. The promotion looks great on paper, but once we send it forth into the world, anything can happen. Marketers should have their finger on the pulse of every campaign, all the time. The metrics addressed in this chapter will provide the essential data the marketer should look at each day to understand results and improve results in real time.

We have a phrase: "Marketing hell is conducting a back-end analysis to find out why a campaign didn't work." There is no reason to wait until a campaign is over to figure out what went wrong. In fact, for the powerful interactive media, such as inbound and outbound telecontact, problems should be diagnosed and triage administered in real time.

The Pulse of a Campaign

If you cannot feel the pulse of a campaign, you don't know if it's dead or alive. In our experience, most marketing information systems need an overhaul. Some provide too little information too late. This makes it impossible for you to do your job. Others are notable for the sheer volume and weight of data dumped on marketers. One of two things happens here: either the marketer is trapped in "analysis paralysis," or stops looking at all data altogether, figuring if something is awry, someone will let them know.

Agility should be your watchword. Timely receipt of net data. Immediate diagnosis and rapid implementation of remedial action. Will this save every campaign going south? No. But they won't go down without a fight.

If You Don't Know, You Can't Act

Surprisingly, many e-marketers are not measuring their campaigns. According to the report, "The State of E-mail Marketing: Perfecting the Appropriate Mix of Art and Science," from Jupiter Research,[1] "marketers do not effectively use metrics to optimize their e-mail campaigns."

Additional perspective is provided by a Yankee Group study[2] that researched customer behavior commonly tracked at Web sites. This study found that only 14 percent of Web sites worldwide were tracking shopping cart abandonment rates.

Most marketers track how long a visitor spends at their site, which browser they used, the click-stream progression through the site, etc. But the only ones that directly relate to the bottom line are conversion, average sale—and shopping cart abandonment rate. Some of the other indicators are important, but only one is directly related to whether your campaign generates more or less revenue. And only 14 percent of us track it.

Marketing Is an Investment in Revenue Generation

Companies invest money in marketing to generate revenue. Direct marketing, because it can be easily measured, can be leveraged to maximize the return on investment. Doug Rose of QVC offers a particularly clear-eyed view of the situation:

> **Marketing is held to the same standard of payback as any capital investment. A media dollar is held to the same standard and accountability as an upgrade on a fulfillment operation. If we have a million dollars to spend, is that money better spent on running magazines ads or is it better spent improving the through-put of our warehouse? One is going to broaden our audience and bring new customers to QVC. But the flip side is that the million dollars spent at our warehouse is going to deliver a 6 percent improvement in the fulfillment operation, and that, based on everything we've learned, will increase customer satisfaction and customer trust.**

The following sections will specify the data you need, identify the key indicators, and suggest tactics for the real-time improvement of both productivity and quality.

Source Coding

Source coding is an essential prerequisite to metrics and reporting. It enables the tracking of results for each important element of a campaign: the list, the test cell, etc. Catalog companies have trained us all very well to recognize source codes: "It's the code that's on the back of your catalog in the yellow box." When the rep captures the source code and keys it in, the computer can generate reports that tell the marketer the results of a campaign. The results reporting can be as finite and as detailed as the source codes assigned.

Thus, each medium that is deployed should be considered a source. Additionally, each test cell within each medium is a source. To enable basic reporting, each of these media components should be assigned a unique source code.

The capture, reporting, and analysis of these source codes will enable you to determine the productivity of each individual source. Comparison of each individual source or media component to both goal and result will help the marketer determine which are most productive, and thus vary marketing investment per potential return.

We suggest a seven-position alphanumeric code so you can easily tell the medium, test cell, list, month, and year of the source being tracked. (First we'll go through the rationale for the seven positions, and then review an example.) You may find that seven positions are too much. If so, we suggest installing an algorithm that translates a shorter source code that may appear on promotions back to these seven positions:

Position 1 = Medium

Which single medium within the mix does this represent?

- P = Print advertising
- D = Direct mail
- E = E-mail
- F = Fax
- W = Web
- B = Bounce back

And so on.

Position 2 = Test

Are you conducting a test of a variable such as list, offer, or format?

- A = the A version of A/B test
- B = the B version of A/B test
- Z = no test

And so on.

Position 3 + 4 = List

List is the primary factor in success. The results of each list should be coded and tracked separately.

- 01 = Customer file
- 02 = D&B

And so on.

Position 5 + 6 = Month

This is a two-position code given the 12 months.

- 01 = January
- 02 = February
- 03 = March

And so on.

Position 7 = Year

This is a one-position code; however, marketers can easily expand this to two positions.

- 4 = 2004
- 5 = 2005
- 6 = 2006

And so on.

The Capture Rate

For example, if the code is DA01114, it's the A version of a direct mail piece sent to the house list/customer file and mailed in November 2004.

There are two critical success factors at work here. First, source codes should be prominent and easy to find on the promotional piece. Second, they must be captured and reported. It must be a mandatory field on all transactions (including "e").

As explained in the previous chapter, it is important to increase the source code capture rate in the customer care centers through training, setting capture rate objectives, and consistent feedback. Unless source code capture is a mandatory behavior and consistently tracked, the capture rate is often 30 to 40 percent. This limits your ability to track results and determine what is working and what isn't—you're making decisions on information that includes less than half the results.

We know of a colleague who worked in a Call Center where commissions were not paid unless the rep reached a 75 percent threshold for valid source codes. That may be slightly draconian, but the take-away is this: do everything you can to ensure the accurate, timely capture and reporting of source codes.

The recommended goal is 65 to 75 percent source code capture rate. The key is that the source code captured has to be real versus something made up because the rep can't clear the screen unless he or she enters a code (yes, in undisciplined environments, we have seen instances where communicators have simply filled in the source code field with random numbers so they could move on to the next call).

PR and Direct Response Print Advertising Metrics

While God may be in the details, most marketers view an in-depth discussion of metrics on a par with meeting their maker. We'll try to make it as easy and palatable as we can, providing explanations and examples along the way.

This first section describes the metrics recommended for PR and Direct Response Print Advertising. They are so similar, we will present them together. The only difference is that advertising can potentially generate response via an 800 number, response device (e.g., coupon or business reply card that is mailed in), fax, e-mail, or Web site. Since there is no potential for offering a response device with PR, it can only generate response via an 800 number, e-mail, and the Web. These slight differences will become apparent as we get to the section detailing metrics.

There are two major reasons marketers deploy PR or advertising:

- When the end result is a sale
- When the end result is a registration or entry for an event, or lead generation

The illustrations we'll use will be the metrics for an entire program versus a specific test cell.

We recommend that metrics reports for PR and Direct Response Print Advertising should be analyzed daily at the beginning of the campaign, then weekly.

Throughout, "total universe" refers to the circulation of a publication.

Scenario One: Sale or Lead Generation

This is when a product or service is directly offered for sale and/or when the marketer is trying to generate sales leads.

Metrics Detail

The first thing you want to know is the total number of responses that came in and the percentage of those responses to the total universe. Then, break out the total number of responses by how the responses came in. For each response medium, you want to know the number of responses that came in, the percentage to total response, and the percentage to total universe. Potential response media include:

- Inbound/800 number
- Reply card (e.g., coupon)*
- Fax*
- E-mail
- Web

*Remember, these do not apply to PR.

Next, you want to know how many sales came in: the number of sales, the average dollar volume of a sale, and the average units per sale. Then calculate the number of sales as a percentage of the total universe, and as a percentage to total response. The last figure is your sales conversion ratio.

Illustration

We will illustrate with an overview of the marketing situation: Company A makes widgets. They have placed print ads to sell the widgets direct to the consumer. Responses that don't generate an immediate sale are ranked as leads according to their propensity to buy. The total universe or circulation is 100,000. To date Company A has received 1,000 responses and 200 sales. Each sale comprises two units. Each unit costs $100.

Therefore, 1,000 responses divided by the total universe of 100,000 yields a 1 percent response. Here's the breakout by response media:

- 100 reply cards sent via first class mail (e.g., coupon) responses
  Reply cards = 10 percent of responses
  Reply cards = 0.1 percent to total universe
- 400 inbound calls
  Inbound = 40 percent of responses
  Inbound = 0.4 percent to total universe
- 200 faxes
  Fax = 20 percent of responses
  Fax = 0.2 percent to total universe
- 250 e-mails
  E-mail = 25 percent of responses
  E-mail = 0.25 percent to total universe
- 50 Web
  Web = 5 percent of responses
  Web = 0.05 percent to total universe

The promotion generated 200 sales and $40,000. Average sale was $200. Given $100 per unit, the average units per sale was two. What does this mean? See the section below, "Thoughts on Analysis."

You always want to know:

- The ratio of marketing expense to revenue (E:R) to understand the productivity of the promotion. E:R benchmarks appear later in this chapter.
- The number of referrals and leads generated. These are statements of future business.

Referrals are generated by satisfied customers in response to questions such as: "Are there friends or colleagues who would also benefit from our product or service?" Referrals have substantial sales potential. In our experience, referrals may convert 100 to 200 percent better than other prospecting lists. Please note we are not implying that advertising, per se, creates satisfied customers. We are merely defining the term.

Leads are those responses that did not turn into a sale, which, given the propensity to buy scoring model discussed in Chapter 3, have been categorized as an A, B, C, or D lead.

Thoughts on Analysis

Given that this is our first time walking down "metrics" lane, we'd like to give you some of our thoughts on what to make of the above numbers. Let's say the ad cost $10,000 to insert in the publication, including development costs. Thus the E:R ratio is 25 percent. Stated otherwise, every time you put a quarter on the table, you make a dollar.

In accordance with the E:R guidelines later in this chapter, the target range for this type of pilot program is 20 percent. But 25 percent indicates potential and is acceptable. An obvious leverage point in increasing sales revenue is the conversion rate. Only 20 percent of responders bought. Any increases here will fall straight to the bottom line.

To increase the conversion rate, we suggest testing:

- Is the offer we are extending both compelling and competitively differentiating?
- Strategies to increase the percentage of inbound or the 800 number response. The rationale is that sales skills can be used within an interactive conversation.
- Body copy: Are we giving a compelling description of the benefits?
- Format (including the visual portrayal of the widget).

Thus, the key metrics indicators of success are the initial response rate, the conversion rate (the percentage of responders who bought), average sale, and the E:R ratio. Each of these directly affects the bottom line. If you only had time to look at a few metrics, this is what you'd analyze.

Scenario Two: Registration/Entry

This is when the ad or the PR story invites the customer to register for a seminar or event, or to enter a sweepstakes or drawing.

Metrics Detail

As in the sales and sales lead scenario, the first thing you want to know is the total number of registrations or entries that came in, and the percentage of those registrations or entries (which we will now refer to by the much shorter term "response") to the total universe. Then, break out the total number of these responses by how the responses came in. For each response medium, you want to know the number of responses that came in, the percentage to total response, and the percentage to total universe. As in the first scenario, "Sale or Lead Generation," potential response media include:

- Inbound/800 number
- Reply card (e.g., coupon)*
- Fax*
- E-mail
- Web

*Remember, these do not apply to PR.

If the goal of the PR or ad was registrations, bottom-line efficiency is measured by the percent registration to the total universe as well as the number of attendees as a percentage of the folks who registered. The latter is referred to as the "show rate." Your targets should be double-digit response (registration or entry) and a 75 to 85 percent show rate when guided by the Consensual Marketing Opt-In Process.

While we always want to hit home runs, success in metrics analysis means consistent singles. A wise friend once said, "What if we could sell just one more?" That's the reward. Understanding the percentage response and show rate by response medium will help you achieve "just one more." For instance (and this is a likely scenario), if you find that the show rate from inbound responses is significantly higher than other response media, you'd guide more folks to the 800 number.

Illustration

Company B makes balloons. They have placed print advertisements offering a free seminar on balloon making. The total universe for this vertical publication is 100,000. To date, Company B has received 100 registrations from avid balloon enthusiasts.

Therefore, 100 registrations equal a 0.1 percent response. Here's the breakout via other media:

- 20 reply cards
  Reply cards = 20 percent of registrations
  Reply cards = 0.02 percent to total universe
- 50 inbound calls
  Inbound = 50 percent of registrations
  Inbound = 0.05 percent to total universe
- 5 faxes
  Fax = 5 percent of registrations
  Fax = 0.005 percent to total universe
- 20 e-mails
  E-mail = 20 percent of registrations
  E-mail = 0.02 percent to total universe
- 5 Web
  Web = 5 percent of registrations
  Web = 0.005 percent to total universe

The 100 registrations generated 50 attendees. Therefore, this promotion generated a 0.1 percent response or registration rate and a 50 percent show rate. "Best in class" standards for response are double-digit, and guidelines for show rates are between 75 and 85 percent.

However, 50 percent of the attendees converted to sale, or 25 sales. Each sale consisted of 50 units, or 1,250 units total, with the unit price being $10. Therefore, the program generated $12,500 based on a marketing investment of $10,000. The E:R ratio is 83 percent versus guidelines of 15 to 20 percent. Based on these numbers, the results suggest that print advertising was not effective.

Neither the number of referrals nor leads generated is likely to change this picture.

The key metrics indicators here are the percent response (registrations or entries), the show rate, and the E:R ratio. As we become more sophisticated in analysis, the average number of attendees per location or company will become another key indicator of success.

Direct Mail/Fax Metrics

In this section we will look at the metrics recommended for direct mail and fax. They are the same and so we present them together. But before we go through the response metrics, we need to stop and talk about the merge/purge metrics.

Merge/Purge

As explained in the section on direct mail in Chapter 4, the different lists selected for a direct mail or fax campaign are combined and deduplicated according to an electronic process called merge/purge. This process can generate a lot of statistics, most of which are for the list and data processing folks. We're going to suggest a sharply curtailed list of metrics for the marketer.

The marketer needs to know how many names—overall and by list— we start with, before the merge/purge. Within the mix of lists, it's likely that the marketer's customer list is present. The marketer wants to know which outside list has the highest match rate to the customer list. This may be an indication of opportunity: it may indicate that the outside list with the highest match rate has the most prospects that have the same characteristics as existing customers. They may have a higher propensity to buy.

After the merge/purge, the marketer wants to know the number of multibuyers. Multibuyers are individuals whose names appear on more than one list. Again, this may be an indication of opportunity. Assuming the marketer has selected the lists with care, these are individuals who seem to have more of the characteristics the marketer is looking for. They may have a higher propensity to buy.

Finally, the marketer wants to know how many net promotable names there are, overall and by list. Promotable names are unduplicated names with deliverable addresses.

Metrics Scenarios

As with PR and advertising, there are two major reasons marketers deploy direct mail and fax, and thus two metrics or reporting scenarios:

- When the end result is a sale
- When the end result is a registration for an event or lead generation

Also as with PR and advertising, the illustrations we'll use will be the metrics for an entire program versus a particular test cell.

Metrics reports for direct mail and fax should be analyzed daily.

Scenario One: Sale or Lead Generation

This occurs when a product or service is directly offered for sale and/or when the mailer is trying to generate sales leads.

Metrics Detail

The detail of the metrics for direct mail and fax uses measures that are common to PR and advertising because our basic indicators didn't change, the medium changed. The first key indicator is the total number of responses that came in and the percentage of those responses to the total universe. Then, break out the total number of responses by how the responses came in. For each response medium, you want to know the number of responses that came in, the percentage to total response, and the percentage to total universe. Potential response media include:

- Inbound/800 number
- Response device (e.g., reply card: business reply card or envelope—we'll refer to this generically as BRC response)
- Fax
- E-mail
- Web

The next key indicators refer to how many sales came in—the number of sales, the average dollar volume of a sale, and the average units per sale. Then calculate the number of sales as a percentage of the total universe, and as a percentage to total response. The last figure is your sales conversion ratio.

You always want to know:

- The ratio of marketing expense to revenue to understand the productivity of the promotion. E:R benchmarks appear later in this chapter.
- The number of referrals and leads generated. These are statements of future business.

Within direct mail and fax, you also want to know the number of "nixies" or undeliverables. Nixies are the mail that has been returned as undeliverable (assuming you are following the recommendation in Chapter 4 to use USPS First Class live stamps; undeliverable mail with Third Class or Bulk postage is not returned). With fax, nixies are those with a bad fax number—the faxes that didn't go through.

Nixies are an indicator of list quality. For instance, if you're mailing your customer list, the percentage of nixies to the total universe should not exceed 2 percent. If you're mailing a prospect or rental list, the percentage of nixies to the total universe should not exceed 5 percent.

Illustration

Company C is a PC manufacturer. They have sent out a direct mail offering to sell the PCs directly to the consumer. Responses that don't generate an immediate sale are ranked as leads in accordance to their propensity to buy. Each list, customer segment, and test cell is coded separately. For this illustration we'll look at the metrics from a direct mailing. Detailed analysis should break this down and consider the results of each individual list, customer segment, and test cell.

The total universe for this mailing is 100,000. To date this mailing has generated 10,000 responses and 2,500 sales. Average sale is one unit. Each unit costs $2,000. Thus the promotion has generated $5 million in sales. Marketing expense was $250,000 (including postage).

Therefore, 10,000 responses is a 10 percent response rate. Here's a breakout by response media:

- 1,000 BRC responses
     BRC = 10 percent of responses
     BRC = 1 percent to total universe
- 4,000 inbound calls
     Inbound = 40 percent of responses
     Inbound = 4 percent to total universe
- 2,000 faxes
     Fax = 20 percent of responses
     Fax = 2 percent to total universe
- 2,000 e-mails
     E-mail = 30 percent of responses
     E-mail = 3 percent to total universe
- 1,000 Web
     Web = 10 percent of response
     Web = 1 percent to total universe

The sale figure is 2,500, or 2.5 percent of the total universe. Based on 10,000 responses, this constitutes a 25 percent conversion ratio, which for a high-ticket sale appears good. The final test is the E:R equation. The program cost $250,000 and generated $5 million. The E:R ratio is therefore 5 percent. The suggested E:R guidelines for this program are 5 to 10 percent. At 5 percent this program was a winner!

Scenario Two: Registration or Lead Generation

This occurs when the customer is asked to register for a seminar or event, or to request sales rep follow-up.

Metrics Detail

The following is almost identical to the registration/lead generation example for PR and advertising. First, marketers need to know the key indicators: the total number of registrations or leads that came in and the percentage of those registrations or leads (e.g., "response") to the total universe. Then, break out the total number of these responses by how the responses came in. For each response medium, you want to know the number of responses that came in, the percentage to total response, and the percentage to total universe. Potential response media include:

- Inbound/800 number
- BRC
- Fax
- E-mail
- Web

If the goal was leads, the number of responses is your net return. In the case of registrations, bottom-line efficiency is measured by the percent registration (to the total universe) as well as the show rate (the number of attendees as a percentage of the folks who registered). Again, your targets should be double-digit response (registration or lead) and a 75 to 85 percent show rate when guided by the Consensual Marketing Opt-In Process.

To fine-tune the program going forward, you should break attendance down by response medium. A hint: while referrals are usually a small percentage of overall registrations, they usually present a large percentage of attendees.

Here too you want to track the number and percentage of nixies as a gauge of list performance.

You always want to know:

- The ratio of marketing expense to revenue to understand the productivity of the promotion. E:R benchmarks appear later in this chapter.
- The number of referrals and leads generated. These are statements of future business.

Illustration

Company D is a training company. Their direct mail invites you to a free "Webinar" showcasing their training capabilities. Folks who attend are then screened and qualified, and assigned a lead category. Each list, customer segment, and test cell is coded separately, so we'll look at the metrics from the overall mailing. The total universe is 10,000. Marketing cost was $13,500 (including postage). To date, Company D has received 1,500 registrations.

- 1,500 registrations = 15 percent response
- 200 BRC responses
    - BRC = 13 percent of registrations
    - BRC = 2 percent to total universe
- 500 inbound calls
    - Inbound = 33 percent of registrations
    - Inbound = 5 percent to total universe
- 50 faxes
    - Fax = 3 percent of registrations
    - Fax = 0.5 percent to total universe
- 250 e-mails
    - E-mail = 17 percent of registrations
    - E-mail = 2.5 percent to total universe
- 500 Web
    - Web = 33 percent of registrations
    - Web = 5 percent to total universe

The 1,500 registrations generated 1,125 attendees for a show rate of 75 percent (11 percent to total universe). Of the 1,125 attendees, 450, or 40 percent, enrolled in a subsequent training session with an average price of $150 per program. This 40 percent conversion ratio generated

$67,500 in revenue. The E:R ratio is 20 percent, which is at the high end of the E:R guidelines.

However, the 1,500 registrations generated 50 referrals (3 percent). Of the 50 referrals, 40 (80 percent) attended. Of the 40 attendees, 20 enrolled in a session, generating an additional $3,000, reducing the overall E:R ratio to 19 percent.

E-mail Metrics

It is distressing, as noted earlier in this chapter, that many marketers are not effectively using metrics to optimize their e-mail campaigns. This approach is shortsighted and based on a false sense of security. We once heard a misguided marketer say, "Maybe we should just send this to everyone. It's so cheap. If we get two orders, we paid for the e-mail."

Unwanted, valueless e-mails will erode the responsiveness of your customer lists. You should use e-mail primarily as a retention tool, and then only in accordance with customer preferences.

Given the plethora of measures available through technology, we are only going to recommend the key indicators or most important metrics.

Metrics Detail

Here are the key metrics that should be tracked, and an explanation of each:

The number of e-mails sent. This is your total universe. Like direct mail, your total universe should be composed of several list sources and/or customer segments and test cells that have gone through the merge/purge process. This is your net opportunity.

The number of e-mails opened and their percentage to the total universe. We can't expect a customer to respond or buy if they don't open the e-mail. As the recipient is deciding whether to open an e-mail, all the input he or she has is the value they attach to the sender's name (primary) and the value they see in the subject line (secondary). Match the open rate to industry standards (distressingly low) and establish your own baselines. Like response, the open rate should be double-digit.

The number of click-throughs and their percentage to both e-mails sent and e-mails opened. Was our offer compelling? Were our copy and design inspiring? Did the customer click-through to take action? A click-through should be viewed as a "response" (e.g., direct mail). Likewise, the click-through rate from opened e-mails should be double-digit.

Many marketing articles focus only on the above metrics: the open rate and click-through rate. Marketers should also focus on the bottom-line metrics of conversion and sales.

For Scenario One—sales—you should track and analyze: the number of sales, the total sales dollars, average dollars per sale, and average units per sale. Calculate the conversion rate as a percentage of e-mails sent, e-mails opened, and click-throughs. True sales conversion is the percentage of sales to click-throughs.

And please track the number and percentage of folks who drop out of the shopping cart before completing the transaction. If there's a hole in the bucket, let's fix it.

For Scenario Two—registration or lead generation—marketers should track and analyze: the number of registrations or leads as a percentage of e-mails sent, e-mails opened, and click-throughs. You should calculate the show rate as the percentage of attendees to the number of registrations.

Metrics common to both scenarios:

- The ratio of marketing expense to revenue to understand the productivity of the promotion. E:R benchmarks appear later in this chapter.
- The number of referrals and leads generated. These are statements of future business.
- The number of nixies (undeliverables) and their percentage to total universe—this is an important indicator of list quality. The same rule applies as for direct mail: If you are using your customer file, nixies as a percentage of the total universe should not rise above 2 percent overall and by segment; if you are using external and/or rental lists, nixies as a percentage of the total universe should not rise above 5 percent overall and by individual list.
- The expense to revenue ratio.

Internet Metrics

Technology affords the marketer the ability to track any number of statistics regarding a Web site. As with e-mail, given the plethora of measures available through technology, we are only going to recommend the following key indicators:

The number of visitors is your total universe or total opportunity. Track how many of them are motivated enough to enter the shopping cart. In IDM terms, we'd call the percentage of visitors who enter the shopping cart the response rate. Your goal should be double-digit response.

How many visitors complete the transaction? Measure this by the number of sales, the dollar volume of sales, the average dollars per sale, and the average units per sale. The number of sales divided by the number of responses, expressed as a percentage, is your conversion rate.

Also measure the number and percentage of visitors abandoning the shopping cart before they have completed the transaction. This is a warning signal and represents lost opportunity. Make sure you understand the most frequent reasons that customers abandon and that you are aggressively addressing these issues. If this reaches double-digit, you're in trouble.

You always want to know:

- The ratio of marketing expense to revenue to understand the productivity of the promotion. E:R benchmarks appear later in this chapter.
- The number of referrals and leads generated. These are statements of future business.

Customer Care Center Metrics

Customer care centers may contribute the greatest dollar volume of all direct response media. The following reports provide the real-time data required to increase productivity and revenue. Customer care center metrics comprise both inbound and outbound telecontact. These are unique media because of their ability to:

- Leverage significant response and sales
- Generate significant customer satisfaction or dissatisfaction
- Incorporate revised tactics in real time to generate real-time improvements

Therefore, we recommend that at the beginning of a campaign, metrics are read and analyzed hourly, and daily thereafter.

These reports become more useful if you establish baselines—or the average result over time for each key line item. Baselines should eliminate as many variables as possible. For example, seasonality is one of the most common variables—sales vary by season for many businesses (e.g., a ski resort may sell less rooms in August). To eliminate, or minimize, the effect of seasonality, we suggest averaging results from the same time period (e.g., June through August) from previous years.

Baselines are essential for understanding trending. This, in turn, enables a more effective diagnosis of current results. Comparison of current results to baseline shows:

- Results per specific tactics
- Cumulative improvement
- Further opportunities for improvement

With this knowledge, marketers can set daily and weekly goals. We recommend establishing an aggressive target, then breaking it down for the customer care center representatives as follows:

- **Conservative.** This is the minimum level of expected improvement. "This is what we pay you for."
- **Middle of the road.** This is about half the aggressive target. It takes effort to get here, and you should consider rewarding effort.
- **Aggressive.** This is 100 percent of your target. As one senior executive said, "If I'm climbing Everest, these are the guys I want to be roped to." This level of effort should be rewarded.

Inbound Telecontact

The purpose of the Inbound Daily Productivity Report (Figure 7.1) is to provide a comprehensive view of the net productivity of the inbound center and the variables that affect performance. As you implement this report, a glossary of terms should be developed and circulated so that everyone who receives the report, or is measured by it, has a clear understanding of it.

The columns (vertical) are straightforward. They show the days of the week and the number of reps. Let's quickly walk through the rows (horizontal) together.

The first block of information deals with time allocation and utilization. The rows answer the following questions:

- How much time are you paying a rep for each day (e.g., 8 hours)?
- How much time per day is the rep in his or her seat, logged in and available to take inbound calls (e.g., they are available to take a call, but not on a call)?
- How much time per day were they actually in conversation with a caller?
- What is their "customer time"?

Customer time is an important new metric. It represents the percentage of paid time that is spent talking with customers or waiting for a call. Here's the formula:

Customer Time = Talk Time + Available Time ÷ Total Paid Time

As an illustration, let's put some real numbers in the formula. Let's start with "best in class." In our experience, the best customer care centers, on average, pay their reps for 8 hours a day, and the sum of their talk time and available time is 6.5 hours (1 hour for lunch, two 15-minute breaks). Leaving time for training and coaching, we arrive at 5.5 hours.

$$5.5 \text{ hours} \div 8 \text{ hours} = 68.75\%$$

We find that at many corporations, the reality of the numbers is far different from the expectations. In our experience, these corporations pay their reps for 8 hours a day. In reality, the sum of their talk time and available time is, at best, 3 hours. This sounds artificially low, but we assure you this is our experience among sophisticated, successful organizations. It seems as if the more sophisticated and complex the sale, the lower the sum of talk time and available time, especially for outbound strategies. Training, order processing, faxing, research, planning, team meetings, composing e-mail, computer issues, etc., all seem to consume at least half the day. Previously, corporations have not used a metric such as customer time to gauge the effectiveness of their customer care center. This metric provides a point of comparison and, thus, the rationale for improvement, as in the illustration below, where customer time actual is 37.5 percent versus "best in class" at 68.75 percent.

$$3 \text{ hours} \div 8 \text{ hours} = 37.5\%$$

IDM Inbound Service Daily Productivity Report

(Today's Date)   (Time Period Covered by This Report)

	Mon. (date) # Reps	Tues. (date) # Reps	Wed. (date) # Reps	Thurs. (date) # Reps	Fri. (date) # Reps	Week Total	MTD Total	PTD Total
Total Paid Time								
Total Time Available to Take Calls								
Total Talk Time								
Customer Time								
Average Monitoring Score								
Total Calls Offered:								
% Abandon								
Average Time in Queue								
Total Inbound Contacts / Calls Answered:								
Average Time to Answer								
Average Talk Time								
Outcomes:								
# Misdirect								
# Calls Transferred								
# Irate								
# Inquiries								
# Customer Service								
# Do Not Mail / Fax / E-mail / Call								
# Send Information								
# Other								
# Sales (Registrations)								

Units
Dollar Volume

Total Leads

A Leads
B Leads
C Leads
D Leads

Conversion rate
Contacts/Hr/Rep
Sales/Hr/Rep
Revenue/Hr/Rep
Units per Transaction (UPT)
Average Order

Figure 7.1 Inbound Daily Productivity Report

The average monitoring score is picked up from the results of Call Quality Monitoring, which we'll discuss in the next section. Bringing that information gives the marketer added perspective regarding quality. (Of course, we must allow the rep time to benefit from Call Quality Monitoring coaching.)

Information about calls offered comes from the Automated Call Distributor (ACD), which is the electronic switch that all calls pass through. This switch, among other things, will route an incoming call to the next available agent within a specific group or skill set. The ACD also has the ability to generate metrics that give insight into the call flow.

Calls offered represents the total of all inbound calls as logged by the ACD. Calls that were answered are the total inbound contacts. The calls that were not answered, or abandoned calls, are represented by a percentage. The average of these abandoned calls should not exceed 2 percent—for both customer satisfaction and net profit reasons.

Let's take as an example an inbound customer care center handling 500 calls per day. That's 2,500 calls per week or 10,000 calls per month. If they manage to keep their abandon rate to 2 percent, they experience 200 abandons per month. If the rate goes to 5 percent, they experience an additional 300, or a total of 500 per month. Let's look at the extra 300.

Our experience is that 25 percent of these 300 will not call back again. That's 75 lost opportunities. If you typically convert 25 percent, you've lost 19 sales this month. If average order is $100, that's $1,900 monthly; $22,800 yearly in lost sales. Combine this with the fact that all additional 300 customers called us but were so dissatisfied by something that they hung up before they reached a rep. That can't be good for customer satisfaction or lifetime value. It becomes very compelling to manage the abandon rate.

The next section of rows in Figure 7.1 details the outcomes, or results of the inbound conversations. Why did these customers call? How are our reps spending their time? This information does not come from the ACD. Rather, this is gathered by the contact management software.

The sum of all the outcomes will always add up to more that the total inbound contacts or calls answered. That's because one caller may have several things on his or her mind and combine customer service with a sale. For instance, a caller may have a billing issue with leased equipment and wish to purchase consumables.

Then we get to the bottom line:

- Number of sales
- Number of units
- Dollars generated (volume)

Leads represent identified future potential. The lead grade is based on your propensity-to-buy scoring model. Inbound reps gather the information to determine propensity to buy and set follow-up steps as appropriate. Within the illustration of the propensity-to-buy formula in Chapter 2, one component of an A lead might be a referral, and, experience tells us, referrals may convert 200 percent better than any prospect list. Given the importance of referrals, you may wish to set a goal for the center and call it out separately on the metrics report.

The calculated fields that follow give a better understanding of productivity:

- Conversion rate, or the number of sales divided by total inbound contacts, is a measure of sales ability (and list quality).
- Contacts/hour/rep is used in capacity planning.
- Sales/hour/rep and revenue/hour/rep are important to sales projections.
- Units per transaction, as applicable, is a lever to increase average order size.

Outbound Telecontact

The Outbound Daily Productivity Report is shown in Figure 7.2. Its purpose is to provide a comprehensive view of the bottom-line performance of the outbound center and the variables that affect performance. As you implement this report, a glossary of terms should be developed and circulated.

Again, the columns are straightforward. It's the days of the week and the number of reps. Let's quickly walk through the rows together.

The first block of information deals with time allocation and Call Quality Monitoring scores. The purpose and definitions of these rows are identical to the inbound report.

IDM Outbound Service Daily Productivity Report

(Today's Date) (Time Period Covered by This Report) (Total Records / % Complete) (# Reps)

	Mon. (date) #Reps	Tues. (date) #Reps	Wed. (date) #Reps	Thurs. (date) #Reps	Fri. (date) #Reps	Week Total	MTD Total	PTD Total
Total Paid Time								
Total Time Available for Outbound								
Total Talk Time								
Customer Time								
Average Talk Time								
Average Monitoring Scores								
Total Attempts:								
# Wrong Number								
# Disconnect / OOB / No Listing								
# Duplicate Record								
# Busy / Unavailable								
# Refused								
# Voice Mail								
# Not Reached / 4 Attempts								
Total Contacts:								
# Service Inquiry								
# Irate								
# Inquiry								
# Customer Service								

Do Not Mail / Fax / E-mail
Do Not Call
Send Information
Completed Presentations
Sales
Units
Dollar Volume
Other

Reach Rate
Total Leads
A Leads
B Leads
C Leads
D Leads
Referrals

Attempts/Hr/Rep
Contacts/Hr/Rep
Reach Rate
Conversion Rate
Sales/Hr/Rep
Revenue/Hr/Rep
Units per Transaction (UPT)

Figure 7.2 Outbound Daily Productivity Report

Attempts are the same as "dials." The number of attempts equals the number of times reps dialed the phone. The result of the attempt can give us some important feedback regarding the list. For instance, we can lump wrong number, disconnected, out of business, no listing, and duplicate record under the banner of "unproductive attempts." Thus, list quality guidelines (and you'll notice they haven't changed from the acceptable range cited for nixies) are:

- Customer list: percentage of unproductive attempts to list size should not exceed 2 percent.
- Prospect list: percentage of unproductive attempts to list size should not exceed 5 percent.

One of the categories is "not reached after four attempts." Here's what it means: Testing has shown that the most profitable use of outbound is when the list penetration reaches approximately 75 percent. List penetration is defined as list size divided by the sum of contacts and unproductive attempts. "Not reached after four attempts" is an early indicator of this threshold—so we only want to try an individual four times, then close the record and move on.

Total contacts are the sum of conversations. The outcomes below tell you the details of the conversations. Outcomes help us to understand how many times reps are "up at bat" and how effective their sales skills are.

Within the outcomes of total contacts or conversations there is a critical metric, the number of "Do Not Call" requests. If this number rises above 0.5 percent of contacts, something is wrong—your audience is not finding value and is expressing their displeasure by opting out. Stop what you are doing and find the problem before you continue.

Another important indicator is "reach rate." The ratio of contacts to total list size expressed as a percentage equals the reach rate. On a high quality list, you should reach, or speak to, 60 to 65 percent of the total list.

The last section includes calculated fields, which, as with the inbound report, displays hourly figures for outbound reps. Setting goals, and managing to reach those goals, leverages productivity. For instance, the industry standard for attempts/rep/hour for B2B calling is 15 to 20. What is your actual?

(Outbound / Inbound) Telemarketing
Reasons for "Not Interested Now"
(Week of)

Reason	(Week of)		Program to Date	
	#	%	#	%
Prefer the competition				
Does not have the features I need				
No need				
No reason				

(Reasons are compiled and ranked, highest to lowest)

Figure 7.3 Reasons for "Not Interested Now" Report

Reasons for "Not Interested Now"

As detailed in Chapter 6, capturing and analyzing the reasons for "not interested now" (see Figure 7.3) enables us to prepare and refine effective rebuttals in the questions and objections script. Analysis may also indicate modifications to marketing materials. This report should be generated and analyzed weekly.

Call Quality Monitoring

IDM Call Quality Monitoring is designed to provide you with a real-time qualitative and quantitative evaluation of rep growth/performance and a "window into the marketplace." You can hear both sides of customer conversations and glean Voice of Customer input from the discussion and reactions to your company's products and offers.

The accompanying process consists of monitoring and scoring the behaviors required for a professional, customer-sensitive sales conversation. Based on the results, you should then make real-time improvements to training, scripting, and procedures to increase productivity and quality. This process applies to both inbound and outbound conversations. The process and form should be adjusted accordingly.

The Monitoring Process

Each rep, whether inbound or outbound, should be monitored for a minimum of 10 *completed calls* per week. The results of Call Quality Monitoring should be discussed with the rep. Completed Call Quality Monitoring forms should be kept as part of each rep's permanent record.

Test calls, whether placed by Call Center management or executive personnel, should also be graded in accordance with this monitoring process.

Suggested IDM Monitoring Form

In the following form:

Y = Yes
N = No
NA = Not Applicable

Y, N	1. Used appropriate opening (identified your company, said name)
Y, N	2. Asked for customer's name and company name in the beginning, and used it throughout the conversation
Y, N, NA	3. Asked for and verified source code (as applicable)
Y, N, NA	4. Probed for the customer's needs and requirements (to enable proactive call handling)
Y, N, NA	5. Showed guidance/consultative value (presented benefits and solutions)
Y, N, NA	6. Attempted to complete profiling questions on the phone
Y, N, NA	7. Attempted to answer fulfillment questions on the phone (e.g., "send me something on your quality processes")
Y, N	8. Demonstrated excellent product knowledge
Y, N, NA	9. Asked for the sale!
Y, N, NA	10. Determined reason(s) for "not interested now"
Y, N	11. Verified/built all relevant database information, which may include name, name of other decision makers, company name, title/functional responsibility, address, phone, fax, and e-mail numbers

Y, N	12. Actively listened to the customer
Y, N	13. Used proper phone etiquette (minimal "dead air," asked permission to place on hold, stated "please" when asking for information)
Y, N	14. Controlled the call
Y, N, NA	15. Used appropriate scripting
Y, N, NA	16. Used competitive differentiators in positioning your company versus competition
Y, N, NA	17. Used defusing skills with an upset customer
Y, N, NA	18. Responded to questions and objections with benefit and value
Y, N, NA	19. Asked for referrals
Y, N, NA	20. Generated leads for future follow-up
Y, N, NA	21. Defined next steps (determined date and time of follow-up, as appropriate)
Y, N	22. Used appropriate closing (gave customer their name, extension, and e-mail, as appropriate)

Comments

Strengths: _____

_____

_____

_____

_____

_____

Weaknesses: _____

_____

_____

_____

_____

_____

Suggested Grading

Number of No's	Grade
0 to 1	Very Good
2 to 3	Good
4 to 5	Needs improvement
6 or more	Unacceptable

IDM Sales Dashboard Report

(Today's Date)   (Time Period Covered by This Report)

	Day			Week			PTD	
Actual	Goal	Delta	Actual	Goal	Delta	Actual	Goal	Delta

Inbound
Customer Time
% Abandon
Sales / Contacts
Leads / Contacts
Referrals / Contacts
Average Sale
Average Units per
  Transaction (UPT)

Outbound
Customer Time
Attempts/Hour/Rep
Contacts/Hour/Rep
Reach Rate
Sales / Contacts
Leads / Contacts
Referrals / Contacts
Average Sale
Average Units per
  Transaction (UPT)

Figure 7.4 IDM Dashboard Report

The Daily Dashboard Report

The Marketing Daily Dashboard Report is a summary of key metrics for management. The concept is to put everything you need to know, all the key indicators, on one page. The other metrics reports are available should you need to dig deeper.

The report, shown in Figure 7.4, provides the daily results by line item, along with the goal for that line item and the delta—or difference—between the daily results and the goal. This report should be issued and analyzed daily.

Constructing a Projectable Testing Matrix

The IDM Philosophy

Testing is a critical success factor and should be part of every promotion. It is essential to continuous improvement—it provides a reality test. You may think a list or an offer is "working" because all the analyses are written in black versus red, but what does the marketplace think? Without testing, you are operating by assumption, not fact. A consistent program of testing major variables will yield better overall results with a higher degree of confidence that you're doing the best you can. This section will provide the guidelines for successful testing.

Significant Variables to Be Tested

Lists and database: these are the major contributors to success. They represent about 65 percent of your potential.

Offer. Is it both compelling and competitively differentiating?

Price. Obviously, this affects the bottom-line profitability.

Content. Few people read. Have we presented the important material in an easy-to-digest, easy-to-skim style? Are we presenting benefits versus features? Which variations work the best?

Package, or the physical piece such as a direct mail package. One productive test is a number 10 personalized envelope versus a self-mailer. To yield the greatest productivity, results must be analyzed by expense and by revenue.

Design or graphics. Is it html versus text? Customers will tell us if it's just easy on the eyes or if it generates results.

Media mix. The correct combination of media leverages big dollars in expense and in revenue. The media mix should be plotted out over time, as in a contact management calendar of events, and constantly refined with regard to results. We recommend that the percentage investment in a medium should be roughly equal to the percentage of revenue it generates.

Two considerations:

First, test against control packages (also called controls—the executions that have "worked" over time). In the case of direct mail, profitability is based on the performance of this package.

Second, consider that sometimes test results indicate a major change in "business as usual," such as when testing has shown that package A did better than the control. When you're faced with such a large decision, validate results through ongoing testing. This is called a "back test." Here's an example:

Company E distributes and sells TV sets. For years they have put together and mailed out a self-mailer with all the new models. It generated a lot of response and traffic. They tested a new package in a personalized outer envelope and found that it generated more response. The store was jammed and sales attributed to the new package were significantly higher.

Correctly, the marketing manager decided to change horses and go with the personalized outer envelope package as the new control. We suggest he also begin testing the former control to confirm results over time.

Constructing the Testing Matrix

The way to manage the testing process is to first construct the testing matrix. To do this you have to determine the variables you want to test. The variables you select should be significant and have the potential to increase results.

Test one variable per cell. That means that everything else has to be equal. A simple example would be an e-mail test that compares customer segment A to customer segment B. Each cell must have the same quantity, receive the same copy and graphics with the same offer. Both must be sent at the same time. Isolate the variable or if there's a change, you'll never know what caused it.

Make sure you have a control cell. This is a representative sampling of the general universe—your control with no tests. This is your anchor. Test everything against this.

Source coding, as we mentioned earlier, is essential. There must also be a corporate mandate and definable goals for the capture of source codes. Without this, testing and reporting are impossible.

Determining Quantities per Test Cell

There are three ways to establish quantities for each test cell:

1. Reference the published logarithmic probability tables (e.g., the DMA Library). Based on the target response rate, acceptable range of error, and degree of confidence you need in the results, these tables will establish quantities per test cell.

2. The formula for determining sample, or cell size, is:

$$\text{Sample Size} = (R)\,(1 - R)\,(C)^2 \div E^2$$

where:

R = Projected response rate, expressed as a decimal

$1 - R$ = Projected rate of nonresponse

C = Desired level of confidence, expressed as a number of standard deviations

E = Desired error limit

For instance:

- Assuming a projected 10 percent response (0.1), we would have a 90 percent rate of nonresponse (0.9)
- 95 percent confidence is desirable
- 1.96 standard deviations, assuming a 95 percent confidence level
- The desired error limit is 0.5 percent (0.005)

$$\text{Sample Size} = 0.1 \times 0.9 \times 1.96^2 \div 0.005^2$$

$$= 0.1 \times 0.9 \times 3.8416 \div 0.000025$$

$$= 0.345744 \div 0.000025$$

$$= 13{,}830$$

3. Establishing your comfort level is required whether or not you use the logarithmic tables and/or equations. Central to your comfort level is the answer to the question: Will the percentage response rate swing with the addition or subtraction of one or two responses?

Here's a simple example: We are testing a new list. We will send this list the same promotion as we send to our database, at the same time. Our database is 100,000 names. How many names should we test from the new list?

Historically, our database has generated a 10 percent response rate from similar promotions during similar times of the year with similar economic conditions. Therefore, a new list must generate the same or a greater level of response to be seen as successful. If we selected 5,000 names from this new list, the range of projected results might be:

% Responses	Number Responses
9	450
10	500
11	550

Although lower than the result of the equation, 5,000 "feels comfortable" because each increment of response requires a substantial number of responses.

Using the same example, what followings is a pro-forma testing matrix. Please note that of the 100,000 database, we have selected a 5,000-name database control cell. Within the list test, this allows us to compare the results of cells with like quantities, eliminating any potential variable. We are comfortable that we have sufficient names to also conduct a list test and an offer test.

	Control Cell	Offer Test	Total
Database 95,000 Names	95,000		95,000
Database Control Cell 5,000 Names	2,500	2,500	5,000
List Test 5,000 Names	2,500	2,500	5,000

Constructing a Response Curve for Forecasting

If you've ever seen response to a direct response program plotted on a graph, it looks something like a parabola. It starts at zero, when the promotion is released, and moves up sharply in an arc, then peaks and trends downward with a long tail. The vertical axis is the number of responses.

The horizontal axis is calendar days. Each point on the arc is the number of responses received that day (days are numbered consecutively beginning with the date when the promotion is released).

A response curve gives the mathematical equivalent of that parabola. It tells you what percentage of total response has been received on a single day. If we plot the response for many similar campaigns and average out the mathematical equivalency of the percentage response received on each day, we have a powerful forecasting tool. For instance, if we were planning to release a similar campaign in a similar time frame and wanted to staff the inbound customer care center properly, we'd look to the response curve for an educated guess on the projected volume of daily calls.

Think of a response curve as a spreadsheet that will tell you the percentage response expected for each day following release of your program. The response curve is used to forecast response and inbound calls (as well as sales and revenue) from a given promotion. For example, the response curve developed by a client shows that Week One of response equals 32.14 percent of total call volume:

Monday = 4.82 percent of total call volume
Tuesday = 6.41 percent of total call volume
Wednesday = 7.59 percent of total call volume
Thursday = 6.53 percent of total call volume
Friday = 4.88 percent of total call volume
Saturday = 1.91 percent of total call volume

Week One also represents:

- 27.29 percent of total sales
- 27.18 percent of total revenue

The first step is to track the response patterns of current promotions. Similar promotions (e.g., target market, media mix, offer, time frame) should be grouped.

Over time, cumulative information continually refines the response curve for similar promotions. The response curve then becomes a reliable predictive tool.

The response curve should track by day:

- Response
- Volumes (such as inbound call volumes)
- Sales
- Revenue

Expense to Revenue Guidelines

All efforts should be measured by net contribution. A fast and easy way to understand net contribution is by the ratio of marketing expense to revenue generated—also called expense to revenue, or E:R.

Here are guidelines/benchmarks for your CMO programs:

- Lead generation pilot: 15 to 20 percent E:R
- Lead generation rollout: 5 to 15 percent E:R
- Direct sell pilot: 10 to 20 percent E:R
- Direct sell rollout: 5 to 10 percent E:R

Points to Remember

"God is in the details."

Timely receipt of key metrics enables you to make real-time improvements, thus maximizing return on investment. Source coding is an essential prerequisite to metrics and reporting. Ensure the accurate, timely capture and reporting of source codes. Analyze key indicators daily for:

- PR
- Direct Response Print Advertising
- Direct mail
- Fax
- Inbound daily productivity
- Outbound daily productivity
- Call Quality Monitoring
- Reasons for "not interested now"
- E-mail
- Internet

Testing is a critical success factor and should be part of every promotion. To ensure successful testing, follow the suggested guidelines for developing a projectable testing matrix.

Construct a response curve as a forecasting tool.

Measure your promotions against the expense to revenue (E:R) guidelines as the net metric of sales efficiency.

Step Seven: Checklists to Help You Implement Consensual Marketing

T HERE ARE TWO PARTS to the seventh and last step in the Consensual Marketing Opt-In Process. Each is a checklist and both are essential to bringing this new discipline to your company and "going live" with CMO. Part I is a checklist for managing organizational change, and Part II is an executive checklist for implementing the CMO process.

In Part I we'll address the following issues:

- How to handle the "rubber band" of resistance to corporate change.
- Increasing your effectiveness as a "Change Agent."
- Why CMO programs fail (and how to succeed).
- The psychology of change management: four conditions for lasting change.

Part II is a step-by-step outline for building your own CMO plan and focuses on the 15-point Executive Checklist for implementation.

We'll conclude this book with the final "best in class" Consensual Marketing case history from IBM. (The first case history, described in Chapter 1, concerned IBM's Focus 1:1 effort and how it generated $594 million over the control group.) The case history at the end of this chapter concerns the IBM Software Premier Club and how it generated $310 million in incremental revenue. It presents the latest evolution of CMO at IBM.

Part I: Checklist for Managing Organizational Change

"We are confronted with insurmountable opportunities."—*Pogo* (comic strip) by Walt Kelly[1]

"Consensual Marketing is a richer process—real business process innovation, consistent with the view of great marketing which is to really meet customers' needs and satisfy them and not harass them and not manipulate them. I am definitely a believer."—Philip Kotler, S. C. Johnson Distinguished Professor of International Marketing, J. L. Kellogg Graduate School of Management

Your ability to successfully implement the Consensual Marketing Opt-In Process hinges on two challenging issues:

- Managing the organizational change process to ensure lasting improvements
- Becoming a successful CMO Change Agent

These issues are linked: to succeed as a CMO Change Agent, you must be able to actively manage organizational change.

The journey of managing the change process begins with understanding organizational resistance. Said without frills: *Corporate culture will actively resist change, regardless of the potential benefit of the change.* Each individual may benefit by accepting the change, but collectively they will fight tooth and nail. Needless to say, resistance to change is the most frequent cause of failure. Corporate culture is lethal to change.

Corporate culture behaves like a rubber band. No matter how you stretch it, it wants to snap back to its original shape. And when it snaps back, someone gets stung. A wise client of ours said, "Corporate culture eats change for lunch." He was correct—we are frequently our own worst enemy.

"We have met the enemy and he is us."—Pogo, Walt Kelly [2]

Portrait of the Successful CMO Change Agent

As the CMO Change Agent you must be a visionary. The project is your company's future and you are the champion. You also will need to be:

A Great Communicator

Show coworkers and management the vision. Be persistent and persuasive. Help team members to understand:

- "What's in it" for them
- How this change is relevant to what they do.
- What, specifically, they should do.
- How they will be measured.
- The consequences.
- What tools and support are available.

Keep team members fully informed of progress and results.

Keeper of the Flame

Look out for the grapevine of negativity. Confront negativity with personalized benefits (here's what's in it for us and especially for you). Be watchful and take immediate action when (not if) regression/insurrection begins.

Garry Dawson, Manager of Marketing Communications Strategy, Americas Enterprise Systems Group for Hewlett-Packard, shares a step-by-step guide for the CMO Change Agent:

> **First, a marcom evangelist must lead the way to educate and inform the marcom and marketing team members. Someone with the passion to lead, train, persuade, manage, and measure the campaign must take charge. Also, you must involve visible executive sponsorship to make the tough decisions to stay the course when things heat up.**

Second, the campaign "team" must buy into CMO, IDM, and VOC Research, and the measures associated. The CMO leader owns this requirement.

Third, expectations must be set on length of implementation time, program results, roles/responsibilities, and other key items. The process requires discipline, patience, and proper planning and implementation. For most people this is very new and different. Behavior must be modified; otherwise, poor results will follow.

Fourth, the implementation must be tightly managed. Attention to detail is critical. No shortcuts!

Why CMO Programs Fail (and How to Succeed)

What follows is a synopsis of the major speed bumps that have led to program failures. We'll point each out so you can see it coming. We'll also suggest the most successful tactics for making it over the speed bump and continuing on your way.

Channel Conflict (or Turf Wars)

"If I was the advertising manager I would torpedo this. My budget is going to be lessened because your method works better than mine."— Philip Kotler

Unfortunately, interdepartmental conflict is the norm. Organizations are structured in silos, each of which has different and conflicting goals and measures. The manifestation of interdepartmental conflict varies from guerrilla warfare to open hostilities. The most common is the traditional rift between Marketing and Sales.

No one wins here. The corporation experiences lost productivity and lost opportunity. The customer is confused by conflicting messages.

There's no way around this speed bump—you have to go over the top. The only way to overcome conflict between Marketing and Sales is to integrate Field Sales into the process from day one. The same is true for all other resources necessary for implementation. You must form a cross-functional team that steers implementation from the planning stage through measurement and refinement. We'll talk more about cross-functional teaming in Part II of this chapter.

Success of this cross-functional team, and thus the project, depends on agreement and commitment to the following rules of the road:

- Traditionally, Marketing feels ownership of the customer base. Traditionally, Field Sales refers to "their" customers. The customer relationship is owned by the company—not by Marketing, Field Sales, or any other department.
- Shared goals. Everyone marches to the same drum, contributing their talents and resources to the common good.
- To defuse intersilo rivalry and ensure that everyone plays nice in the sandbox, measurement must be aligned. All are measured by the same metrics: gross revenue and the ratio of expense to revenue (E:R).

No VOC Input

"Everything today is built on a supply chain model. I make a bunch of stuff. I think I add value. I have no clue as to what the customer wants, so I don't know how they define value. We need to look at demand chains. What do customers want and how do I match my organization up to what they want and what they need? The customer today is managing you to fit you into what things work for them."— Don Schultz

Voice of Customer Messaging and Communication Research is a unique process that helps us understand how customers define value and what customers find compelling. The goal of this methodology is to bring customer messaging and communication needs and preferences to the marketing planning table. The findings will help you avoid making significant mistakes. As we saw in Chapter 3, VOC Research:

- Generates powerful, directional, qualitative marketing intelligence regarding:
  o Awareness/perception of your company
  o Business issues/drivers

      o Decision-making process, roles, and responsibilities
      o Barriers to purchasing/switching to your company
      o Media mix and sequence
      o Optimal contact preference and timing
    • Allows you to pretest critical parts of your strategy:
      o Positioning
      o Messaging
      o Creative
      o Offers

So if we don't have the customer-driven information that VOC brings, the customer is not at the planning table. Everything else is "best guess."

No Project Champion

The change process requires a member of senior management to provide visible support and sponsorship.

Implementing the Consensual Marketing Opt-In Process involves a great deal of change, both overt change that can be seen and internal change that can't. Both are wrenching. Both create pressure. The CMO Change Agent is the focus of the pressure. The manifestation of the pressure is resistance, which can be overt or covert.

Resistance can and will compromise results. Only visible, sustained, proactive senior management support can break up the logjams of resistance. Choose your sponsor carefully.

Another reason to choose your management sponsor carefully is that change does not happen from the bottom up. The troops must see that the new initiative is important to the "person who signs their check" or it won't be important to them.

Sudden Agendas

The most typical sudden agenda goes like this: "Sales are below quota—we need to take action now. We'll do this CMO later, when we have time. Let's get busy doing things the old way. But let's try to do it faster."

These sudden agendas derail long-term change and innovation. All stakeholders must agree to goals and deadlines. The CMO Change Agent must help everyone keep his or her eye on the brass ring. Remember, it's the old way of doing things that led to sales being below quota.

Lack of Field Integration

As Eric Borchers, Imaging and Printing Commercial Customer Marketing Manager, Hewlett-Packard, notes:

> **There are always going to be customer "ownership" turf wars. Reps are often unwilling to allow or support a direct marketing touch to their most important asset: They may believe that marketing may mess up a potential deal, or promise more than the rep and product can deliver.**
>
> **One way to avoid this is to involve the reps, sales management, product management, and research in program setup—this establishes the necessary connections and buy-in up front.**

Within a corporation, and specifically within the Marketing department, there is a general lack of recognition that there are two kinds of customers. There is the big C Customer, who buys the products and services. Then, there is the small c customer, Field Sales.

Field Sales often has had no input regarding the strategy and execution of a marketing program. Thus, it is no wonder that Field Sales feels no ownership and exhibits no buy-in. Integration of the field from day one is the only answer. Following are the highlights of our tested eight-step process for successfully integrating the Field, as discussed in depth in Chapter 4.

1. The Field must be a key member of the IDM cross-functional team.
2. The Field contributes to IDM Voice of Customer Messaging and Communication Research.
3. The Field contributes to offer development.
4. The Field reviews creative.
5. The Field contributes to database development.
6. The Field defines lead criteria.
7. The Field designs lead management tracking systems.
8. Shared metrics for Marketing and Field Sales.

These steps were developed and refined over the course of many programs. We offer them to you as a proven path to success.

Conflicting Measurement

Here's Don Schultz again:

> **There are two real issues in all of this. The first is organizational structure—we've created these silos. Consumers don't have any silos. The second one is compensation—we continue to compensate people on unit sales. We talk about becoming customer-focused. But then we give salespeople a volume goal. If I give you a sales goal and I'm going to evaluate you at the end of every month on whether or not you've met that sales goal, I can tell you what happens to customer focus. It goes right out the window. I'm going to rape and pillage everyone I can to make my sales goal if I want to keep this job. The way to make Consensual Marketing work is to compensate these people for managing income from customers, not from flogging products.**

Traditionally, Marketing is measured and rewarded based on gross response—inquiries and leads. Field Sales, however, is measured by net sales and dollars. This creates enormous tension. To achieve lasting change, all areas must be measured and rewarded based on revenue contribution, customer retention, and lifetime value.

Ineffective Lead Criteria and Classification

As the cross-functional team votes on the information that comprises a lead, the most important votes are from Field Sales—because what's at stake is their sales efficiency and compensation. This is their area of expertise and it is their skin in the game to deliver.

Field Sales must also drive the classification of leads (e.g., A, B, C, and D). When is it appropriate to invest their time in following up a lead? Which leads are to be nurtured via other media?

Ineffective Lead Tracking

Full-loop lead management is an area where most companies fail. The reasons for failure are usually similar: the process was not designed and/or fully supported by Field management. The manifestations are usually similar as well. Individual reps see the process as administrivia, and administrivia is not what they get paid for. Field Sales, as a department, views the process as a police action instigated by Marketing.

Field Sales must champion the process of lead tracking both as a concept and in practice. Not only must Field management be visible supporters, they must also educate the reps as to the ultimate value of lead tracking—more sales. Everyone on the team is now measured and rewarded by net revenue. Feeding results back into the system will fuel continuous improvement, which will generate more qualified sales opportunities, a higher close ratio, and more net revenue.

The Psychology of Change Management

The following excerpt from *The McKinsey Quarterly*,[3] an article titled "The Psychology of Change Management," presents the view that there are three levels of change:

> **On the most straightforward level, companies act directly to achieve outcomes, without having to change the way people work; one example would be divesting noncore assets to focus on the core business. On the next level of complexity, employees may need to adjust their practices or to adopt new ones in line with their *existing* mind-sets in order to reach, say, a new bottom-line target. An already "lean" company might, for instance, encourage its staff to look for new ways to reduce waste.**

> **But what if the only way a business can reach its higher performance goals is to change the way its people behave across the board? Suppose that it can become more competitive only by changing its culture fundamentally—from being reactive to proactive, hierarchical to collegial, or introspective to externally focused, for instance. Since the collective culture of an organization, strictly speaking, is an aggregate of what is common to all of its group and individual mind-sets, such a transformation entails changing the minds of hundreds or thousands of people. This is the third and deepest level: cultural change.**

Consistent with the above article, there are four conditions that must be met to achieve meaningful, lasting change at this third and deepest level. The conditions are:

- Employees must see the vision and internalize the vision.
- Support structures and recognition systems must reinforce the behaviors consistent with lasting change.
- Employees must be trained over time in the new skills they will need to succeed.
- Role models must be consistent, visible, and include management.

Employees Must See and Internalize the Vision

Change is both scary and difficult for human beings. Employees approach corporate change with the deadly FUD factor—the combination of fear, uncertainty, and doubt. If you address this early, you'll win converts.

Employees need to understand how the business community they live in will change and why it is changing. The rationale is as important as the mechanics of the change. Show them the future state and why it is better for the company. Show them specifically why it will be better for them— answer the unspoken question, "What's in it for me?" And last, be very clear about the behaviors that will deliver the future into their hands; specifically, what is expected of them.

Reinforce Behaviors Consistent with Lasting Change

Organizational structure, measurement, and compensation must be consistent with the goals of the change. They must nurture and reward the change.

For instance, if your focus is implementing the Consensual Marketing Opt-In Process, but the organization only measures and compensates unit sales and product revenue, change may fall apart once it gets near the end of the month and folks get concerned about quota. However, if the corporation's measurement and reward structure is based on changes in Customer Lifetime Value, you will reinforce the behaviors consistent with lasting change.

Train New Skills, and Train Them Over Time

If you stood up in front of all your company's employees and announced that from this day forward the corporation would become "customer-centric," there might be head-bobbing and handshaking, but few individuals would have a clear idea of what they would be required to do differently. There's only one answer: you must train them and give them the specific skills required for successful change.

As you consider training, also consider that training is a process rather than a single event. People need time to listen, think about, and test the concepts and skills. People retain little from a core dump, also referred to as "drinking from the fire hose."

Vary the training format. Sometimes a classroom or lecture situation may be appropriate. As much as possible, train through group interaction. When people in a nonjudgmental environment are encouraged to exercise and apply the new concepts, it's more likely that they will retain and internalize those concepts.

Train over time. Improving skills and learning should be a recognized part of the fabric of corporate life. Cover fewer subjects in more depth per session and you will increase retention and application of the new information.

Role Models Must Be Consistent and Visible

The bottom line is that employees must see that the organization is consistent in rewarding those who successfully model the change behaviors, and that management consistently "walks the talk." If the organization fails at this, the other three conditions don't mean a thing.

It is important that at each level of the organization, within each department, employees see a person of influence who is a role model for the change behavior. And most of all, they must see management as consistently living and breathing the change behavior. They must see that the "person who signs my check" is committed.

Part II: Executive Checklist for Implementing the CMO Process

"Consensual Marketing is the wave of the future. I don't think there has ever been a time when marketers have been more convinced that 'business as usual' isn't going to work anymore."—Al Ries, Chairman, Ries & Ries

Let's Start at the Beginning

As we prepare to walk you through the executive checklist for implementing the Consensual Marketing Opt-In Process, it is helpful to reexamine the fundamental strategy behind the CMO process and the linkage between its component parts: Integrated Direct Marketing (IDM) and Voice of Customer (VOC) Messaging and Communication Research.

CMO is both a philosophical point of view and a strategic process, challenging management to reexamine how we *value a customer* and how we engage with the customer, both long and short term. To truly value customers, companies must expand corporate goals from just sales and revenue to also include customer retention and Lifetime Value as strategic measures.

IDM is the most effective tactical go-to-market process because of its focus on the precision integration of multiple media. IDM embraces the belief that relationships can only be achieved through ongoing, increasingly relevant touches over time—using multiple media, deployed in accordance with individual preferences.

VOC is a highly specialized process that allows us to pretest strategies, value statements, media mix, and offers in terms of what prospects and customers find *competitively differentiating*. We may have done a great job at the planning table, but before we go live, we need to understand customer preferences and requirements.

Now let's put them all together and bring the benefits of the Consensual Marketing Opt-In Process to your company. David W. Ralls, Vice President, HMI Marketing & Advertising, speaks to this subject:

> **Consumers and businesspeople alike are sending a message loud and clear: We are drowning in too many irrelevant communications. Communication overload. The lazy marketing "shotgun" approach, blindly trying to communicate with anyone and everyone, is dying a well-deserved death. It is wasteful and disrespectful.**

> **We believe in "appropriate communications" . . . and that's as defined by our clients' business goals as well as their prospects' and customers' preferred communications channels. Consensual Marketing is the ideal—individuals self-select and self-identify, they tell us what they want to hear, when they want to hear it, and how they wish to receive the message. We owe it to our clients to make them aware of the Consensual Marketing philosophy and how they can best deploy it to reap the benefits.**

Build Your Own CMO Plan Step by Step: A Checklist

The following executive checklist has been put together based on our 20 years of implementing IDM, VOC, and CMO programs. The checklist takes our experience, integrates it with the important action items from the chapters, and sequences them for a step-by-step process. It is designed to help you succeed.

1. Identify Members of Your Cross-Functional Team

Begin the change process by forming the CMO cross-functional team. This team should consist of representatives from each of the resources required to implement CMO. The following areas, at a minimum, should be included. Each representative contributes to the planning and implementation given his or her area of expertise. And as everyone is measured by net revenue and increased Customer Lifetime Value, each area has skin in the game:

- Executive sponsor
- Product management
- Customer service
- IS/Database
- Print advertising
- Electronic media
- PR
- Telecontact/Telesales
- Creative
- Field sales
- Marketing
- Direct mail
- Finance
- HR
- Legal

Here's an important perspective regarding the workings and deliberations of the cross-functional team, voiced by Vincent Amen:

> **Executive leadership must make it clear that no one division, product group, sales force, etc., owns the customer . . . the customer is an asset of the entire organization.**

2. Define Your Goals and Objectives

"Consensual marketing is mandatory for industry-leading firms. We no longer have the luxury to 'spray and pray' our marketing messages."—Garry Dawson, Manager, Marketing Communications Strategy, Americas Enterprise Systems Group, Hewlett-Packard

Goals should be strategic and broadly stated. Examples include:

- Develop and implement a "best in class" program in line with the CMO process.
- Introduce Integrated Direct Marketing (IDM) as an alternative channel of distribution, complementing traditional channels.

The objectives are tactical, specific, and measurable. Examples include:

- Generate double-digit response.
- Increase market share by 20 percent.
- Achieve an E:R ratio under 10 percent.

3. Carefully Select Your Product or Service

The product or service selected as the focus of a CMO campaign must have strategic importance to the corporation. Management must care about the product or service, or even the best results will go unnoticed.

One other suggestion: carefully research competitive issues before finalizing the product selection. The product or service must have clear competitive differentiation and compelling benefits.

4. Define Your Target Market

As you select your target market, consider the important issue first raised in Chapter 2: you may not be spending enough on your best customers. These are the customers who have stayed the longest and bought the most. Marketing dollars spent against your top-tier customers will generate the highest return on investment (ROI). They have the highest potential—the greatest propensity or likelihood to buy.

Figure 8.1 is repeated from Chapter 2. It consists of two triangles. The one on the left represents your customer file. It is likely that the top 10 to 20 percent generates 80 to 90 percent of your revenue. They have

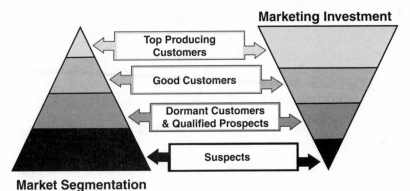

Figure 8.1   IDM Investment Pyramids

the highest propensity to buy. Therefore, a high proportion of the marketing budget should be deployed against this group.

Of course, you may select a different target market, depending upon your strategic goals. Either way, make sure you:

- Establish the potential universe size, your market penetration, and the market penetration of your key competitors.
- Prioritize market segments. Implementation is a continuum, not a shotgun blast. Thus, we suggest you learn by starting with a mid-tier segment. Once systems and performance are up to snuff, move to the top tiers.

5. Implement the SWOT/GOAST Planning Process

SWOT/GOAST is an effective planning process that structures and sharpens thinking.

SWOT stands for Strengths, Weaknesses, Opportunities, and Threats. The way to implement it is for the cross-functional team to evaluate and list the strengths and weaknesses of your strategy and product or service. First from your point of view, and then from the point of view of your key market segment.

Next, detail the Opportunities and Threats that are apparent, based on the strengths and weaknesses. Again, do this first from your point of view, then from the point of view of your key market segment.

GOAST stands for Goals, Objectives, Audience, Strategies, and Tactics. Now, bring in the work the team has done on defining goals, objectives, and the audience or target market. The cross-functional team should review and isolate the most important items identified in the SWOT portion. With these in mind, and using the previously determined audience, the team should develop the strategies and tactics that will achieve the goals and objectives.

6. Conduct VOC Messaging and Communication Research

Implement Voice of Customer Research, following the guidelines in Chapter 3, to define and/or validate:

- Target market/key market segments
- Decision-making process
- Strategies
- Media mix
- Appropriate messages by key market segments
- Offers
- Creative

7. Define Database Structure

Your database will represent 65 percent of your potential success. According to the guidelines in the section on building the consensual database in Chapter 2, consider the following as critical success factors. As you and the cross-functional team develop solutions, remember that the most important requirement is responsiveness of the database.

What information must be stored in sortable fields? And, thus, what data inputs are required?

- Is this your customer base? Does it need enhancing, perhaps to add demographic data? What are the sources you would turn to?
- Are you using external rental lists? If so, follow the direct mail guidelines in Chapter 4. Some of those guidelines include:
  - o The List Broker, who can be an important ally—choose them carefully.
  - o No one list will satisfy all your needs!
  - o Testing should become a standard operating procedure.
- For each input to the database, define the:
  - o **Source.** Specifically, which lists; one list equals one source.
  - o **Sortability requirements.** B2B examples of sorting or seg-

menting the list include company size, number of employees, by annual sales. B2C examples include age, income, and interest.

o **Accuracy.** Since lists and/or database comprise 65 percent of your potential success, the accuracy—including completeness and recency of update—is a leverage point.

How should the information be organized? We suggest that organization be based on your ability to respond. The following simplified organization, will get you started:

- Product purchased/installed
- Industry/application or use
- Geography
- Business driver(s)

What linkages are required? Database linkages (and we define a linkage as real-time access to key data) should include:

- Telecontact/Telesales
- Marketing
- Field sales
- Customer service
- Technical assistance
- Fulfillment

Define the necessary systems. Where will you "house" the database? Is your current database capable of housing the database? Is there bandwidth or are the daily requirements of the existing database overwhelming? If not internal, what are your options? Consider that in many cases you're better off operating outside of the legacy system. No matter what the capabilities of the legacy system are, its priorities are to be running mission-critical applications. And that puts your program at the bottom of the food chain.

8. Get Folks to Opt In

How will you stimulate customers and prospects to participate in your Consensual Database? For inspiration, and guidelines, let's look at how IBM achieved this for Focus 1:1.

IBM's target for this Consensual pilot consisted of 221 large customers who acknowledged their need for information but had expressed dissatisfaction with the irrelevant messaging and communications they were receiving. The cross-functional team targeted five to seven contacts per account, and with the help of Field Sales, identified key executives from each account. In total, 1,394 participating customer contacts were generated from the 221 original accounts, or 6.3 contacts per company.

Direct mail was sent to the key executives, briefly describing the goals of the Consensual pilot and announcing in advance the value of Field contact. Field Sales was deployed to make face-to-face contact with each of these senior executives to enlist them in the Consensual pilot and gain their endorsement, which would then greatly increase the buy-in of the other decision makers in the company. Reps were armed with a detailed discussion guide regarding the rationale for the Consensual pilot, and a formal Customer Interest Profile that verified all contact information, established media preferences and aversions, and requested important information such as key issues confronting the corporation today and how technology can support their longer-range plans.

With senior management on board, the balance of enrollment was accomplished via direct mail, e-mail, and the SPOE agents (e.g., inside salespeople).[4]

9. Define Field Requirements

We've laid a solid foundation for integration of Field Sales in Chapter 4 and in Part I of this chapter when citing lack of field integration as one reason for program failure. Use these guidelines to build tight linkages to Field Sales. As the CMO Change Agent, help the field take the lead on critical deliverables such as:

- Definition of qualified lead criteria
- Follow-up procedures according to lead grade
- Structure for a closed-loop lead management system

10. Define the Deployment and Synchronization of Media

"The new model starts with touch points. That is where people come in contact with your company, products, and services. We must try to manage these touch points. And that in essence is Consensual Marketing."—Don Schultz

The deployment and synchronization of multiple media is so critical to success that we have devoted fully a third of this book to providing insights, guidelines, and "how to" information. The following chapters should be your bible in selecting and deploying media:

Chapter 4. Step Three: How to Integrate Media and Message
Chapter 5. Step Four: Let's Get Real about E-marketing
Chapter 6. Step Five: Rethinking Customer Care

Select, invest in, and synchronize the deployment of each medium based upon its role and its potential contribution in accordance with the principles of Integrated Direct Marketing (IDM). Our goal is to understand how customers want to receive information, then to surround them with messages of value and compelling offers. Your palette of media includes:

- PR
- Direct Response Print Advertising
- Direct mail
- Inbound/Outbound telecontact
- E-mail
- Internet
- Field Sales

I I. Establish the Rules of Participation

"The rules of participation, which may involve the combining or suppression of communications, is not really an issue as long as every business unit believes that it will get its fair share of the highly qualified opportunity."—Yvonne Brandon, former Direct Marketing Manager, Worldwide e-Business on Demand, Operating Environment Initiatives, IBM

There is some pain in transitioning from traditional to Consensual Marketing. Traditionally, within a corporation each profit center is free to choose its own target market, and some competitiveness between the profit centers was considered good. As illustrated in the IBM Focus 1:1 case history in Chapter 1, the result is often marketing waste—unsolicited messages sent to the customer base that do not satisfy the needs of some customer segments. In fact, some customers consider the messages irrelevant. That is a recipe for customer dissatisfaction.

Within CMO, messages are sent to customers based upon their expressed interests—when they opted in.

Here's an example: Let's say you're an ice cream manufacturer specializing in vanilla, chocolate, and pistachio. Each flavor is a profit center. Customer A only buys vanilla—it's all he likes and all he wants. And he happens to prefer your brand. However, because he is an ice cream lover, he is also targeted by the chocolate and pistachio profit centers. Traditionally, they'd send him messages—his preferences didn't matter, and the marketers were arrogant enough to think they would change his mind. The customer, however, threw the messages away and became irritated with the company. (Customers do not see or care to see the different profit centers. They see one company.)

To move to Consensual Marketing, the marketers of chocolate and pistachio would have to either forgo or combine their message with vanilla, and be subordinate to the vanilla message. Hence the pain. You may get the different profit centers to cooperate once based on corporate citizenship. More than once will require some compelling reasons. The compelling reasons we suggest are:

- Visible senior management support providing "aerial cover." The troops need to see that senior management is supportive and actively engaged. Senior management can swoop in and easily break up logjams.
- A customer advocate position that reviews marketing plans in line with a Consensual view and has the power to recommend, mediate, and arbitrate, as required.
- The metrics and results reporting that will show each profit center that they're getting their fair share of the opportunity.

12. Metrics: Projections and Results

Without metrics you are flying blind. They're the instrument panel in your marketing rocket ship. Metrics enable in-flight corrections. We urge you to install the metrics and reports contained in Chapter 7. Some hints:

- Establish baselines. A comparison of current results to baselines will answer the question, "How are we doing?" at a glance.
- Based on experience, project results—by medium.
- Identify variables that may compromise results tracking.

And please, as we saw in Chapter 7, consider testing as a critical success factor. Testing will keep your program at maximum effectiveness. Consider testing with every campaign.

13. Define Ongoing Communications Strategies

Ongoing communications is the term we use to signify the stream of messaging and communications that takes place during the growth and retention period of the Customer Life Cycle (Figure 8.2). The goal of ongoing communications is to nurture these customers until they come back into the presale phase of the cycle. Interactive communications allow you to listen and learn how your customers' needs and requirements have changed over time, which then enables you to offer value.

> *"Traditionally, we have always used an outbound message distribution communication model. The new model is inbound—how do I get you to ask me for information or things that you need or you want? And then how do I respond?"*—Don Schultz

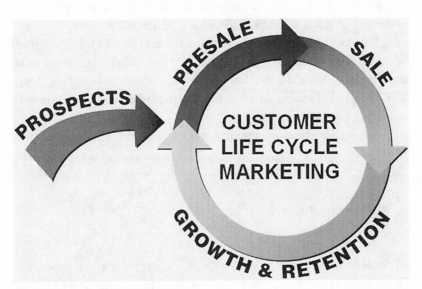

Figure 8.2   Customer Life Cycle

14. Define Resource Requirements and Linkages

Leadership is synonymous with being the CMO Change Agent. And as the leader, it is essential that you define your resource requirements and necessary linkages as early in the process as possible. Refine your projections periodically. Key areas include:

- **Human resources.** How many people, with what skills and performing what functions, does the process need to succeed?
- **Technology.** Treat this as an enabler, not a show stopper. Key message: Don't let technology bog you down. Evaluate good off-the-shelf solutions. Outsource as necessary.
- **Scalability.** How should these resources be scaled when the Consensual pilot is rolled out? For instance: If we needed 10 people for the pilot, how many do we need for the rollout?
- **Budget**

15. Establish Implementation Timelines

Implementation must be timeline driven. We suggest that prior to the first meeting of the cross-functional team, the CMO Change Agent prepare a pro forma implementation timeline. That timeline should tackle the major tasks to be accomplished and estimate how long they will take. Time intervals should be by the week. Consider what tasks are linked (e.g., you cannot undertake B until A is finished) and what tasks are independent.

Then, as planning progresses, refine the timeline. Let the individual or group responsible for a deliverable or a task detail what needs to be done and develop their timeline. Let them commit to how long it will take and when it will be done. Refine the implementation timeline until all stakeholders are satisfied.

Your implementation timeline should have the following column headings:

- Task
- Responsibility
- Due date

Include a column that says "Status." Suggest issuing this implementation timeline weekly, as an ongoing status report. This brings several benefits:

- The status report is a strong project management tool. It has no friends and no enemies. It simply tells the team where the project is, what projects have been completed and which are open, and what's on time and what's not.
- The report serves as a communication tool, letting all team members know exactly where things stand.
- It shines a light on problem areas quickly, before permanent damage is done.
- It keeps the program on track.

Case History: IBM Software Premier Club

We'd like to share with you another important Consensual Marketing Opt-In Process case study. The first IBM case, in Chapter 1, was about the Focus 1:1 effort and how it generated $594 million over the control group. The case history of IBM's Premier Club built on the findings of Focus 1:1 and generated $310 million in incremental revenue.

Yvonne Brandon, former Direct Marketing Manager, Worldwide e-Business on Demand, Operating Environment Initiatives, IBM:

The IBM Software Premier Club is a relationship direct marketing initiative targeted toward senior software decision makers and influencers in IBM's largest accounts worldwide. Today the program regularly communicates with 21,000 members in 49 countries and in 13 languages. Members represent over 90 percent of IBM's software revenue.

Exclusive to loyal customers (and by invitation only), the club keeps members informed and educated regarding the IBM Software Group's strategies, brands, and offerings. The target audience for the Premier Club is companies with over 1,000 employees who have spent $2 million or more on IBM software to date (or $1 million or more on IBM software within the calendar year), over multiple industries. Targeted decision makers are:

- CIO
- IT executives
- Data processing managers

Targeted influencers are:

• Database administrators
• Project managers
• User support groups
• Network managers

The objectives of the IBM Software Premier Club include:

• Maximizing revenue from IBM's best software customers—increasing revenue by 10 percent per year versus 2 percent annual growth for the overall customer base
• Maintaining value-based relationships with IBM's best software customers and increasing loyalty
• Improving executives' perception of IBM as a leader in software solutions
• Delivering the "right message to the right customer at the right time," using the best available electronic methods

IBM received guidance from Voice of Customer Messaging and Communication Research, which included data from 32 countries, including countries in Europe, the Middle East, Africa, North America, Latin America, Asia, and the Pacific Rim. A significant question in the VOC was: "What can IBM do to strengthen its relationships with you?" Yvonne Brandon provides insight regarding key findings:

Information overload: "Research found that the problem was much worse than we thought. Customers identified the sheer volume of untargeted communications as a major point of dissatisfaction."

Need for targeted information: "Customers said that their information needs are complex and that they vary by market and by individual. It was important that our communications match their needs."

High-tech/high-touch approach: "Customers were looking for help in evaluating optimal business solutions to business problems."

Peers (internal and external) are the best source of IT knowledge: "The IBM Software Premier Club should provide opportunities for participants to interact with each other."

Business department heads are important decision makers but don't feel a close relationship with IBM: "They wanted more attention from IBM."

IBM Issues

In implementing the Premier Club, IBM needed to strike a balance between short-term and long-term goals. The core of this issue is the (seeming) conflict between immediate revenue generation and customer retention and loyalty. The solution began with understanding each client's long-term business needs. This enabled IBM to help software decision makers plan for the future while making them aware of products and services that, if purchased today, would help them achieve their long-term goal.

To address customers' needs while eliminating marketing waste, IBM had to actively manage the content of the communications. That meant cooperation between every profit center, across all divisions. All the folks who were used to lobbing in whatever communications they wanted had to agree to combine or perhaps forgo a communication, based on a customer's profiled requirements. Analysis of the customer profiles enabled IBM to "map" the opportunity for each profit center to show them exactly which customer segments wanted their information and which did not. As Yvonne said earlier, each profit center had to be convinced that it was getting its fair share of the opportunity.

The Consensual Profile

The IBM Software Premier Club enabled a customer to profile themselves on four levels:

Level 1: Regional. Support content was relevant to the customer's physical location (e.g., the IBM services available locally).

Level 2: Language. IBM's goal was to support its global audience on its own terms—positioning IBM as a leader in global software strategies. Reaching out to non-English audiences in their specific language or dialect gave IBM a competitive advantage. Languages and dialects included U.S. English, Brazilian Portuguese, French, Canadian French, Spanish, Italian, and German.

Level 3: Areas of interest. This allowed IBM to discreetly position campaign tactics based on the user's declared areas of interest. For the customer, this meant ease of use for content navigation while offering access to a full library of articles. The IT categories, or customer interest areas, drove presentation of all "articles," which composed the bulk of site content.

Level 4: Industry. This adds a level of personalization, discussing not just technological innovation but how that innovation relates to a specific industry.

Strategies and Tactics

Communications were conducted electronically, encompassing both Web and e-mail. Why did the Premier Club communicate primarily through electronic media? Yvonne says:

> **Solutions in the information industry change rapidly. Lead times for the development, translation, and distribution of hardcopy could be as long as six weeks and were never shorter than four weeks. Our member customers needed to receive essential and timely information conveniently and immediately. With "e," information could be sent or posted as soon as it was available. Additionally, IBM coined the phrase "e-Business"—"e-implementation" proved not only that IBM "walked the talk" and used the tools it sells, it also served as a model to help customers see the value of e-Business in their own companies.**

Outbound e-mail was customized and matched to the individual's Consensual profile and contained technology information, member-only benefits such as special events, Webcasts, and special offers like "try and buy" software. As in Focus 1:1, there were also "full wave" e-mails that contained a broad array of information and went to everyone. E-mail was deployed in 21 languages.

The Web site was built with 100 percent IBM architecture and allowed members-only access. Customer information was immediate and timely. As soon as it became news, it was posted. The Web site also served as an executive portal to a variety of other IBM and industry sites.

Here are some of the tactics deployed in this multitouch/multimedia program:

- **An Internet Users Group was formed,** aimed at three different segments: technical influencers, IT managers, and IT executives. The spectrum of discussion ranged from pure technical to business-oriented applications of the technology.

- **An Internet Starter Kit was created** for nontechnical business development heads and senior executives to give those less technical people access to information from the IBM Software Premier Club and other IBM Web sites.
- **Customized Internet information page:** Customers said they wanted access to the right information, fast. Thus, a customized Internet information page was set up for each IBM Software Premier Club member, built to accommodate the customer profile.
- **Trend news:** Research showed that there was strong demand from customers for IT-related information going beyond products, to give business-oriented information, trends, strategies, and solutions-based news. Non-IT customers showed a strong preference for hardcopy over softcopy media. The deliverable IBM provided was a four-color, hardcopy eight-page booklet-style magazine, translated into six languages.
- **Customer-focused seminars and events:** "Customers said that hearing how other customers solved their business challenges through IT was important to their work, and to their choice of IT solutions," Yvonne Brandon says. "For some customers and cultures, 'in-person' contact was critical. The seminars we built were an in-person complement to the Internet Users Groups. They were part-day meetings and events where customers shared their IT solutions and strategies for success with other customers."
- **Audio teleconferences and Webcasts:** As a complement to the face-to-face events, and to minimize the inconvenience of lost office time, IBM sponsored a series of events that customers could participate in from their desk. Content and subject matter varied by target audience.
- **Software seed program:** The research also indicated that technical executives liked having access to early examples of leading edge technology before they recommended it to their companies. On the profile, customers indicated whether they wished to receive advanced copies of software, and if so, what type of products they were interested in.
- **Consultative sales mailers:** "Once intelligence was gathered on a customer's immediate needs," Yvonne, says, "a series of mailers and other deliverables were built in order to facilitate the next-step discussions. Once we'd nurtured the relationship and proved to

customers that we were listening, we'd earned the right to ask them to take the purchase cycle journey with us."

- **Software Account Manager (SAM) customer contact kit:** SAMs cringed when they learned that mailings and other information were being sent to their customers without their knowledge. The customer contact kit provided the SAM with periodic information on IBM Software Premier Club events and activities and contained mailing pieces they could send to their customers regarding special event notifications and other value-added information.

Yvonne Brandon:

The IBM Software Premier Club is viewed by customers as a single point of contact into IBM for anything they need. Members are recognized for their value to IBM and receive special treatment. The program recognizes spending signals or buying triggers and alerts the appropriate IBM representative so they can immediately address the opportunity.

Based on a Consensual Database, IBM Software Premier Club sends only the information that is of interest to a particular member. This saves customers time and saves IBM marketing dollars by not sending unwanted information.

The IBM Software Premier Club uses the principles of the Consensual Marketing Opt-In Process to enable each individual member to identify their own specific preferences and software interests. Thus, the club establishes a Consensual relationship and maintains an ongoing dialogue with each member to introduce new solutions and stay abreast of changing needs.

We use both an e-mail digest for regular push communications and a password-protected members-only Web site (i.e., an executive portal) so that members have an electronic community with 24-hour access to information about IBM software solutions.

In addition, members are able to communicate with each other and have access to industry research, a complete calendar of IBM

conferences, shows, and seminars, and IBM software experts to answer questions.

Results

- $310 million in incremental revenue
- 35 percent of members said they made purchases of IBM software products they would not have otherwise considered
- 28 percent increase in opt-in membership, while the opt-out rate is less than 1 percent
- 179 percent Web traffic increase since the Web site's inception
- 19.7 percent average annual click-through rate worldwide, versus single digits for other nonconsensual e-implementations
- 90 percent member satisfaction

What Customers Say

Germany: "Easily readable and presented in an easily understandable manner. . . ."
Denmark: "It's an easy way to get specific information."
USA: "They seem to target the audience very well: they supply the right kind of information."
UK: "I can quickly read e-mails and get more details as I require. It saves me a lot of time."

Assessment

The final lessons and steps to success, according to Yvonne Brandon:

- "Align your objectives with those of the top executive in your company or business unit. Make sure they 'own' your program."
- "Include members of the field sales force in all your planning. Doing so will give your program greater credibility in the eyes of the salespeople."
- "Once you launch your program, make sure you get regular feedback from customers on how well you are meeting their objectives."

- "Establish a strong cross-divisional editorial team. These people should be your regular source of information and offers for your customers."
- "Build and report measurements regularly."

Conclusion

Stephen J. Kimmerling, Conference Program Manager, Direct Marketing Association:

> **Business is always about relationships and connections. These are fragile, yes, but they're also flexible and organic. A business that treats its customers and the market with integrity, honesty, and flexibility can buck downward trends in the long term by creating greater loyalty and value per customer.**
>
> **The Consensual Marketing Opt-In Process represents a best business practice and brings permission and relationship marketing to the next level. Business is as much about people as it is about revenue and expenses. While it is true most businesses cannot be the "corner grocer," it is also true that customers want to be treated respectfully and personally.**

The last item on your executive checklist is intestinal fortitude. Stick to your guns. Your mission is to help shape the future of your company. There are speed bumps and land mines in your path. Not everyone is ready or willing to enter the Promised Land, and they will actively resist. CMO challenges how corporations are structured, how they value the customer, and how they organize and compensate their personnel. CMO changes the marketing paradigm from an outbound or "push" model to an interactive dialogue.

You must persevere. You must lead the way. In the current world of short-term thinking, the Consensual Marketing Opt-In Process represents viability for the long term, and that is worth the sacrifice.

Your leadership, perseverance, and sacrifice will bring your company this magnitude of increased results:

- A minimum 15 percent reduction in marketing waste
- 12 to 19 percent response or higher
- 100 percent increase in field follow-up to leads
- A minimum 21 percent increase in sales
- A minimum 15 percent increase in customer satisfaction

NOTES

Introduction

1. Philip Kotler is the S. C. Johnson Distinguished Professor of International Marketing at the J. L. Kellogg School of Management. He is the author of over 35 books, including *Marketing Management, Principles of Marketing*, and *Marketing Insights A to Z*.
2. John Carroll, "Know Thy Customer," *American Way*, July 15, 2003.
3. searchCRM.com, August 26, 2003.
4. Don Peppers and Martha Rogers, "Interconnectivity Is the Future," 1to1 Magazine, August 22, 2002.
5. "The Blueprint for CRM Success: Outcomes of a Comprehensive Study Identifying Best Practices Leading to ROI and Factors Contributing to Failure," CRM Guru, Caribou Lake Customer-1, and Mangen Research Associates, December 5, 2002.
6. Seth Godin, *Permission Marketing* (New York: Simon & Schuster, 1999).

Chapter 1

1. Direct Marketing Association.
2. CNN.com, 2003, Associated Press.
3. *Direct Newsline*, Direct Marketing Business Intelligence, August 25, 2003, Primedia Business Magazines and Media.
4. eMarketer, July 2, 2003.
5. *Direct Newsline*, Ibid.
6. 2003 Response Rate Study: Direct & Interactive Marketing Campaign Metrics.
7. The e-tailing group, as reported by eMarketer, July 29, 2003.

Chapter 2

1. Ray Schultz, "With Lester Wunderman," *1to1 Magazine*, May 2000. *Note:* Wunderman also coined the term "direct marketing."
2. Two in-depth sources you should also consider in learning more about IDM and how it has performed for both large and growth companies are the following books by Ernan Roman: *Integrated Direct Marketing: The Cutting-Edge Strategy for Synchronizing Advertising, Direct Mail, Telemarketing, and Field Sales*

(NTC Business, 1995) and, *Integrated Direct Marketing: Techniques and Strategies for Success* (McGraw-Hill, 1988).

Chapter 3

1. Quoted in Ernan Roman, *Integrated Direct Marketing: The Cutting-Edge Strategy for Synchronizing Advertising, Direct Mail, Telemarketing, and Field Sales* (NTC Business, 1995).
2. Ibid.
3. GeneAmp is a registered trademark of Roche Molecular Systems, Inc.

Chapter 4

1. "Multichannel Retail, Infrastructure Strategies to Maximize Customer Value," Jupiter Communications, Commerce Infrastructure, vol. 3, 2000.
2. Mr. Ries ran an advertising agency in New York City for 27 years (Trout & Ries) and is now a principal of the Ries & Ries marketing consultancy.
3. eMarketer, September 5, 2003.
4. eMarketer, June 18, 2003.

Chapter 5

1. eMarketer, August 26, 2003.
2. eMarketer, Radicati Group, June 16, 2003.
3. "What Spam Costs, Service Providers Debate the Financial Impact," DIRECTnewsline, May 15, 2003.
4. eMarketer, June 10, 2003.
5. eMarketer, April 23, 2001.
6. "Response Rate Study: Direct & Interactive Marketing Campaigns," Direct Marketing Association, 2003.
7. eMarketer, February 4, 2003.
8. eMarketer, June 11, 2003.
9. "A Failing Grade for E-mail Replies," *Target Marketing*, June 1, 2003.
10. "Inside 1to1 Report," Carlson Marketing Group, June 1, 2003.
11. eMarketer, September 5, 2003.
12. eMarketer, April 29, 2003.
13. eStatNews, eMarketer, August 8, 2003.
14. eMarketer, April 29, 2003.
15. eStatNews, eMarketer, September 8, 2003.

16. eMarketer, June 25, 2003.
17. The section "Web Site Promotion and Search Engine Optimization" was contributed by Bret Giles, cofounder of Sitewire Marketspace Solutions, a leader in SEM.

Chapter 6

1. Target Marketing, North America Publishing Company, September 2003.
2. eMarketer, November 11, 2003.
3. James L. Heskett et al., "Product Number 4460, Putting the Service Profit Chain to Work," *Harvard Business Review*, March–April 1994. Many thanks to Michael Miller of the Cathedral Corporation for bringing this article to our attention.

Chapter 7

1. Kate Maddox, "E-mail Marketers Missing the Mark," BtoB e-mail, Marketer Insight, August 11, 2003, Crain Communications, Inc.
2. eMarketer, April 29, 2003.

Chapter 8

1. James B. Simpson. *Simpson's Contemporary Quotations.* New York: Houghton Mifflin, 1988.
2. Ibid.
3. Emily Lawson and Colin Price, "The Psychology of Change Management," *The McKinsey Quarterly*, 2003 no. 2.
4. SPOE, or Single Point of Entry, is discussed in Chapter 6, in the section "Inside/Outside Partnership with the Field," and is addressed in Chapter 1 in the section "Case History: IBM Focus 1:1."

Index

About the Authors

Ernan Roman is the award-winning founder and president of Ernan Roman Direct Marketing. The pioneering author of several influential books, including the landmark *Integrated Direct Marketing: The Cutting-Edge Strategy for Synchronizing Advertising, Direct Mail, Telemarketing, and Field Sales*, Roman created the Integrated Direct Marketing methodology and Consensual Marketing Opt-In Process. His articles appear regularly in *Direct*, *Advertising Age*, *DM News*, *Target*, and other prominent publications.

Scott Hornstein is the award-winning senior partner and principal of Ernan Roman Direct Marketing. Hornstein has been central to the development of both the Integrated Direct Marketing and Consensual Marketing Opt-In Process methodologies. A popular industry speaker, he has written for and been quoted in numerous prestigious regional and national publications.